In God's own
IMAGE

SECOND EDITION, THIRD PRINTING

Personal Growth and Basic Counseling Skills

SIMON PETER KYAMBADDE

WORKBOOK PRESS LLC
187 E Warm Springs Rd,
Suite B285, Las Vegas, NV 89119, USA

Website: https://workbookpress.com/
Hotline: 1-888-818-4856
Email: admin@workbookpress.com

Ordering Information:
Quantity sales. Special discounts are available on quantity purchases by corporations, associations, and others.
For details, contact the publisher at the address above.

ISBN-13:   978-1-958176-97-9 (Paperback Version)
                        (Digital Version)

REV. DATE: 07/04/2022

In God's Own Image

Personal Growth
and Basic Counselling Skills
in the Light of Scripture

Simon Peter Kyambadde

To my mother Pilmiva who gave me life and taught me love

Acknowledgements

The production of this book would have been impossible without the contribution in different ways of the following people: Rt. Reverend Joseph Willigers MHM who authorised the payment for my studies and Fr. Daniel O'Sullivan who contributed to that payment.

This work has been written in loving gratitude to the Institute of St. Anselm, Cliftonville, England, where I was first exposed to the process of seriously looking within self and of systematically getting involved in the growth of others. It is in gratitude to the founder of the institute, Rev. Len Kofler MHM, DD. DSoc. PhD and all his staff team. It is written in appreciation of the warm friendship from the participants coming from practically all over the world, some of whom became intimate friends. The various group work and community interactions that within nine months turned a collection of individuals from so many different countries into a tightly bonded group of friends, who openly shed tears at the saying of farewells, convinced me that the effort spent in community building is worthwhile.

I am also grateful to Sr. Lillian Sullivan CSC and Mrs. Joyce Parmeter for proofreading this work and for their encouragement, to the parishioners of St. Jacobus parish, Puchkirchen, Austria, to Mrs. Zalka Likozar of Cleveland Ohio, for their support.

Contents

INTRODUCTION 8

CREATED IN THE IMAGE AND LIKENESS OF GOD 11

INTRA-PERSONAL REFLECTION OF GOD'S IMAGE.....................13
    The Body *14*
    The Consciousness..*17*
    The Unconscious...*18*
    The Higher Faculties...*19*
    The Spiritual Self...*22*
    The Embodiment...*26*
    The Self..*27*
    The beauty of the self *29*
INTER-PERSONAL REFLECTION OF GOD'S IMAGE......................31
    Male and FEMALE, he Created Them *33*
TRANSPERSONAL RELATION WITH GOD AND THE UNIVERSE 40
    Relation with the Universe..*40*
    God's Image of Me..*41*
    My Image of God *42*
    Relation to God and the World *47*

THE TARNISHED IMAGE OF GOD IN ME...................................49

THE FUNDAMENTAL IMPORTANCE OF CHILDHOOD 50
    Laying the Foundations of Personality in Childhood *51*
    Effects of Childhood Experiences on Adult Life...........................*53*
    What to Do about The Effects of Childhood *61*
THE MID-LIFE CRISIS..63
    General Description *64*
    Symptoms *64*
    Meaning *65*
    Coping with the Midlife Crisis...*66*
'DISAGREEABLE' EMOTIONS 67
    Anger..*68*
    Fear..*78*
    Regret...*80*
    Anxiety..*84*
    Negative Emotions Related to Love and Sexuality *86*
    Conclusion...*90*
DEFENSIVE MECHANISMS 91
    Projection *91*
    Prejudice *93*

The 'Destructive Critic' 95
Other Defensive Mechanisms 97
POST-TRAUMATIC STRESS DISORDERS 100
Meaning 102
Causes 102
Immediate and Short-term Effects 103
Long-term Effects 104
Personal Coping with Trauma 106
Helping others cope 107
Expert Treatment 109

**RE-CREATED IN THE IMAGE OF GOD: PERSONAL
GROWTH 111**

THE ROLE OF THE SELF 113
It is important to want to be well again 113
Listening to the body: Burnout and self-care 114
Self Knowledge through the Intensive Journal 122
Listening to the Unconcious: Self Knowledge Via Dreams 131
Listening to the Higher Faculties: the Voice of Conscience 134
Managing Money Stress 136
THE ROLE OF OTHERS 142
THE ROLE OF THE ENVIRONMENT 149
THE ROLE OF GOD 152
Private Prayer 152
Liturgical Prayer 166

**RE-CREATING IN THE IMAGE OF GOD: HELPING AN
INDIVIDUAL 168**

EVERY HUMAN ENCOUNTER COUNTS 169
HELPING USING COUNSELLING SKILLS 171
Counselling in General 173
Working Alliance 174
Time Management 176
Prayer in Counselling 177
Attending 178
Listening 179
Advanced Empathy 184
Feed back 187
Paraphrasing 190
Exploration 191
Reluctance and Resistance 196
Immediacy 200
Self Disclosure 201

Decision Making and Problem Solving *202*
Helping Others Solve their Problems *208*

RE-CREATING IN THE IMAGE OF GOD: HELPING A GROUP 209

WORKING WITH GROUPS 210
The Necessity of Cooperation *211*
What is a Group/Community? *214*
Formation and Running of a Group *215*
Some Elements of Group Process *218*
Stages in Group Development *226*
Dimensions of Behavior & Intervention Strategies *229*

EPILOGUE **232**

INTRODUCTION

There is a Greek myth about a man called Midas that loved gold more than anything else, or so he thought. When he went to an oracle to make a petition, he asked that whatever he touched may become gold. The petition was granted. Whatever Midas touched became gold. He was thrilled. He scooped up dust, and it flowed from his hands as the finest golden dust. He went home and touched his plates and cutlery turning them all into golden utensils. Like a king, he sat down to eat with the golden gear. The first piece of food he put into his mouth turned into gold! Suddenly, he wasn't so amused. Each piece of food he touched became gold. As he could not satisfy his hunger, he tried at least to drink. He poured some wine in the cup turned golden, and the wine oozed out in the form of a pure golden liquid. Midas began to panic. Disconsolate, he went and sat down. His dearest daughter came in, cheerful as usual, and ran straight into his arms. Instantly, she turned into a statue of gold. Midas now knew that he had made the greatest mistake of his life.

In the Bible, Solomon was a lot wiser than Midas. In a dream at Gibeon, he, too, was confronted with the offer to ask for anything, but he was smart enough not to go for the obvious targets like riches, conquest, or a long life (1Kings 3:4-15). He asked for wisdom to make the right decisions. He got this as well as the things he had not asked for, as a bonus.

Not many of us anticipate such an offer in our life. And yet, we can all think of what it is we consider to be the greatest value in our lives. What we would sacrifice everything to get. Unless we choose wisely, we can easily value something which, if obtained, would be disappointing; if not downright our ruin the way gold was the ruin of Midas.

The greatest value we have is ourselves, and the greatest thing we can do is to become as close to our ideal self as possible. There is nothing as important and as difficult in the life of every person as growth into mature beings capable of exploiting to the full the human potential. All around us there is so much to admire, to be proud of, to thank God for, if you are a believer. A homeland, intimate friends, social order, technological development; all these are good things that we enjoy and are thankful for or take for granted. However, there is also so much that we wish would be different. When you hear of wars in different parts of the world, of violence, of famines that could be avoided if it were not for the greed of some, of injustice and oppression, you wonder why we human beings never learn from experience, for these are as old as humanity, and there has been enough time to learn of their tragedy and futility. However, every social evil we see is born and incubated in the human heart. Any authentic desire to change the world outside must begin with the world within.

What we see in the world around us mirrors the world within us. There is so much good in us whether we are aware of it or not: our existence, our talents, our hobbies, our virtues, all the things with which we make the life of others more joyful constitute part of our inherent goodness which we cultivate to a greater or lesser degree. There are varying degrees of goodness in each of us, but goodness is there in each one, however minimal. Side by side with this goodness is much we wish were different. Unfulfilled aspirations, little habits that we may not be fully aware of but which are annoying to others, failures that we regret but continue to fall into, potentials that we know we have but never quite develop as fully as we know we could, all constitute part of the important but difficult journey towards human maturity. Often, the negative within us prevents us from fully appreciating the goodness there is.

This book offers a set of suggestions in that perennial struggle for human growth. Integrating modern psychological insights with Christian biblical teaching, it is useful to the individual or group seeking personal growth, as well as to a counselor, or spiritual director assisting others in that all important journey.

The material is arranged under five parts. Part I describes the ideal: what God meant us to be. Part II describes the reality: what we actually are with both our original beauty and our fallen nature. Parts III to V are concerned with our struggle to restore the tarnished image of God in us. Part III focuses on the personal growth of an individual, part IV regards how we can help another person grow, and finally part V describes how we can facilitate the growth of others in a group.

The work may be of great value to individuals who have the courage to embark on the arduous but most important journey of growth and who are in search of some guidelines, particularly those who, for one reason or another, have no possibility of attending a full-fledged counselling course. It is also intended for people who in one way or another have something to do with formation or facilitating groups and communities, but who have not had any course on group facilitation and counselling: people in schools, universities, institutions, novitiates, seminaries, and other groups and associations. It is particularly helpful to those who have had some basic training in personal and group development counselling and who are called upon to assist others in that field. For them, it is a source of easy reference to material they may have covered or touched upon in their training but have since forgotten or cannot apply to the present situation in a coherent manner. For them the book offers a simple one-volume reference. It can also be used by those who have attended some course of human growth and must continue their growth process on their own. It can be used to incorporate in support groups others who have never attended a counselling course, using the material in this book for their initiation.

The work has no pretense to giving professional and expert information and skills, yet one cannot rule out the possibility that even expert counselors and therapists may find in it some elucidation and guidance, for wisdom is often embedded in very simple things. It is amazing to see to what extent the most sublime teaching is just common sense. But perhaps this is because the law of God is written in our hearts. "The word, that is the faith we proclaim, is very near to you, it is on your lips and in your heart..." (Romans 10:8).

Part I

CREATED IN THE IMAGE AND LIKENESS OF GOD

Certain truths, even fundamental ones, can fail to impress us simply because we have heard them over and over again. When in the very first lectures of a counselling course I heard that we are made in the image and likeness of God, this did not sound at all new. It does not sound new to anyone who has been a Christian for any considerable time and who is familiar with the scriptures, particularly the book of Genesis. It is much less striking for one who spent eight years of major seminary training and twelve further years as a priest and whose job is to teach theology.

What I found more striking was an exercise in the same course the main content of which was to answer the question "who are you?" We were divided in pairs. Your partner had to have a blank sheet of paper and a pen and ask you the question, "Who are you?" Whatever answer you gave, the partner wrote down and asked again the same question, "Who are you?" Each time, you had to give a different but truthful answer about your identity. The exercise went on for several minutes. At first, the answers came easily enough. For the majority, the first answers we thought of included the name, the profession, the sex, and the nationality (for we were quite an international assortment!). However, it was explained that all these answers did not quite define one's identity. For example, in spite of the undeniable importance of a name, it is still something outside of me. It was given me after I already existed. Its choice had something arbitrary about it. I could have been called by a different name. Moreover, quite often people are identified by several different names. A name helps humans in their limitations to differentiate one person or one thing from another. It does not really define what that thing is in itself. Other descriptions also put us in one category or another, they do not define us. My profession, my vocation, my nationality, all these do not exhaust my identity.

"God created man in the image of himself, in the image of God he created him, male and female he created them. God blessed them, saying to them, 'Be fruitful, multiply, fill the earth and conquer it. Be masters of the fish of the sea, the birds of heaven and all living animals on the earth." (Genesis 1: 27-28)

The mystery of who we really are is closely linked with the mystery of how we really came to be and with the mystery of our destiny. In the natural course of events, parents do not have a choice in determining whom the child will resemble. God, on the other hand, made a conscious choice of creating us in his own image, like an artist who chooses to paint a self-portrait. God said, "Let us make man in our own image, in the likeness of ourselves..." (Genesis 1:26). Immediately when a believer affirms this truth, a series of questions present themselves: who is this God? in what sense are we made in his image? and how does one account for the vast differences between us, not only of physical appearance but also moral and spiritual differences?

Part I of this work is a reflection on the beauty that is the human being. It further examines in the light of revelation and of faith, the source of this beauty and wonder. We are created in the image and likeness of God. This means that no matter how deformed we are, there is in every human being something good and beautiful. Our growth is geared towards reclaiming that image of God in us. We can view our likeness to God from two perspectives: the intra-personal which focuses on the "inside" of each individual, or the inter-personal, which views the human being from the perspective relations to other human beings. We shall conclude this part by looking also at the world outside of us, as well as at God who, having created us in his own image, remains at the same time one who is totally "other."

INTRA-PERSONAL REFLECTION OF GOD'S IMAGE

In trying to comprehend the complex reality of our being, the immediate problem we encounter is the limitation of human understanding and expression. Realities that are otherwise simple have to be partitioned so that we understand them bit by bit. And so we go…

The Body 14
The Consciousness 17
The Unconscious 18
The Higher Faculties 19
The Spiritual Self 22
The Embodiment 26
The Self 27
The beauty of the self 29

If instead of the question "who are you?" I had been asked "what constitutes you?", I think I would have found it easier to answer, and I think I would not have been alone. It is easier to talk of what we have than what we are. If we forget for a moment the thought of "have" in the sense of having possessions and consider it in the sense of what makes me me, then this can help us towards an understanding of who we are.

THE BODY

I have a body. I can think of its different parts. I have a head, I have a torso, and I have legs. I can think of my eyes and ears, my nose and mouth, my neck and back. I have fingers and toes, hair and nails. With my tongue, I can speak and turn the food in my mouth. With my knees, I can kneel and genuflect, bend my leg to kick and to walk. I have many internal organs which I know are there even though I have never seen them. I can feel my heart beat, my belly grumble, and my lungs expand and contract as I breathe.

I know that the different parts of my body function in perfect harmony and not as individuals. My blood flows through all of them. My bone structure or skeleton holds everything together, protects the tender organs, and gives me my shape. My nervous system makes the whole body capable of sensing, warning me against any danger so that I can take the appropriate measure to protect my body. My brain controls all the bodily functions and is the bridge to the higher faculties yet to be discussed. I can talk of different systems all in the same body: the respiratory system, the digestive system, the reproductive system, and the nervous system. All are coordinated. Even what seem like individual limbs have a function that serves the whole. The eye sees not for itself but for the whole body. I have only to remember what happens when I walk in darkness and have to grope around. The hands move all over the place feeling the surroundings. The feet slow down and drag. The whole body is slowed. I can think of the many things I couldn't do without hands: from not being able to scratch myself to not dressing myself; from not being able to type or write to having to be fed. And, if I have ever lain in bed because of something that had happened to my leg or seen someone else on crutches, then I know how important the legs are for the whole body. Every tiny part of my body has some function for the whole. In scripture, perhaps there is nowhere else where the importance of each part of the body comes out as in St. Paul's analogy of the body to the mystery of the Church (1Corithians 12: 12-30).

I have senses: with my body I can perceive. I can smell good food, the aroma of a flower, and the repulsive stench of rotting carrion. I can taste good fruit or enjoy a refreshing drink. I can listen to soothing music, to the voice of a loved one, to the singing of birds, as well as to the honking of a coming car that warns me to be clear of the road. With my body, I can bask in the morning sun, enjoy a warm bath, a cool breeze, and a swim in a pool or lake. I can play a game, do my work, and fulfill my dreams. I enjoy my sleep as I listen to gentle rain falling on the roof. My body preserves me from all sorts of danger, from what is too cold or hot. I pull away from fire, and I do not walk bare-footed in the snow. When I become sick, I know that a part of my body needs some repair, and I procure it. When I am hungry or thirsty, I know that the body needs replenishing. When I am tired, I know that my limbs need a rest in order to recuperate lost energy. The urge to go to the toilet helps me to dispose of what the body no longer needs. Sexual desires remind me that I am made with the capacity to propagate other humans, as well as with a capacity to be complemented and fulfilled by another.

In my body, I experience emotions. I experience the joy of meeting a long-awaited friend, as well as the sadness and grief at the death of a loved one. I know the wonderful experience of falling in love. I can understand the hope and anxiety an expectant mother experiences. I have experienced the disappointment of investing so much energy and time in a project that later flopped. I know the frustration of suddenly losing a computer document that I have worked on for hours or even days. I know the hurt of being betrayed by a person I trusted, as well as the elation of being commended by someone significant in my life. I remember the times when I went into a rage when someone trampled on my rights taking me for a fool. I can feel sympathy for the pain caused to a defenseless little child. I can feel moody when things do not go my way, and I can feel enthusiastic when engaged in an activity that I really like.

I can see that all these feelings and emotions act as a bridge between my material nature and something spiritual. They all have something physiological about them. I acquire them primarily through some experience. But, they are not altogether material. For one thing, I can often keep them to myself and hide them from the outside world, because they are in themselves imperceptible.

I also know that I have something higher than feelings and emotions. I can think and reason. I can choose even against what I desire at the moment. Even though many times I am swayed by my feelings and I act according to how I feel, there are also times when I take charge of them. I have a higher faculty which can govern my feelings. I know when it would be inappropriate to show anger or to sulk. I can say that what I really want now is to go to bed, but I have to finish off that letter, so I choose to write it and postpone going to bed. I do not need to be taught that this is a higher faculty. I know it, and others know it, too. By this faculty, a good person is differentiated from a bad one, and reputations are built. Anyone can admire in another human being such qualities as endurance, industry, kindness, sympathy, generosity, and self-sacrifice. All these qualities are based on the capacity to overcome natural inclinations: of giving up when things are difficult, of laziness and of selfishness, and of subjugation of feelings and emotions to the intellect and will.

Through our bodies we have the capacity to realize our full potential as human beings. When we think of a fruit, we think exactly about that: the fruit. We often do not think of the seed that germinated at the beginning, the roots that held the plant in place and continued transferring water and the necessary minerals to it, the stem that kept it standing permitting it to remain exposed to the sun which is necessary for its growth, the branches on which the leaves were attached in order to gather in the light and to facilitate photosynthesis, nor the flower, which later turned into fruit and which in due time will turn into seeds to begin the whole plant cycle anew. All these elements constituted the plant from which this fruit was plucked. Depending on where we live in the world, we may not even know how the plant from which a pineapple, a banana, or an apple grows or what it looks like. And yet, every part of the plant was important in the formation of the fruit we enjoy. So does the body act as a matrix of all that constitutes us.

This body, so beautiful and complete in its complexity, has suffered and continues to suffer so much degradation. The meaningless killings, torture, and maiming in wars, all sorts of defilement, the subjugation of this body to all sorts of addictions, as well as the pampering it gets to the extent of forgetting the higher values for which it is called—all these make it comparable to a plant that is hindered from bearing the fruit it was meant to bear, in this case fruits of goodness. It is like a plant which is ravaged and trampled on, or one which is over-manured to the extent of bearing many leaves but no fruit at all. However, God who created us in his own image has also shown us that no matter how low we have sunk, we can always be elevated to that original dignity. This he did by assuming a body like our own in Jesus Christ. By this, he showed us that whatever social rank we are, we have the potential to rise to our full potential as human beings. He showed us this by his own example, by his words that teach us the way, and by the merits of his own sacrifice through which what is damaged in us becomes whole again.

THE CONSCIOUSNESS

You are conscious of what you are reading. If you stop and reflect a little, you also become conscious of the fact that you are reading. If you make further reflection, you become conscious or aware of many other things: of the sounds around you, of the things that are in your range of vision, of the thoughts within your head, of the feelings you have, of any possible pains you may be suffering at the moment. With further reflection, more and more things may be added to your range of consciousness. At the same time, however, when more details come into your consciousness, some of the things you were conscious of a little while before may start slipping from your range of awareness. The ensemble of things you are aware of at any particular moment are your conscious self.

Quite often we identify ourselves with what we are conscious of, particularly with our sensations and feelings. I can say that I am hungry or sleepy or weak or tired or that I am angry or lonely or happy or worried. The fact is that I am conscious of these sensations or feelings, but they are not me, even though they are a part of me. Usually, they last only for a time, but that does not mean that I constantly change. Detachment means that I am not a slave of my feelings, thoughts, emotions, sensations, etc. I may be angry now, but I am more than my anger. I can observe the feeling of my anger and can take a distance from it. I can, for instance, examine why I am angry, what is the reasonable thing to do about it, etc.

Although my consciousness is by far the smaller section of what is me, it is within it that I act, that I can knowingly and deliberately effect my own growth. Although expert psychotherapy deals much with what lies in the subconscious, amateurs are usually advised to restrict themselves to material that lies within the conscious. It is relatively easier to handle. This book, which is intended for the non-expert, will also focus mainly on the conscious even while taking into account the unconscious which we cannot afford to ignore in an effort towards any meaningful healing and growth.

In our consciousness, we reflect the image of God in a very little way. Ancient philosophers defined God as "self-thinking-thought" or "eternal consciousness." They perceived him to be perfectly conscious, not only of all that is past, but of all that goes on in the present and all that is to happen in the future, all at the same time, but also of everything in him, so that nothing ever slips out of his consciousness.

THE UNCONSCIOUS

As we make an effort to be aware of the things in our consciousness, we also become keenly aware of the fact that things slip out of it. Anyone who has ever tried to concentrate and exercise mental prayer or meditation knows also the experience of distractions, of constantly losing vision of what you want to focus on. It is not difficult to see that what we are conscious of constitutes a much smaller fraction of the things that we know. You cannot hold present at the same time all the things that happened to you since you woke up this morning. Even if you could, that would still be a small part of all the reality that you know. This reality also includes all the things that happened to you each hour and moment of yesterday. What about all that happened each day of last week? Then consider all that happened to you the whole of last year and all the other years of your life! Many of these things you can remember although in various degrees of accuracy. You could bring them into consciousness. If you set your mind to it, you could write a lot about your life, even to your own surprise.

That was my experience at that counselling course I mentioned before and that I will refer to over and over again in this book. At one stage of the course, we were required to write our life history. The idea was to recall as much of one's past as possible, because much of our healing and growth entails completing any unfinished business of our past. I started the exercise without much enthusiasm, but then I gained interest. One was required to take a summary of about 3 to 4 pages to one's growth facilitator to process. But, once I had warmed up to the exercise, I just went on writing long after I had discussed the summary with the growth facilitator. It became like writing one's autobiography. Each day, I found time to add a few episodes. One recalled incident led to another. Thanks to the invention of the computer, one can always insert a new recollection exactly where it fits in the life history without upsetting what has already been written. Eventually, I was amazed at how much I had written: it had accumulated to five hundred typed pages. What is more, I had come to the realization that I could write much more, if I put my mind to it. Much of this was stacked away in the subconscious.

If you simply listed the people, you have ever known, you could come up with a very long list of names, even without describing anything else about them. All this is hidden in the unconscious. There are also things that are hidden there that you cannot bring to consciousness—things you have forgotten. Consider all the dreams you ever dreamed all your life, many of which you never recalled at all. Think of the things that might have happened to you before you were three years old. There are many things about you that you are not aware of but which keep affecting your conscious actions. It is said that the mind may forget but the body never does. Everything that has ever happened to it has left an effect. Scientists can gauge the age of certain trees that grow for hundreds if not thousands of years by counting the number of rings each winter season leaves in their stem. The bodies of these trees store "memories" of each passing season. Our bodies store memories of whatever happened to us. If the unconscious were compared to a deep pit in which all sorts of things are thrown, there would be those nearly at the surface that can be recovered by simple rummaging through the knick-knacks, as well as those that are too deep to be recovered easily. But, each of the items regardless of depth would contribute to the overall size and weight of the pit's contents. So does the subconscious. For better or for worse, it is part of all that which goes to make me, me and you, and you.

THE HIGHER FACULTIES

We did not have a radio at home when I was a little boy. My earliest memories of coming close to a radio were when I was about four or five in the home of an uncle whom I had been taken to visit. I was fascinated by this queer little speaking box with knobs. And, it did not speak in one voice but many. I longed so much to look at the little people I imagined to be inside who could not only speak in full-grown men's and women's voices but could also sing and play music. In fact, my uncle told me as a joke that there were such people inside, and perhaps he did not realize that I believed him.

One day my uncle chanced to change the batteries, and I had an opportunity to look inside. You cannot imagine my disappointment!

There were no Lilliputians moving about. Instead, there were a few metallic objects and things which were fixed even as the radio "spoke," for my uncle allowed me to look inside while the radio was switched on. Still, the fascination remained. How on earth could metals and wires make such intelligible sounds without ever making any movement?

Even as an adult, I have never stopped to wonder at the marvel of technology. The knowledge that the radio itself does not produce the sounds but only acts as receptacle does not dispel the marvel. Only, it broadens its scope so that one wonders not only at the ingenuity of human beings who thought of transmitting and trapping radio waves, but also at the power that created the waves and made them capable of transmitting sounds. It is fascinating to realize that the words we say, the sounds we make are never really destroyed but move out in form of waves and can be captured and heard elsewhere given sufficient technology. The reality of human ingenuity for which a radio is evidence, as well as the capacity to perceive and wonder at the marvelous, are pointers to our higher faculties, which were briefly mentioned in the description of the body above. These higher faculties of intellect and will are closer to our core by which we reflect most the image of God in us.

With the exception of these higher faculties, what we have considered so far is shared by other creatures, even though perhaps in different ways. Every living organism has a body just as we have—one that is a beautiful complex interaction of systems. Even a tree has a respiratory system, a digestive system, a reproductive system, even a defensive system of its own. Some have thorns for their protection, others have sap, others height. Because many fruits are sour while they are growing, many predators including human beings leave them alone, thus giving time for the seeds within to mature. When these are ready to propagate the race, the juice turns sweet, inviting the predators to assist in the job of propagation. Even a dog has a nervous system. It, too, has feelings. You can tell when it is angry or happy or afraid. It must have an unconscious, and that is probably why it can learn through conditioning. And so, the perennial question: what is it that sets us human beings apart from the rest of other creatures on earth? Let us look at these higher faculties that bring us closer to God.

"...God is love; and he that dwells in love dwells in God, and God in him." (1 John 4: 16)

We are in the image of God, because we are created to love and to be loved. Love is a fundamental factor in the life of every human being. Happiness or the lack of it depends largely on our reception and giving of love. God is love, and he created us to love and be loved. The very idea of trinity implies love. They are three, all different and yet all one, united in love. Love in its pure sense in which one's focus of attention is the good of the beloved rather than the self belongs to the realm of the higher self.

We are in the image of God, because we are free beings. Other creatures live by instinct. Humans, too, like other creatures are guided by instinct, of course, but we have more than that. We are free to change our destiny even though this may be very difficult at times. We are conditioned by so many things: our parents and parent figures, our environment, our genes, the traumas we encounter in our lives…and yet all these things can only influence us. They do not determine us. It is always possible to change. We are free, because we have both the higher faculties of knowledge and will. We can discern what is good and what is not and decide to do one thing or the other.

Like "Love", the concept of "Freedom" is one that is easily misunderstood. To be free is not to do whatever one wants or desires. Similarly, to choose what is right even when this is very painful is not lack of freedom. The choice according to what we desire and in contradiction to what is right or really good, leads to the very opposite of freedom: inner slavery to our desires, and in extreme cases, even to addiction (see "Nature of Addiction" on page 143). The Compendium to the *Catechism of the Catholic Church* defines freedom as follows:

> Freedom is the power given by God to act or not to act, to do this or to do that, and so to perform deliberate actions on one's own responsibility. Freedom characterizes properly human acts. The more one does what is good, the freer on becomes. Freedom attains its proper perfection when it is directed toward God, the highest good and our beatitude. Freedom implies also the possibility of choosing between good and evil. The choice of evil is an abuse of freedom and leads to the slavery of sin.[1]

Activity 1: Experiencing willpower

> *Try to recall when you tried to reach a goal against an obstacle, inner or outer. This experience brings you close in touch with your willpower as it struggles against resistance.*

---

[1] English translation published by, St. Paul Publications/Daughters of St. Paul, Nairobi, 2006. No. 363.

> *Next time you encounter an obstacle or a difficult task, try to catch*
> *your will in action to experience it consciously. As you struggle,*
> *recall that you are exercising the will and that the more it overcomes*
> *the stronger it becomes.*

In many contemporary psychological schools, the will is given little room. This may be partly because of the portrayal of it in many religions as stern, the source of repressions, neuroses, etc., but in Psychosynthesis[2] the will is of paramount importance.

I exercise my will whenever I say I would like to do this, but I had planned to do that, so I do that instead of this. When I exercise my will, even amidst difficulties and resistance, it is strengthened a little more. The next time I find myself in similar circumstances, the choice will be slightly easier. If, on the other hand, I choose to obey the feeling rather than what the intellect tells me, then the next time under similar circumstances the will finds it slightly harder and so on.

The strengths gained in repeated use of the will can be used in other aspects as well. In this sense, we can understand the value of fasting, for instance. Fasting does for the will what jogging does for the physical body. An athlete who runs every day finds it much easier to endure during the actual race, because the body is used to the discipline. Similarly, a person who exercises the will in some voluntary act, say of fasting or abstinence, is building a "spiritual muscle." When it comes to the need of this muscle in some other action that requires doing something that is contrary to his or her desire, the action will be a little easier.

The constant and proper exercise of our higher faculties brings to the surface of our Spiritual Self. "Proper" means living by the truth that we know.

THE SPIRITUAL SELF

Part of our self is spiritual. The spiritual self which we all have by virtue of being human is more or less developed from one individual to another. For that reason, while some may be very much aware of it, others may find it more difficult to be in touch with it. But because we

---

[2] For a general introduction to the psychological model of Psychosynthesis one can visit the website http://www.aap-psychosynthesis.org/psychosy.html .

all have it; we are able even to detect it in others who have developed it to a higher degree than ourselves. If you are one who enjoys literature, you might recall a novel or a movie with a particularly heroic character that moved you to tears, simply because you got in touch with the beautiful spiritual self in that character which echoed the potential within yourself. It may be that it evoked feelings of fidelity, of selfless love, of courage, of nobility. At that moment you glimpsed at the spiritual self of another that was 'more exposed'. But we can also sense it within ourselves. Prayer and meditation help us to get in touch with our spiritual self. According to Psychosynthesis we know of the spiritual self because of the urge towards altruistic love and hope. We know of the higher needs like love, respect of each other, self-actualization, intimacy, self-transcendence, etc. All these point to the spiritual self. We also know about the experiences of the mystics. Another form of evidence is the call from above, especially in the religious life. Many have experienced the fact that they fought and sought to resist this call, and in spite of everything found themselves choosing it. This spiritual self shows more clearly than the other aspects of our being, how we are created in the image and likeness of God.

I look up at your heavens, made by your fingers, at the moon and starts you set in place – ah, what is man that you should spare a thought for him, the son of man that you should care for him? Yet you have made him little less than a god, you have crowned him with glory and splendour, made him lord over the work of your hands, set all things under his feet. Psalm 8:4-6.

There are other ways of looking at our higher self. In the first place we realize that every human being is important. One of the things counselling should do for people is to help them regain their sense of importance, of dignity. Basically, every human being is important in as far as he or she is created in the image of God and is destined to an eternal life with God. Unfortunately, quite often people do not feel important about themselves as much as they should for several reasons. It may be because of having been wounded in the past, particularly in their childhood. It may be because others do not treat us as important and we let ourselves be led by their opinion of us. It may also be due to our own weaknesses that create in us a sense of guilt or of self-disdain, and erodes our esteem. Because we do not consider ourselves important, we can waste our existence. We can waste it by brooding over past hurts without doing anything about them, by focusing on small and insignificant issues while ignoring the more important ones. One with a healthy sense of self-importance knows too that life means much more than such things as money or power, which are a trap for so many. This importance we do not see only in ourselves but in every other human being, for they too are created in the same image of God.

The more a person's spiritual nature comes to the fore the more that person is able to radiate a kind of inner light. People who have lived with saintly people or met them often describe them as radiating an inner light. Different people who heard Jesus made such comments as that he spoke with power and authority; that no one has ever spoken like him; that their hearts were burning from hearing him speak. Spiritual people radiate inner light as it were. They touch the lives of those they meet, and this is done through love. The spiritual person brings peace and happiness in the

You are the light of the world. A city built on a hill-top cannot be hidden. No one lights a lamp to put it under a tub; they put it on the lamp stand where it shines for everyone in the house. In the same way your light must shine in the sight of men, so that, seeing your good works, they may give the praise to your Father in heaven. (Matthew 5:14-16).

lives of others. These in turn enkindle the lives of those they meet making them radiate also. It may even be argued that a spiritual person radiates physical beauty. Physical beauty is increased by virtue, and conversely vice mars physical beauty. It is reported that in apparition of Mary the mother of Jesus at Medjugorje, she was asked by one of the children who were privileged to see her, how come she was so beautiful. She smiled and answered that it was because she loved.

While on the one hand we need to strive to let our inner light shine, on the other hand this shining is not made through a willful act on our part. It is the spontaneous emanation from a saintly life. Those who radiate inner light may not even be aware of it; while those who strive to radiate with their own effort may not go very far if their life is not such as can radiate.

A spiritual person is capable of perceiving greatness in what others consider very ordinary things: in the delicacy of a flower, the simplicity of a child, in the sunset or sunrise, in the wonders of nature. Spiritual people are capable of wonder and worship.

To be spirit is to acknowledge that there are many things about reality which we do not know fully. Amid his pain and questioning of God's justice Job received as answer from God, not a rational explanation. Rather he was invited to look at mystery, at the many things he did not know about. In the end Job answered "I know that you are all-powerful: what you conceive, you can perform. I am the man who obscured your designs with my empty-headed words. I have been holding forth on matters I cannot understand, on marvels beyond me and my knowledge…" (Job 42:1-3).

…The wind blows wherever it pleases; you hear its sound, but you cannot tell where it comes from or where it is going. That is how it is with all who are born of the Spirit…" (John 3:8).

Unless a wheat grain falls on the ground and dies, it remains only a single grain; but if it dies, it yields a rich harvest. Anyone who loves his life loses it; anyone who hates his life in this world will keep it for the eternal life. (John 12:24-25). Anyone who does not take his cross and follow in my footsteps is not worthy of me. Anyone who finds his life will lose it; anyone who loses his life for my sake will find it. (Matthew 10:38-39).

Essential to bringing our spiritual nature to the forefront is acceptance of suffering. None of us likes to suffer. We know that there is something psychologically defective with people who seek suffering for its own sake. Everyone has the right and the obligation to alleviate suffering when this is in their power to do. And yet we also know that there is suffering that is constructive. There are so many sayings that express the wisdom entailed in suffering: "there is no gain without pain", "nothing ever comes free", "determination is the key to success", etc. Quite often it is clear that in trying to avoid legitimate suffering we actually suffer much more in the long run. If we want to grow, to be converted, to live the paschal mystery, to be integrated, to be Christian, to be human, the call is to suffering. There is a distinction between neurotic suffering and constructive suffering. The neurotic tries to avoid facing legitimate suffering, say by repressing painful emotions. Another neurotic does the opposite: he wallows in suffering as if it is good in itself, because he finds in it some perverted compensation. Suffering is part of the path to happiness but it is not good in itself. "Was it not ordained for the Son of Man to suffer and hence enter into glory?" (Luke 24:23).

A spiritual person is adventurous, is one capable of exploring, not only the environment, but understanding even the much harder task of exploring the self and the relationship with others. In this journey of adventure there comes a time when the person needs to surrender to God in trust rather than depend on personal resources. A spiritual person is one who can accept the richness of the possibilities even in the darkness and agony of the soul. Abraham is a good example: even when his situation seemed hopeless, for he was an old man without heir, he could still believe in the promises of God of a multitude of descendants (Genesis 12:1-2). The spiritual person believes in that potential in spite of the gloominess of the present situation. The spiritual person is one able to listen to the inner movements of the soul: to the voice of conscience, of memories, of duty, even listening to the voice of beauty of others that gives a sense of interconnectedness with the others and with the world.

It often happens that the darkest hours in our life are also moments of great potential for learning. Great personages attained their greatness precisely in the most painful circumstances. Consider Gandhi or Nelson Mandela. It does not feel that way at the time; only when we have the courage to go through trials with hope and perseverance do, we see how graced these moments were when we emerge from them.

Another characteristic of the spiritual nature brought to the surface is joy. Joy and happiness are part of the authentic life. Life is meant to be enjoyed. "Rejoice in the Lord always: and again, I say, Rejoice." (Philippians 4:4). Even in the midst of our troubles and difficulties we can find reason to be cheerful and to laugh. A spiritual person is one who can also laugh at personal mistakes. When we are able to laugh at our own follies, then we acknowledge ourselves as having limitations. It is okay to laugh even at our foolishness.

While the spiritual self comes closer to our core, still it constitutes only a part of the complex reality that is our being, for we are more than our core. This reality encompasses all that we have seen above, and even goes beyond, for we are more than the sum total of all that constitutes our being. We now look at that total.

THE EMBODIMENT

At this stage we return to the body with which we started. All the components that constitute our being are embodied; that is to say they function within our bodies. It is vital to appreciate the importance of our bodies. For the full realization of our potential everything that constitutes our being is important: our physical body and all its members, our sensations, conscious and unconscious, our feelings and emotions, as well as our higher faculties. Each element is important in as much as it affects all the other elements and we cannot ignore any without having to pay in some form or another.

That means in the first place that the care for our bodies is also the care for our entire self. We look after our bodies in so many ways: through procuring the necessary nourishment in the appropriate measures, giving the body the necessary physical exercise, dedication to work with the appropriate moments of rest and relaxation, having sufficient sleep, acquiring appropriate medical attention when we need it, paying attention to our feelings and making the proper responses to them, setting time aside to pray as well as to play. We also take care of ourselves by striving to be true to our values and convictions.

THE SELF

Does all this bring us any closer to answering the simple question "who are you?" Yes, you know you have a name, a nationality, and perhaps a profession or a vocation or both. You have a body with its complex of functions; you have sensations and emotions; you have a character with interests and dislikes; you have ineptitudes as well as talents and skills, virtues and flaws. But who are you that have all this? There is the 'you' that remains through the passing of the years of your life. You were you when you were one day old without many of the things mentioned above that you now have. Not a single cell of the body you had then still exists in you today, since according to science the cells of our body are constantly dying and getting renewed, and in about seven years we have a complete turnover of cells. It is true that you have changed, but the very fact that we can talk of you changing means that there is 'a you' that has changed; otherwise, there would be more than one person.

It is almost impossible for the self to disembody itself from all its modes of identification. The different identifications are like clothes for the Self, and it is never naked. That may give the impression that it is therefore not there, an abstraction, the sum total of your sensations, thoughts, feelings, emotions, at any one time. But this is not true.

The fact that the Self may give the impression of being unreal may be demonstrated by the parable of the ten fools. Ten fools once crossed a river. On the opposite bank one of them suggested to check and see whether they were all there, and none had drowned. He counted his friends and found that they were nine. He was worried and the others asked him why. He explained that he thought one of them had drowned. Each of them counted his friends and each time they were nine. None of them could tell who had been drowned, and yet it was a fact that they were ten when they started crossing the river, and now each could only count nine. At last, a passer-by met them and they explained their predicament. He understood their problem and told them that each time he points to one the one pointed at mentions a number in their chronological order. They did that until they could count ten. Then they were happy.

Similarly, the self is part of you so much so that it becomes very difficult for you to contemplate it independent of its different manifestations. This does not mean that it is not there. It is you!

Faith teaches that this "you" that persists through changes of physical growth, that is constantly modified by the circumstances you go through as well as the choices you make, in fact also persists through the ultimate physical disintegration which is death. It is *immortal*, and this is one other quality by which you are made in the image of God who is *eternal*. In other words, unlike God we have a beginning but like him we have no end.

THE BEAUTY OF THE SELF

Tests of people's self-esteem reveal that it is rare to have an accurate estimation of our self-worth. Sometimes people may have an exaggerated self-image, but the usual tendency is to have a low self-image. We tend to emphasize the negative aspects of ourselves; our failures may loom larger than they actually are. We are weighed down by guilt, whether real or exaggerated; whatever its cause may be. We can also have a combination of both: we can think we are greater than we are in certain areas and think we are less than what we actually are in other areas. Growth consists in forming a more and more accurate concept of our selves.

It was you who created my inmost self, and put me together in my mother's womb; for all these mysteries I thank you: for the wonder of myself, for the wonder of your works. (Psalm 139: 13-14).

It is important for us to recognize our self-worth. Even apart from all that we do, we are something beautiful simply because we are creatures of God, and not just any creatures of God, but human beings made in his own image, redeemed in the blood of his Son, and destined for eternal life. In Genesis it is said that at every stage of his creation God looked at what he had made and saw that it was good, but when he had made the man and the woman, he looked at what he had made and said it was *very* good. It is important for us to see what God saw, or sees.

Even when we are tarnished by what we have done in the past with our lives, the realization of that which we were in the beginning and that which we can become when we want to, is itself the beginning of healing. One of the things counselors do while helping those who are depressed is to help them realize their own self-worth and the capabilities they have.

Today there are all sorts of tests to check the level of one's self esteem. Such tests are also available on the Internet. In a counselling course students may be asked to answer a questionnaire for testing each one's self-image. The results are then communicated by each one's growth facilitator and processed for each one's growth in a one-to-one forum. Below is set of questions to help us appreciate more the good in us.

Activity 2: Recognize the Beauty that you are

Recall a task that you did well lately
What skill have you finally mastered?
Recall a weakness that you have overcome

29

What would your enemies respect you for?
Write one quality that you like about yourself
Recall when you pleasantly surprised yourself
What bodily features do others admire in you?
When you are at your best what do you usually do?
Think of the most positive thing ever said about you
What particular quality do your friends admire in you?
What bodily features of you do you admire of yourself?
Recall an incident when you pleasantly surprised people
What particular fault could people not convict you about?
What is it that others find difficult but you do fairly easily?
If you were asked to count your blessings, what would you say?
If you were to say something good about self, what would you say?

2

INTER-PERSONAL REFLECTION OF GOD'S IMAGE

Having considered the constitution of the human being as a beautiful creation in God's image we now turn attention to a person's relation to other human beings. From the very moment of conception in the womb we are made to be dependent, at this stage on the mother who supplies all that we need for our growth and nutrition. Other animals are less dependent on their mothers than human beings. Mother hen lays her eggs and incubates them for a number of weeks, (three, I think). But she permits herself moments of respite to look for something to eat. Her developing young one can go on living in the shell even in the absence of the mother. The human embryo on the other hand depends on the mother for every breath until it is "hatched". Even after that it is more dependent than many other infant creatures. One who has lived on a farm knows the amazing experience of watching a calf or goat-kid stagger to its feet a few moments after its birth, and soon after that look for the udder of the mother animal. The little one of the human being requires months to get on to its feet and cannot get to the nipple of the mother unaided.

Our dependence extends far beyond the biological needs and becomes more and more sophisticated as we grow older. The child's growth into a full normal human being depends primarily on the mother or mother-figure, but as well as that on the immediate family. If this baby is accepted in a warm, welcoming, loving, caring network of relationships - father, mother, grandparents, sisters, brothers, uncles and aunties - the child has the potential to be a happy, healthy and lovable person that is capable of loving. Also, in our adult life we find happiness and fulfillment in relation to other human beings. One has only to consider the modern world: the things that we consider essential to our lives bring us into contact with so many other people. The food we eat is grown by so many different people, sold by others, cooked by others. The clothes we wear were made in different factories. The raw materials were processed by others and so on. There is no end to the list of dependence. It includes culture, religion, social status… Just stop reading for a moment and look around you. Notice each and every human-made object and consider how many people were involved to bring it to the stage it is now: the clothes you are wearing, the shoes, the watch, the chair, the book you are reading… even the thoughts you are thinking and the language you speak.

Because we are essentially relational, valuing, cherishing, and promoting every human relation is closely connected to our own happiness and wellbeing. One way of looking at God's commandments is to consider them as basic requirements for our true and lasting happiness. Loving others as ourselves is a commandment, but it is also the key to our own happiness. Self-centeredness may seem to be the quickest way to personal fulfillment, but we discover the disillusion sooner or later. We saw in the last section that we can uplift our self-image by focusing on the positive in us. Similarly, we can uplift others by focusing on the good in them and by making them aware in different ways of this goodness. One way of doing that is through positive well-meant complements or affirmation. In Transactional Analysis this is called giving each other positive strokes.

One day during a lecture on Transaction Analysis we were asked to sit in groups of fours. After a brief reflection one would start, looking in the eyes of any of the other three who would in turn look back. The giver of the stroke would begin with "I like you because…" and mention a quality which he or she liked in the recipient. Everyone was required to try and think hard in order to give strokes which were actually meant. Then the recipient would reflect for a moment on the stroke received, symbolically swallow it by swallowing saliva, and then say "thank you." Each. Each of the four members of the group was to receive strokes three strokes, one from each of the three participants. Later on, during the evaluation, the facilitator asked all the participants to write down the strokes they had received. Some of the strokes had been forgotten. This was an involuntary indication of the stroke filters that we all have. We take in only some of the complements given to us by others.

How do we reflect God's image in our fundamentally relational nature? We are called to live in relation to each other just as there is relationship in the Holy Trinity. God speaks to people through other people. In this way we reach our destiny through the manner in which we relate to others. Each one of us can become a means for another to get acquainted with God.

Jesus replied, 'This is the first: Listen, Israel, the Lord our God is the one Lord, and you must love the Lord your God with all your heart, with all your soul, with all your mind and with all your strength. The second is this: You must love your neighbor as yourself. There is no commandment greater than these.' (Mark 12: 29-31)

Our inter-dependence, rather than being a defect, is on the contrary, a gift. By it we can exercise that greatest of God's gifts which at the same time makes us most conformed to his image: we can give and receive love, thus complementing and completing each other. Our uniqueness means that there is something that we alone can give; while our limitations mean that we can receive from others that which is lacking in us.

MALE AND FEMALE, HE CREATED THEM

Among the different relationships of interdependence between human beings, one deserves special treatment because it was made special right from the time of God's creation, and it continues to be so. It is the relation between male and female. Within this relationship God put the mechanism by which the human race, indeed every living creature, is propagated. There is a mutual complementarily between the genders that finds its fulfillment in marriage. But in order to reach that, it too, like all other truly human acts, must be guided not only by feelings and sentiments, but also by the higher faculties of intellect and will. In every successful marriage there must be such human qualities of fidelity, of endurance, of tolerance, of understanding and selfless love.

That marriage relationship usually begins, although not always, with mutual attraction followed by 'falling in love'. It is true that not all successful marriages begin with falling in love. We know of many cultures in which marriage was considered something too serious to be left to the sentiments of young people; cultures in which marriage was always arranged by the elders. It is equally true that not all incidents of falling in love are the beginning of a marriage relationship, or even an ordinary intimate relationship. People fall in love when they are not yet ready for marriage. They fall in love when they are already married, or committed in some other way. They fall in love with the most unsuited people: culturally, socially, or from the point of view of a difference in belief. In many cases of falling in love the wisest course of action is to postpone or even exclude the possibility of marriage. Yet this reality, beautiful as it is, is the cause of much turmoil in the lives of many that it is worthwhile to give it a little more space.

At a certain stage of the counselling course, I mentioned at the beginning, we were asked each to write our own love story. We were not required to share this in public or even with the growth facilitator, unless one chose to. But it was sufficiently made clear that it is ok even for celibates to fall in love. It is something that happens to all those who are normal. It is what we do with our feelings that determines their morality. If a celibate has never fallen in love, it is not by particular merit of theirs that they have not. Below is part of the story I wrote.

> Rose never even got to know that I loved her! Unless of course, she got to intuit it as womankind is known to do more often than her counterpart. I was about nineteen and in the fourth year of college in a boys' boarding school when I first saw her. She was starting college herself in a neighboring day Girls' School. She could have been sixteen or so.
>
> Rose was a relative of our headmaster, and that meant she was classified material to any of the students who cared for his stay in the college. We had a nickname for the headmaster, as we also had for any other of the staff members. The headmaster was called Puncher. I do not know which generation of students nicknamed him Puncher, nor do I know for what reason. This was simply one of the traditions of the place which was passed on from year to year. The road that led to Puncher's home was just above the window of my cubicle.
>
> One fine evening two girls passed by, evidently coming from school. I think one of my comrades drew my attention with an exclamation of amazement at the beauty of one of the girls passing by and I craned my neck like the rest. *And I saw her…!* I fell in love with a thud, or so I imagined. Immediately, I felt offended by those who whistled at her. "Bad manners" I condemned, self-righteously. "Why should they whistle to decent girls passing by?" I asked within myself. But she seemed to enjoy the admiration she was provoking from the boys, for she looked in our direction with a smile, unable to make out who was trying to draw her attention from the dark curtained windows. So, she passed by…

Another encounter was when I had been sent – I do not remember by whom or for what – to the headmaster's house. As I came into the compound, *I saw her again...!* There she was, totally absorbed in her work. She was bent over some laundry, singing a Christmas carol that I have never been able to forget. She sensed my presence, or maybe I coughed to attract her attention; and then she turned and stopped singing. I stated my errand while my head reeled with confusion.

On yet another occasion I had been taking photographs of students near the cassava-like shrub between the dining hall and the chemistry lab. Photography was one of the few envied privileges as well as compensations for being an altar server, or "cassock," as we were nicknamed. And actually, it was not any "cassock" that was privileged to take photographs. You had to be a veteran "cassock", and I had been raised to those ranks after four years of faithful service. And so, having carried out the envied duty I was marching ceremoniously towards the chaplain's home where the photographs were printed and where the camera was kept, wearing the Japanese Olympus around my neck, like any other professional photographer, when I met the nymph. She looked even more beautiful than before. She smiled the angelic smile, the one which melts boys, this time all for me and not to anonymous boys behind dark windows; and asked me totally irrelevantly: whether I snapped photographs. Even I in my state of reverie could sober up enough to notice that she was pretending not to have seen me take the photographs, for she *had* seen me. I saw her see me. It was her way of starting a conversation. I now think though, that her interest was entirely in having her photograph taken, as teenagers are prone to, and not in the photographer. But if anyone had voiced that alternative perspective during those days, he would have risked decapitation. I do recall that as she talked to me and at the same time she wanted to rejoin her friends who had not stopped but walked on, she kept walking backwards, while facing me and I was fascinated to see her so. One corner of my mind registered that even I in my hopelessness had a bait, and that was the camera.

The only problem with my bait was that Father Chaplain did all the printing of the photographs I took, and would definitely ask who the girl was. But I was too much in love to let the chance pass by, so I promised I would take her photographs when I got the chance. Anything to give me a chance to talk to her again! I went on my way with my heart singing as if she had promised to marry me the next day.

From that day onwards Rose was to occupy my mind for much of the time for an entire year ahead, even though the amount of time I saw her during that period hardly adds up to an hour! On that lucky day I was too dumbfounded to fix a day and time to take Rose's pictures. So, after a few sleepless nights I sauntered to Puncher's home like a food-thief in the neighbor's garden on a rainy day. I had gone to Puncher's home only once or twice. No one among us students ever went there for a friendly chart. It was when someone had to answer for some crime committed, that he went into that concentration camp as we perceived it. But this time the penitentiary had been transformed into Eden because Eve had taken aboard in it.

So I hazarded to go to Puncher's home, hoping that I would meet my heart's desire, bent over a basin of washing, singing the familiar Christmas carol. No! Nature is not that kind. This was a different setting. I heard a lot of laughter of women and girls, and I wasn't quite prepared for this. Through much embarrassment and more stammering, I asked her when she wanted to have her photos taken and we agreed on a day…

The long and short of it is that I never got to take her photographs. Nor did I ever make Rose to understand what I felt for her. It was about this time that I had to leave the college, having completed the final year. All I could do was consume myself with love at a distance. When I visited the chaplain again several months later, Rose was gone, and I could not dare ask anyone where. I was a seminarian, and I believed that seminarians never inquired about girls. I never heard of her again.

It is a marvel that about this time in spite of her I could decide to join the seminary. Was it the "pull from above"? The whole first year in the seminary I recalled her constantly. In my first retreat I confessed my love for her, but I was greatly surprised by the priest who said that he saw nothing wrong in what I had said. It was not wrong to fall in love; all depended on what we did afterwards, and I had done nothing wrong.

As I wrote my love story and as I continued attending the lectures on human love and sexuality, I gained a few insights in the matter.

In the first place falling in love is a wonderful experience. It is part of God's plan who created both male and female in his own image, as mutual gifts to each other, and who saw that it was very good. For some it can be a very painful experience as it was in my case, when it has no normal fulfillment. But whatever God allows is for a good purpose. Even in this case I can look back and say that the timing of the experience if anything helped me to realize the price of what I was deciding to give up in order to serve God as a priest.

> *"Yahweh God said, 'It is not good that the man should be alone. I will make him a helpmate.' …So, Yahweh God made the man fall into a deep sleep. And while he slept, he took one of his ribs and enclosed it in flesh. Yahweh God built the rib he had taken from the man into a woman, and brought her to the man…" (Genesis 2: 19-23).*

Secondly, I learnt that falling in love is not love. It is often the beginning of a loving relationship, and it feels very much like love. But love as a virtue, as the greatest virtue, is something conscious, something we choose to do. Love involves knowledge of the beloved. It involves conscious choices that promote our good as well as the good of the people we love. It may or may not be accompanied with loving sentiments. In my case I never got to know Rose apart from seeing her on the few occasions and exchanging a few shy words. It is quite possible that if I had got to know her better, if she had reciprocated that love, and if we had the opportunity, it might have been very difficult for me to make the loving choice, namely of letting her continue with her studies and I with my own, for we were both still very young and I had made the decision to join the seminary and become a priest.

This is not to say that love, even between people who are in some way committed and who cannot marry, is something that must be reduced to

> *"…Ah, why are you not my brother, nursed at my mother's breast! Then if I met you out of doors, I could kiss you without people thinking ill of me. I should lead you; I should take you into my mother's house, and you would teach me! (Song of Songs 8:1-2).*

heroic choices and self-sacrifice. It too can be enjoyed within its own limits. The most unsuited couples fall in love under circumstances in which marriage is socially, economically and morally impossible. A person who has been married for some time discovers for the first time what it means to fall in love; only sadly it is not with the partner but with someone outside the marriage bond, possibly someone who is also tied up with another in an unsatisfactory union. Love may also occur where one or both the partners have consecrated themselves to a celibate life. Instead of being a cause of great joy the phenomenon of falling in love can be a cause of great anguish and suffering. And yet everything that comes from the hands of God is good. Even in this case the two people are called to see in the encounter a challenge for growth, self-realization and self-transcendence.

In practical terms they are faced with about four choices each of which has its own consequences, good or bad. On one extreme they may ignore each other and live as if the other does not exist or does not mean anything to them. That can bring a lot of stress for both. The emotions that are denied and repressed may eventually come out in some unhealthy manner. On the other extreme they may give free reign and go where their heart leads them; forget about what everyone will feel, think and say and get into a new union. In this case they compromise what they believe in, and they hurt so many others in the process. They carry with them the sense of guilt before God and before society. Others may want to take a middle course by compromising and cheating; entering into an illicit and clandestine relationship while outside they give the impression of being loyal to their commitments. They too will experience an illusory happiness which sooner or later will yield bitter consequences. There is a fourth alternative of remaining steadfast to their commitment, drawing out of this new relationship whatever joy and consolation is permissible and honorable, and accepting the pain of staying away from a total union; which pain like all unsolicited but graciously accepted pain, leads to growth and purification.

The wisdom of recognizing misplaced intimacy for what it is is comparable to transplanting in time, a tree seedling that has germinated between the tiles of a roof. It is folly to feel sympathy for the sapling and say: oh, but it is doing so well! If left to grow it will widen the crack and destroy the roof, as well as destroy itself for lack of enough space.

Love and friendship bring joy to our lives. Without them life becomes dull and metallic. It is important to realize that sexuality is much more than genital activity. Intimacy with a friend means that I can laugh or cry, show what I feel without being embarrassed. I can be a fool without being rejected. Love and intimacy which are basic human needs can be expressed in many other ways apart from physical union.

I once found pinned up in someone's shop a paper with the title "101 ways 2 make Luv without doing it." There was no indication of the author. I was intrigued by the list. I took the liberty to select 11 out of these 101 ways which I thought particularly cute. I also took the further liberty of re-arranging them in the order of length.

Play a game
Just be there

Created in the image and likeness of God

Give compliments
Respect each other
Carry out a task together
Give each other pet names
Make sacrifices for each other
Enjoy together the things that you both like
Make a list of things u like about each other
Do things for each other without being asked
Find out what's special for the other person and do it

3

TRANSPERSONAL RELATION WITH GOD AND THE UNIVERSE

Relation with the Universe 40
God's Image of Me 41
My Image of God 42
Relation to God and the World 47

"Trans-personal relationship" simply means 'the relationship beyond the person', beyond fellow human beings. In the first place it is the relationship between us and God. Secondly it is the relationship between us and the rest of the universe. We examine the latter first.

RELATION WITH THE UNIVERSE

From a physical point of view, we are made of the same stuff as the rest of the universe and are part of a continuous recycling of the material of the universe. Our bodies could be broken down to the basic elements of the universe. We grow and are sustained in life through absorbing material from the environment: food, air, warmth. We constantly give off other material that sustains other organisms. When we die our bodies decompose and are taken in by other organisms, both animals and plants, which in turn eventually are imbibed by other human beings for their sustenance.

Blessed be God the Father of our Lord Jesus Christ, who has blessed us with all the spiritual blessings of heaven in Christ. Before the world was made, he chose us, chose us in Christ, to be holy and spotless, and to live through love in his presence... He has let us know the mystery of his purpose, the hidden plan he so kindly made in Christ from the beginning to act upon when the times had run their course to the end: that he would bring everything together under Christ, as head, everything in the heavens and everything on earth. (Ephesians 1:3-4; 9-10).

"I am an individual, who is made uniquely individual precisely to be an essential ingredient of a whole: a whole family, a whole nation, a whole world, a whole cosmos: all inextricably related by the very fact of their uniqueness."[3]

GOD'S IMAGE OF ME

What does God think of me? If we imagine that the great book of Revelation were brought out today and the chapter that regards me was read, what would God say of me? Suppose there were three topics in that chapter: one regarding God's original plan of what he had intended my life to be, another regarding what my life has turned out so far to be and a third regarding what I can still do to come close to God's original plan, what would be the content of these topics? Certainly, if the thoughts of God about me were put in human words in the smallest detail, each of these three topics would be far bigger than a complete set of encyclopedias. We believe that God has a very clear picture of our past, our present and our future.

Even if we can only speculate about what God has in his divine mind regarding each one of us individually, from scripture we have a fair picture of what he thought of his people throughout the ages and what he thinks of us in general. "When I see the stars the work of your hands, what is man that you should care for him; mortal man who is merely a breath. Yet you have made him little less than a god…" (Psalm 8:4-6); "I shall not call you servants any more…I call you friends..." (John 15:15); "Does a woman forget her baby at the breast, or fail to cherish the son of her womb? Yet even if these forget, I will never forget you. (Isaiah 49:15); "…God loved the world so much, that he gave his only Son, so that everyone who believes in him may not be lost but may have eternal life" (John 3:16); "a man can have no greater love than to lay down his life for his friends…" (John 15:13); "Before I formed you in the womb I knew you…(Jeremiah 1:5)" "What man among you with a hundred sheep, losing one, would not leave the ninety-nine in the wilderness and go after the missing one till he found it?…" (Luke 15:4); "…every hair on your head has been counted. So there is no need to be afraid; you are worth more than hundreds of sparrows…" (Luke 12:7).

---

[3] Austin McCormack, Lectures at the Institute of St. Anselm, Cliftonville, England, 2003.

How God sees us: his love, his trust, the potential he has placed and sees in us, his plans for our lasting happiness with him; all this is succinctly captured in a song the name of whose composer I could not find:[4]

> The Love I have for you, my Lord,
> Is only a shadow of your love for me,
> Only a shadow of your love for me,
> Your deep abiding love
>
> My own belief in you, my Lord,
> Is only a shadow of your faith in me,
> Only a shadow of your faith in me,
> Your deep and lasting faith.
>
> The dreams I have today, my Lord,
> Are only a shadow of your dreams for me,
> Only a shadow of your dreams for me,
> If I but follow you.
>
> The joy I feel today, my Lord,
> Is only a shadow of your joy for me,
> Only a shadow of your joy for me,
> When we meet face to face.

MY IMAGE OF GOD

If God used the words he once used through his Son and asked: who do people say I am? We could give whole lectures on the topic: Some say you are Allah; some say you are Three in One, others say you do not exist; just a fabrication of the mind, a consolation for the simple, opium for the poor. Some say you are merciful and powerful; others wonder why so many people suffer innocently and you look on in spite of the prayers of those who believe in you. Some address you as a man, others as a woman, and others as both. Some live in fear of your judgment, some ignore you as irrelevant to their life. Some give their lives for love of you...

---

[4] Joseph Bragotti and others, eds., *We Pray and Sing to the Lord*, Nairobi, Paulines Publication Africa, 1991, p. 435.

And if he turned to us and asked, 'but you, who do you say I am?' Here each one would have to answer for self. For many of us it would not be an easy question. We might rush out with a quick answer from what we have learnt about God from our religion lessons, our catechism or our study of theology, but we would find ourselves answering the first question: "who do people say I am," and still left with the question, "but you, who do you say I am?"

A person who has heard about Australia has a picture in mind of that country. One whose geographical knowledge is rudimentary might confuse Australia with Austria because of the similarity of the names. But the person with more advanced geographical knowledge knows that there is a vast difference between the two countries: the distance between them on the globe, the difference in size, language, landscape, etc. are enormous. One who has read captivating novels, or seen movies set in Australia has yet another picture of the same country. A citizen of the country has yet another. Moreover, there are differences in the picture each citizen has, depending on where in Australia they lived, whether they lived in luxurious or squalid conditions, whether they were happy or sad, and so on. The analogue is intended to demonstrate the difference in the subjective perception of the objective reality that is God. Consider these two representations of God in the bible:

"…Then Yahweh said, 'How great an outcry there is against Sodom and Gomorrah! I propose to go down and see whether or not they have done all that is alleged in the outcry against them that has come up to me. I am determined to know" (Genesis 18:20). The second is this: "Yahweh, you examine me and know me, you know if I am standing or sitting, you read my thoughts from far away, whether I walk or lie down, you are watching, you know every detail of my conduct. The word is not even on my tongue, Yahweh, before you know all about it…" (Psalm 139:1-4).

This is one illustration of how even in scripture there is a variety of God representation. In one we see a God who has heard about what is going on in Sodom, and proposes to go down and *find out*. In other words, he is not sure whether what is alleged is true or not. He is determined to know, so he does not know already. In the second account we hear of a God who knows everything even before it happens. In the same way each of us has a different image of God formed under the influence of several factors.

Our God Representation is simply how we individually perceive God to be. When we talk about God, we all conjure a picture in us about God.

The picture we have of God is largely influenced by our own background and the significant people in our life journey, particularly our parents. We form our understanding of God through different experiences we acquire in the course of our history and which we link with the name of God. Perhaps more than anyone else the mother has the greatest role to play in the early formulation of the God image of the child. The mother-child relationship begins already as the child is still in the womb. It is argued, for instance, that a mother who has attempted abortion may transmit to the child the feeling that it is not wanted. And that even without attempting abortion, the fact of an unwanted pregnancy may be transmitted to the child already while it is still in the womb. This will affect its God image. The birth process is a key moment in the life of the child. Even in a normal birth it must be a frightening moment for the child who leaves the warm and familiar surroundings of the womb to face the rough world. But when the birth process for some reason is irregular, this could be traumatic for the child, and have lasting effects for its later life, affecting its God image as well. The kind of welcome the child receives in the family affects its God image later; whether this welcome is of love and warmth, or whether it is one of rejection. People who have had a stern father are more likely to form an image of God that is stern and judgmental, whereas those who have had a tender loving father may see God in the same light. For the little child the parents are God, for on them it depends entirely. They will largely determine whether the child sees God as joyful, affectionate, critical, compassionate, dominant, understanding, etc., depending on how they were treated as children.

On the one hand there is the objective reality of God: what God is in himself regardless of what we think of him. No human being knows the objective reality of God, for our little being is not capable of containing the infinite which is God. St. Augustine's image illustrates this very well: you cannot hope to contain the whole of the ocean in a little hole dug with your finger. What is taught in theology or philosophy about God aims at this objective reality of God; namely, what God is in himself regardless of what we think of him. But every human discipline simply cannot exhaust that infinite reality which is God.

Then there is the subjective reality of God: God as we understand him to be. This includes what our parents and teachers taught us God is; the important people that influenced our lives right from earliest childhood: our parents and close relatives, what we learnt of God through catechism and later training and the convictions we formed as a result of this learning, the experiences we went through in our lives and how we related to God through these experiences; how God answered our prayers or did not answer them in the way we expected and how this affected our attitude towards him, etc. My subjective God-representation can be positive or negative, healthy or defective. Whereas the objective reality of God does not change, our subjective understanding of him changes constantly; through our experiences, through theological and spiritual training, etc.

Activity 3: My God-Representation
What is the first thing you think of when you mention 'God'?
Describe in detail what is God for you. Has your understanding of God changed over time?
Is there a link between how you understand God to be and the influence of the significant persons in your life: Father, Mother, Uncle, Grandmother, etc?
What do you consider to be the ways of updating your God-representation?

Even if we said earlier on that we cannot have an objective understanding of God, for he is much greater than our capacity to contain him, yet the little we can perceive of him can be more or less objective. This is understandable if we remember that we are created in his image and likeness. Our goal and our spiritual growth consist in making our subjective understanding of God as close to the objective reality as possible; to dismantle the false concepts we have of him and to replace them with the truth that he is. Because the God representation of our childhood is often incomplete, if not downright defective, we need to update it, and we are capable of updating it. People who had a vague and narrow idea about the universe might change their idea about God as well when they discover that the universe is millions of light years in expanse, (a 'Light-year' is the distance that light – which is the fastest thing known – travels in a year at a constant speed of 186,000 miles every second), billions of years old, with hundreds of millions of Galaxies. The immensity of the universe points to the greater immensity of its creator.

In our effort to up-date our understanding of God, God is not an indifferent onlooker. In the question-and-answer simple catechism there is a question "why did God create you?" and the answer "God created me to know him, to love him, to serve him on earth and to live with him in happiness forever". In other words, he created us, out of love, for our own happiness, and is concerned that we should attain to that happiness, through knowing him, a knowledge that generates love of him for he is love irresistible. He intended that through obeying his commandments – which in fact are nothing but the proper path to happiness chosen against other paths that, in the light of our limited vision, seemingly lead to happiness but in actual fact do not – we might attain that everlasting bliss. He knows our limited capacity to know him, and that is all right. What is important in our present state is that we know him sufficiently to keep on the track towards our destiny.

A niece and nephew of mine once had a conversation. Peninnah was six years and Michael was three and a half. She was telling him about the imminent expansion of their family.

"We are soon becoming eight in our family. We have three cows and we are three children. But now the cow is pregnant and mummy too is pregnant. The cow will soon produce and mummy will also produce a baby. Then we shall be eight".

"Yes" replied the little brother, a little mystified by the complex arithmetic. But he had caught a point of interest, so he went on, "but aren't babies bought from the shop?"

"No! Babies are produced by mummy. Don't you see her big tummy? There is a baby inside, and she will soon produce it in the same way as a cow does." Evidently, she had once seen a cow produce a calf.

The dialogue was continuing but then mummy put an end to it by sending the sister to an errand. I do not know whether they picked up afterwards from where they had stopped. But this childish conversation can serve to illustrate our knowledge of God. Michael knew rightly who his mother and father were. But he had not yet known what that really meant. He had no idea that a few years before he had been in his mother's womb. He did not know how much pain, anxiety and love he had cost his mother. He did not know what role his father played in his coming to life, or what he was doing at that time for Michael's growth into a full human being. Probably for him the reason for going to kindergarten was in order to meet other playmates. But it was perfectly all right for Michael to have such limited knowledge about his parents at that stage. All he needed was to know his parents with that knowledge of a child, to love them in the usual selfish way of a child, to obey them in their plans for his well-being, some of which he did not fully comprehend, and so to grow into a happy human being. That is the same way God acts with us.

He created us to know him, but he does not demand a knowledge of him that exceeds our capabilities.

Intellectual knowledge of God has its place in our up-dating of the God-image. But this must go hand-in hand with other ways. We get to know God better through prayer and meditation as well as through the effort to live according to the truth we know already which leads to discovery of more Truth, who is God, and which in turn sets us free. "If you continue in my word, then you are my disciples indeed; and you shall know the truth, and the truth shall make you free." (John 8: 31-32); "O taste and see that the Lord is good: blessed is the man that trusts in him." (Psalm 34:8).

RELATION TO GOD AND THE WORLD

We have seen how each one of us is related to God in whose image we are created, to other human beings in an intricate pattern of interdependence and to the rest of the universe with which we share the same matter in a continuous process of 'recycling'. It follows, therefore, that our happiness and fulfillment are very much connected with the manner in which we relate to all that lies outside of us. This dynamic and life-giving way of relating can best be described as love. But it is love that must be exercised in right proportion. The love for plant life for instance means that I appreciate the fact of the inter-dependence. They give me oxygen and absorb carbon-dioxide. They transpire water vapor which eventually turns into rain. They give me food, medicine, furniture, etc., looking after them well is kindness to myself, to my neighbor and to future generations. The love of human beings is based on the acknowledgement that they are just like me. The desire for happiness, the potential I have, the fear of pain in me, the weaknesses I experience; all these are experienced by the others as well. The love of God is based on the realization that he contains all the goodness which no single creature can ever supply.

Often in the variety of choices we must make there comes conflicts. It becomes important then for me to know the hierarchy of values; not to exchange a lesser value for a higher one. It would be tragic to exchange the love of God for the love of a human being *if the two loves happened to conflict*. It would be equally folly to exchange the love of a human being for the love of a pet, *when the two loves happened to conflict*. The proper balance of our love, guided by our reason and will, our learnt values, our faith, ensures the joy and happiness God intended us to experience in this world of relationships.

Part II

THE TARNISHED IMAGE OF GOD IN ME

If Part I of this work deals with the ideal, Part II, which we now begin, deals with the reality. Whereas it is true that I am created in the image and likeness of God, it is equally true that this image has been tarnished through the common condition of human weakness (or from a theological point of view: original sin), the negative forces that have influenced my development from the earliest moment of my existence to the present moment, as well as my own weaknesses and sins. Each time we compromise on essentials or important values, we lose something of ourselves.

There are many areas one can think of that require 'repair': Relationships damaged where communication no longer takes place, blaming others and failure to take responsibility, loss of spontaneity, acquired false beliefs and scripts, the Destructive Critic, prejudice (e.g. against other people, races, countries, classes, against ourselves, against other Churches and institutions), inferiority or superiority complex, loss of reputation, low self-esteem, vengeance, repressed emotions, sexual mal-adaptation; these are but a few of the possible manifestations of our being tarnished.

Activity 4: Areas for personal growth

List for yourself things about your personality that you would want to change.

Part II examines the different ways in which the beautiful image of God which is our being is tarnished. The tendency is to ask oneself what the solution is, once we have discovered the problem. However, if part II could be compared to a diagnosis, the prescription and cure are relegated to III to V, even though here and there a solution may be suggested in Part II as well.

4

THE FUNDAMENTAL IMPORTANCE OF CHILDHOOD

In dealing with the reality of our life we might as well begin from the beginning of our life after birth, not simply for the sake of order, but above all because it is here that the foundations of what we are to become later are laid, for better or for worse.

There are three major determinants of the main features of our personality. Some features are genetic; they are inherited from our parents or passed on to us through them. Other features are learned, mainly during our early childhood. A third category consists of the habits we develop through our conscious choices guided by our intellect and will. The constant making of similar choices hardens individual actions into the formation of attitudes, into developing of habits, and into personality traits. We are somewhat like the atmospheric environment. Meteorologists compute the daily weather conditions of a place for over 30 years in order to determine the climate of that place. But even after 30 years climates do change.

It the second category that is the subject of our concern in this chapter: how to outgrow those ways of thinking, acting and reacting that we learnt in childhood and that are no longer helpful in the adult environment. Below are the areas considered in this chapter.

Laying the Foundations of Personality in Childhood..........................*51*
Effects of Childhood Experiences on Adult Life..............................*53*
   Wounds of Childhood according to Transaction Analysis 53
   Theory of the 'Inner Child'..59
What to Do about The Effects of Childhood..................................*61*

LAYING THE FOUNDATIONS OF PERSONALITY IN CHILDHOOD

When a tree is for some reason bent at the time when it is a seedling, it is likely to take that shape as it grows to its full size. One may reshape it at an early age by tying it to a straight metal or to a pole. If this is not done at an early stage, later it will not be possible. You might simply break it in trying to give it the shape you want. What happens to a plant physically also occurs to human beings on the psychological level.

Anyone who welcomes a little child like this in my name welcomes me. But anyone who is an obstacle to bring down one of these little ones who have faith in me would be better drowned in the depths of the sea with a great millstone round his neck. (Matthew 18: 5-6)

Practically all psychologists are agreed that what happens to us in our early childhood is fundamental in forming the life we are to lead afterwards. A child who is constantly ridiculed or shamed may grow up into a shy adult with a sense of guilt. A child born of very critical parents may also learn to be critical or to condemn others. Parents who are tolerant and encouraging may raise a patient and confident person. The approval we receive as children may teach us to appreciate and like ourselves. Our very capacity to love may be a consequence of the acceptance we received from those nearest to us while we were children. People who find it difficult to trust anyone may have been let down by their own parents or parents figures, and so on.

How a child takes in the information in its immediate world is clearly visible in its capacity to learn a new language. An adult who has tried a foreign language knows how laborious the exercise is. In spite of all modern aids and in spite of much effort the majority of those who learn other languages as adults never come to speak them perfectly. On the other hand, a normal child learns perfectly whatever language it is born into, no matter how difficult that language may be. This it does without ever sitting down to the drills of a grammar lesson. People that have lived in a foreign land for some years might be amazed to see the child born 'yesterday' speaking the language much more perfectly than themselves, and laughing at their mistakes. In the same way as a mother tongue imprints itself on the mind of the child so do all the 'mother threats', 'mother habits' and 'mother commands'. At the link www.aboutpsychology.com: under the heading *"What is a Personality? What Makes Me, Me?"* I found a beautiful description of how our attitudes and behavior patterns are formed from what happened to us in early childhood.

Imagine a one-year-old child reaching out for something that grabs his interest, as is the habit of a child that age. But his mother (or whoever is raising him) is anxious. Maybe she always is, maybe it's because this is her third child in as many years and she's getting fed up and stressed, maybe it's because her husband just left her, maybe she just left him, whatever. In any event, she barks anxiously at her child in a voice too loud and strident, then rushes over and whisks him into his high chair for safety. Now assume that this is not a single occasion of mom's bad mood, but a common occurrence, her usual reaction to her son's exploration of his environment. What happens to him? Does he say to himself, "Ah, well, Mom's uptight, I mustn't take this personally? I can explore the world later when she's calm or when she's not around?" Not likely. He's barely a year old, remember; all he knows of the world, its dangers, its pleasures, its meanings, comes from this person. No, he does not put mother's behavior into this kind of adult perspective. Instead, he learns that this is the way of the universe: small actions lead to catastrophic reactions.

A parent or parent figure bears great responsibility to know that whatever they say or do to a child has great effect on the child's development. It is particularly required of them not to act from their own negative emotions, or if they do, to try to redress the situation later as much as possible.

Parental love is paramount for the integral development of a child. However, it is also important to know the proper way of expressing that love in a manner that a child can perceive and understand. It requires a delicate balance of sometimes viewing the world from the child's point of view and other times from the adult point; of being gentle and yielding at certain times and firm at others; of recognizing the child as the full person with rights, as well as the child that it is. A few hints are suggested below:

Ways to love a child: give your presence; laugh, dance and sing together; listen from a heart space; encourage; understand; allow them to love themselves; ask their opinions; learn from them; say yes as often as possible; say no when necessary; honor their no's; apologize; touch gently; open up; fly kites together; read books out loud; teach feelings; share your dreams; admit yours; frame their artwork; stay up late together; eliminate comparison; delight in silliness; handle with care; protect them; cherish their innocence; giggle; speak kindly; splash; let them help; let them cry; don't hide your tears; brag about them; answer their questions; let them go when it's time; show compassion; bend down to talk to little children; smile even when you are tired; surprise with a special lunch; don't judge their friends; give them enough room to make decisions; honor their differences; respect them; remember they have not been on earth very long.[5]

EFFECTS OF CHILDHOOD EXPERIENCES ON ADULT LIFE

Different personality theories have different ways of explaining and dealing with the scars on our personality inflicted by wounds received in our childhood. Below we very briefly discuss two of these:

Wounds of Childhood according to Transaction Analysis

People rehearsing a play prepare using a script – the text of the play which they have to learn and to cram. They get to know when they come in, what they have to say, how they have to say it, and the gestures to accompany the words. Later on, when they have mastered the script, they can act in such a way that the observer can hardly notice that what they say and do is from a script. It seems to be spontaneous, coming from them. Transaction Analysis borrows the term "script" in this sense to describe how we act as if spontaneously, when actually we are programmed by what happened to us in childhood.

Zimbardo defines scripts as "clusters of knowledge about sequences of interrelated, specific events and actions that are expected to occur in a certain way in particular settings."[6] Like scripts in plays, our mental scripts outline the "proper" sequence in which actions and reactions are expected to happen in given situation.

A Script is a Life Plan. It is developed before adult thinking. It is reinforced by 'parent' messages. For instance, if my parents ignore me, I may decide that I am not important. Usually when we act from our scripts we are not conscious of it. For this reason, we need to take time to discover our script decisions. Script decisions are based on our interpretation of both external and internal events, which does not exactly correspond to reality. As grown-ups, we sometimes replay the strategies we decided upon as infants. We respond to the 'here and now' reality as if it was the world we imagined in our early decisions. When we

---

[5] Taken from *Cambridge Slim Diary 2004*. (Author unknown).
[6] Cf. Philip G. Zimbardo, *Psychology and Life*, (11th edition) Scott, Foresman and Company, London, 1985, p. 351.

do this, we are said to be 'in script'. Two main factors will invite us to go into script:

o   When the here-and-now is perceived as stressful

o   When there is a resemblance between the present and a similar situation in childhood. The invitation then is to 'rubber band' from the 'here and now' into child ego state.

The greater the stress, the more likely the person is to get into Script. However, stress can never make anyone go into script. The movement is always decisional.

Learning about script can improve my ability to take stressful situations before moving into script behavior. It is also important to understand scripts because it gives us a way of understanding why people behave in the way they do. This is especially important for understanding those behaviors that appear self-defeating. Sometimes people get into the same painful situations over and over again. The reason for this is provided by script theory: it is to reinforce and further the script.

"Rubber banding" is a graphic term relating to us feeling as though we have been catapulted back to early childhood. Our feelings and reactions to an experience are more like a child than that of an Adult. Sometimes we can't make the link, as it may be such an early experience. For example, if I am in a large group and want to ask a question, I may feel like ten years old and be scared of being told that I should know the answer, or that I am stupid. My fear may prevent me from speaking in the group, and it may be that the tutor reminds me of some teacher from the past or a criticizing adult from my childhood. Or I may feel shame or embarrassment and not know why, the experience may have been before language, and the memory is stored in my bodily reaction, i.e., blushing or feeling uncomfortable.

Connected with the theory of life scripts is the concept of "injunctions". There are many injunctions or "Don'ts" which we receive in our childhood and we imbibe in our actions. Don't be childish, don't be late, don't eat in strangers' homes, don't be lazy, don't talk back, don't talk with food in your mouth, don't be naughty, don't be silly, don't be slow… These "don'ts" linger in our later life. The phrasing and even the content of injunctions differs from culture to culture, but all cultures have them in one way or another. Even when we think we have overcome them, they usually come again when we feel vulnerable. Then we rubber band into the don'ts of our childhood. When you come to a place where they are not expecting you, you may rubber band in the sense of not belonging, if you had this in your childhood.

For instance, a frightened parent may have handed you the injunction "don't exist." Maybe you came along too early and the parent was scared that there wouldn't be enough love to go round. You may have heard an angry parent say "I could kill you" or "I wish you hadn't been born" or "I nearly died when you were born". Not everyone decides to take their own life, but some may decide "it's OK for me to exist as long as I: work hard, keep quiet, stay out of the way, please others", etc.

There is also the injunction: 'don't be you; be what I want you to be'. Maybe the parents were set on having a girl and you were a boy or vice versa. Often the name reflects this. Or maybe the child is compared to another: I wish you were clever, like your grandfather, mother, etc.

Again, a frightened or inadequate parent may give the message "don't be a child, be responsible for yourself" or may not know how to communicate on a child's level. The child quickly learns to speak "grown-up" to get recognition. Others from dysfunctional families may decide they have to look after themselves and younger siblings. Oldest children get this message once a second child comes along.

There is also the injunction "don't be well". This message is realized when the child learns that the way to get attention from his/her parents is to be ill. In today's society it is easy to see how it occurs, when so many parents are out working.

Yet another injunction is "don't grow up". This often applies to the youngest child, and the injunction may come to meet the need of the mother who sees no other role in life apart from raising her children, or as puberty approaches it could come from an anxious parent. Many people can identify this injunction in adults who seem to be spoilt or childish. They will often ask the person's number among the siblings, and if the person happens to be the last child, they will nod with understanding as if they have come to the explanation.

The injunction "don't belong" is often passed on to people who have been abandoned at birth, unwanted, fostered or adopted. They may feel a sense of not belonging. Some may experience this by feeling "out of place" within the family.

Apart from "Don'ts" TA also applies the term "Drivers". These are given in later childhood and tell you that you are OK if you do certain things, i.e., they give you conditional "OKeyness".

If one were to picture a person's life like that of a man half way submerged, half way floating on the sea, the injunctions or don'ts are like stones tied on his feet and legs under the water pulling him down. At the same time the drivers are like balloons tied on his hands holding him above the water. For normality one needs to dismantle both the injunctions and the drivers, but this like any other process of growth is to be done carefully, otherwise the man submerges or flies off into the air. The following are some of the drivers.

The driver "be strong, please me" happens especially among people who were brought up by people other than their own parents. It implies not admitting being tired, never refusing other people's requests and satisfying them at one's own expense.

There is also the driver "hurry up". It characterizes people who seem to be ever in a rush, and in spite of it never accomplishing much.

"Permissions" are the chief therapeutic tools of the script analyst, because they offer a chance for an outsider to free clients from the crosses laid on them by parents and significant adults who raised them. Permissions run like: it is okay to be weak, to cry, to feel; it is okay to ask for what you want, to say no, to enjoy yourself. It is okay to lose a game, it is okay to relax.

Activity 5: What are your Permissions?

Identify where in your life you need to give yourself permission.

Divide in groups of four and discuss your permissions. Each one read to the others the permissions he/she has discovered for him/herself.

The other three then read them back to him in turn, while he/she listens attentively to each of them. The reason for this apparently monotonous exercise is to dismantle the habits already ingrained in us.

Another important term in TA is the concept of "Strokes".[7] A stroke is a unit of recognition (attention) which provides stimulus. Strokes confirm the presence of another. It may be positive, genuine, negative, plastic, etc. Strokes can also be non-verbal, in the form of a look, a smile,

---

[7] See also "**Error! Reference source not found.**" on page 35.

a frown, etc. Strokes can also be tangential: these are said 'about you' not to you, i.e., you hear your parents talking about you when you should be in bed but are listening to their conversation. You may overhear good things about you that they won't tell you in case you get 'big-headed'.

We all need strokes. A negative stroke is better than no stroke at all, we need strokes to know we exist in the world. In a supermarket where workers are distressed and serve so impersonally, a word of kindness to the girl at the cashier's table may make a great difference. Little words or gestures of kindness in every sphere of life can make a great difference in our lives. The most effective people are not those who are intelligent or efficient but those who are sensitive.

Claude Steiner who developed this theory from Berne also stated: "Different strokes for different folks". In other words: we all have our own unique stroking patterns.

There are different types of strokes. There are positive unconditional strokes – for being: these are pleasurable strokes without any strings attached. They confirm your Being is OK without having to do anything. For example, 'I love you', 'I enjoy being with you'. There are also positive conditional strokes – for doing: these are also pleasurable, but aimed at something you Do, for example a particular behavior or achievement: 'That was good', 'I like your style of working.' 'I love your cooking', etc. The negative conditional strokes are equivalent to constructive criticism: These strokes are critical in nature and give constructive comments about behavior. 'I know you want to complete this course and you won't be able to study if you go out every night.' These strokes are designed to give valuable feedback and be helpful for personal growth. A fourth category of strokes is that of the negative unconditional – These are powerful messages which both negate and do damage to the receiver. They are not constructive and can be psychologically wounding. 'You are stupid'; 'You're hopeless at this'; 'I hate you.'

The normal life as it begins in childhood is one of giving and receiving of strokes. A mother gives and receives strokes from her child. The smile of a child is a stroke to the mother. Her tender feeding of it is a stroke. At a certain stage there may be an event that upsets the normal exchange of strokes. For instance, in time of bereavement the mother may fail to give the normal attention to the child. The child gives its usual strokes but is surprised to see that they are not returned. If the situation goes on for a long time, it may cause a hardening in the child and influence its future life.

This mutual exchange of strokes is termed "stroke economy". It can be demonstrated with two glasses half filled with water held in both hands. The giving is demonstrated by pouring water from one glass into the other. The receiving glass also pours in the other glass in turn. The normal condition is when both glasses contain roughly the same amount of liquid. A situation of crisis is demonstrated by a cover being placed over one glass. This glass neither receives the water from the other glass nor can it give back. When water is poured from the uncovered glass, it bounces off the lead of the other glass and pours on the flour. Soon the giving glass is near empty, and this stands for the person who gives without receiving strokes in return. Eventually this glass also closes up, for fear of becoming emptied.

This is what goes on also in our adult life. We are familiar with people who never say "thank you" or show appreciation in any form even when you know they are happy about a behavior done to them. There are those who do not seem to be affected by our appreciation or affection. Some people may be neither capable of taking in strokes nor of giving them. When complemented about something they become embarrassed and may brush off the complement with such a comment as "it is nothing" or "you can't mean that". Such behavior can be frustrating in relations and may lead the other partner also to close up even when they know that their companion silently longs for their praises, affection or gratitude. This may be a kind of self-defense they learnt from childhood as a result of giving without receiving strokes. They may make the other person become like them by he or she stopping to give the strokes. The negative thinking process behind the failure to give or receive strokes goes as stated below:

> Don't give them when you have them to give
> Don't ask for them when you need them
> Don't accept them when you want them
> Don't reject them when you don't want them
> Don't give yourself a stroke

There is also a positive readjustment to counter balance this negative attitude which goes as follows:

> It is good to give strokes when you have them to give
> It is good to ask for them when you need them

It is good to accept them when you want them
It is good to reject them when you don't want them
It is good to give yourself a stroke

Theory of the 'Inner Child"

It is not uncommon to encounter a cheerful, joyous child, full of life and freedom at the age of three or four, and after a number of years to meet the same child or young adult totally transformed: reserved, sad, serious, too courteous… You can then wonder what happened to that child you knew, what wrought the transformation. The hassles of growing up have pushed that free spirit of childhood at the bottom of the personality, but they do not destroy it. Many who had a happy childhood can still recall the freedom of that period to express their emotions of joy, rage, playfulness, pain, fear, expectation, love. According to the theory of the "Inner Child" this early spontaneity of our life actually never gets destroyed.

According to the model of the "Inner Child", the inner child is your source of energy, vitality and the inner world of your feelings and emotions. "Whatever you have become, your childhood, in actual, literal sense exists within you now. It affects everything you do, everything you feel… the child you once were, continues to thrive inside your adult shell. Whether we like it or not, we are simultaneously the child we once were, who lives in the emotional atmosphere of the past and often interferes in the present…"[8] Many of us have grown up with highly developed minds and frozen feelings and emotions. And the trouble is that when we stay exclusively in the grown-up world of thoughts, plans and responsibilities, we cut ourselves off from our bodies, i.e., we live in our heads. And living in our heads is one way by which we abandon our Inner Child.

"The Inner Child is present when we have feelings. The Inner Child is the emotional self. It is where our feelings live. When you experience joy, sadness, anger, fear, or affection, your child within is coming out. When you are truly feeling your feelings, you are allowing your Inner Child to be. Your child within is also active when you are being playful, spontaneous, creative, intuitive, and surrendering to the spiritual self."[9]

---

[8] W. Hugh Missildine, *Your Inner Child of the Past*, 1963.
[9] Lucia Capacchione, *Recovery of your Inner Child*, 1991.

This model invites us to pay attention to every one of our emotions, particularly those we habitually ignore, if we want integral growth. Your Inner Child and your adult self are one. Therefore, when you feel negative emotions of fear, anger, frustration or rejection, it is as if your Inner Child is upset, and is demanding your attention. So, you need to attend to it by listening to it uncritically, because if you involve in undue self-criticism or feelings of exaggerated guilt and shame, the child will feel rejected and become rebellious, uncooperative and can even sabotage your plans by getting sick and making your life more miserable. So, in order to develop a relationship with yourself, you need to learn how to love your Inner Child and experience the childlike qualities of fun, playfulness, enthusiasm and creativity, which are available to you at any age. By giving the child today the attention and acceptance it needed long ago, by showing it now the understanding and compassion it wanted then, we begin to heal the old wounds.

The care for the Inner Child does not imply self-indulgence and abandoning reason in order to satisfy the whims of every emotion and desire. One has only to remember, as we have seen above, that bringing up a child well does not mean giving it all that it asks for. It simply means taking time to listen to it and finding out the most loving and appropriate way of responding to it that ensures its well being.

Using the concept of Inner Child as a model for personal growth is not a shortcut to the arduous efforts that genuine growth always demands. For it to be effective one must also go deep in one's past, often with the help of another person, to find out at what stage or stages the Inner Child was wounded and needs healing. Counselors and therapists use questionnaires, among other techniques, to determine at what stage one's inner child was wounded, or, to put it in other words, where one was fixated in the growth process.

For the purposes of this book the model of the Inner Child can be summed up thus: there are three things that help one to give the best of oneself: self-nurturing, discipline and fun. 1) Nurture yourself: never under-estimate your needs at any age or stage of life. Know them and attend to them within the possible limits. You have a need for tenderness, caring and loving attention, for rest and relaxation, etc. 2) Discipline yourself: know the boundaries between self-care, fun and duty. Keep to the agreement you make with yourself. Only a balance of the three will enable you to give the best of yourself. 3) Have fun: remember the saying, "all work without play makes Jack a dull boy." Allow yourself to be creative and to play. Give yourself a break every now and then. The spark of glee kept alive within you will help you in creating and maintaining the kind of inner resource state that empowers you in any relationship.

WHAT TO DO ABOUT THE EFFECTS OF CHILDHOOD

The realization of how fundamental our childhood is in determining what we are today and how difficult it is to undo the harm done can lead to three different attitudes. In the first place it can lead to anger against all the persons and circumstances that we believe led to undesirable aspects of our personality today. Secondly, it may lead to a kind of fatalistic resignation, a feeling that we cannot undo what has already been done. Thirdly – and this is the perspective that is pursued in this book – it can lead to a realistic appraisal of our situation, coupled with a determination to improve it, taking into account all that needs to be done. This third alternative also includes the acknowledgement of anger, resentment and sometimes even hatred of those that have done us harm, but these negative sentiments are brought to the surface as a prelude to genuine healing.

Concretely the focus on the wounds of our childhood and the effects they have had on our adult life teaches us the following truths:

- That since knowing our past is that important in our present growth, it is worthwhile to take pains to excavate it. This may mean the painful opening and submission to the probing of a helper.

- That because we often act from our scripts outside of our awareness, we need the humility to realize that we know ourselves much less than we believe or feel we do. For that reason, the assistance of another person, preferably an expert, is often necessary.

- That we have an enormous responsibility towards children; the basic patterns of whose future are now in the making, especially when these children are in our charge as parents or guardians.

- That we have a great responsibility if we are in position to influence others who must play a key role in the developing of children; that is if as pastors, teachers or counselors, we direct and form present or future parents and guardians.

- Knowledge of the influence of childhood on us ought to bring compassion in us for those who are difficult to live with. We learn to appreciate the fact that often they did not choose the circumstances of their growth. This, of course, does not excuse weaknesses in them, anymore than it would in us. But it makes us aware of the difficulties entailed in the growth process and the patience needed if quick results are not forthcoming.

5

THE MID-LIFE CRISIS

Between the time of our childhood and the time of Midlife there are obviously key stages that are worth looking at, not least of which is the period of adolescence.[10] The present work does not pretend to be comprehensive of all that is important in a person's life. From childhood and its effects in adult life we now move on to mid-life, which is treated under the following sub-headings:

General Description *64*
Symptoms *64*
Meaning *65*
Coping with the Midlife Crisis *66*

---

[10] The 'Mid-life crisis' is but one of the many critical stages of development in life. Erik Erikson isolated eight of these stages, and there may be more. M. Scott Peck lists "some of the major conditions, desires and attitudes that must be given up in the course of a wholly successful evolving life" which are: "the state of infancy, in which no external demands need be responded to, the fantasy of omnipotence, the desire for total (including sexual) possession of one's parent(s), the dependency of childhood, distorted images of one's parents, the omnipotentiality of adolescence, the 'freedom' of uncommitment, the agility of youth, the sexual attractiveness and/or potency of youth… authority over one's children, various forms of temporal power, the independence of physical health, and, ultimately… [earthly] life itself. Scott Peck, *The Road Less Travelled*, London: Arrow Books, 1990, p. 74-75.

GENERAL DESCRIPTION

The Midlife Crisis is the crisis of limits, in the sense that we become more acutely aware of our human limits than before. Jung described it as the "Second Half of Life", the process of individuation, becoming that unique self that we are called to be. But it is important to understand that crises in life are an invitation and opportunity for growth. For men the Midlife crisis is usually between 40 and 45 while for women it is approximately between 35 and 40, but this varies from person to person.

Quite often we have a dream in our early days. We give ourselves into something. For instance one may want to study in order to become somebody. Often it is the case that when eventually we have achieved what we wanted, we discover that we have neglected our own selves. What we strived so much to attain may appear not so important after all. We may then ask ourselves whether this is all there is to life. Another common symptom of the crisis of limits is that what used to give joy becomes a source of burden. We lose the joy of celebration.

By midlife most of us are accomplished fugitives from ourselves. We speak about other things but not about ourselves. We lose contact with ourselves and consequently with others. We speak about many things but miss the people. Many people in midlife are preoccupied with money, security, power, etc. Personal values become casualties on the road. It seems that the increase of success, security and comfort is directly proportionate to the decrease of meaning, self-understanding and personal happiness. To get the balance right is a challenge and a most difficult thing.

SYMPTOMS

Symptoms of the Crisis of Limits include depression, restlessness, frustration, anxiety. One may feel trying to re-create the excitement of earlier life, while at the same time experiencing meaninglessness. Another may have a feeling of having wasted one's earlier life; a realization that I am aging; a realization that death is not far. There is a sense of urgency, what seems to have worked no longer seems to work. The first grey hairs may cause anxiety. Other physical symptoms include wrinkles, a need for glasses, weight in the area of the waistline, greater need of moderation in food; increased fatigue precisely when our duties seem to have increased. These symptoms may not be considered very important in isolation, but the cumulative effect can weigh on us. Midlife may be characterized by a declining tenderness, a reduced sensitivity. A woman in this period may have a peak of sexual desire while at the same time she is aware of her gradual loss of charm. She feels threatened by younger nubile women. She may become moody and restless. A mother may become detached from her children. For parents, the midlife crisis may also consist in seeing their children in whom they had invested so much hope fail. The crisis is all pervasive and can turn all human activity into something boring. One realizes that time flies although nothing really happens. Birthdays begin to cause a depression.

It is important to realize that the midlife crisis is but a stage in the long process of growth. It follows other crises.

MEANING

We cannot fulfill ourselves in our purely earthly condition. We can fulfill ourselves only in our original integrity with the whole of being. Midlife crisis points beyond our earthly condition. We are made in the image and likeness of God, therefore we must work on ourselves to get back to that, where we can experience ourselves as loveable. That unites us with God and with the whole of creation. In this crisis of limits, we discover the radical limitedness of being human. We learn the hard way.

Midlife is the prelude to old age. That may sound frightening; unless we have the courage and the faith to look at the positive side of old age. The usual tendency is to focus solely at the negative side of old age, as the time when one is frustrated with failing faculties, when the beauty of youth is gone, when old acquaintances have died, when health is poor, every day brings pain, so many medicines to take, when the fear increases that a time will come when a person becomes totally dependent, and perhaps even a nuisance. All this can be true, but there is also a positive side. We need to see old age like the moment of transition it is, in the wise plan of God. The sun sets slowly, not abruptly. The airplane must reduce speed before landing in order to avoid a crash. As a person approaches the passage to the next life there is need to get detached from this earthly life. Many of the things that were of utmost value here below must slowly lose their importance. Old age is meant to loosen these ties – to wealth, to health, to beauty, to ambition, etc. – in order to prepare the person for the radical break with the earthly. But it requires wisdom and faith to see it that way. And midlife is the transition to old age.

COPING WITH THE MIDLIFE CRISIS

One of the ways of coping with this crisis is to move more from doing to being; for it is precisely when one has acquired everything they longed for that they feel unfulfilled. In this period spiritual life and cosmic participation are part of our goal.

We have to expose ourselves to and retrieve the original wonder. We come to realize that even if we would gain the whole world life would remain meaningless. We have to come to a stage in our inner realization that ultimately, we have to surrender to God. Once we do that this becomes a release. We are challenged to achieve the fullness of our authenticity, to be perceptive of reality in its true color: the world, others, myself, God. This inevitably requires us to learn to love, to listen to the wider picture. We learn that the "negative" symptoms of midlife are in fact neither negative nor pathological. They call us to the realization that there is more to life than what we know of it. They teach us that we have mistaken merely human values for ultimate values. Feelings of frustration and of failure are fundamentally not wrong. They are healthy indications that a new phase of growth is awakening in us. You may be feeling darkness; welcome it, stay with it and wait. In due course the light of growth will come. The darkness liberates us from merely earthly values and frees us for our most authentic values. Unfortunately, we can spend the rest of our life struggling through the midlife crisis if we don't open ourselves fully to God. But for those willing to take on the risk of growth, the successful outcome of the midlife crisis is the birth of a mature personality.

'DISAGREEABLE' EMOTIONS

Anger 68
   The Value of Anger 70
   Unhealthy expression of Anger 71
   Healthy ways of Dealing with Anger 72
Fear 78
Regret 80
   Description 80
   Value of Guilt and Regret 81
   How We Can Learn to Use Regret Fruitfully 82
Anxiety 84
Negative Emotions Related to Love and Sexuality 86
   Fear of Rejection 86
   Fear of Loneliness 86
   Mistrust 87
   Demanding too much 87
   Possessiveness 87
   Withholding of Self 88
   Irresponsibility 88
   Inability or Refusal to Communicate 88
   Fear of Intimacy 88
   Jealousy 89
Conclusion 90

All emotions are a gift of God and as such they are meant for a good purpose. Every feeling has its purpose in God's wonderful plan. Even in our feelings we reflect God: for God as revealed in his Son, has feelings of love, of mercy, of compassion. But he also experienced such negative feelings as anxiety, fear, anger and rage, frustration, pain, fatigue, discouragement, temptation, humiliation. Even feelings that we consider negative or painful have a purpose. Anger, anxiety, pain, jealousy, fear, passion; all these can serve – are meant to serve – a useful purpose. It is mistaken to consider any feeling as wrong or bad. It is what we choose to do with a feeling that determines its morality. There is nothing wrong for me to be angry or to feel sexually aroused. What is important is how I deal with these feelings. I can deal with them for my well-being or for my harm as well as for the well-being or for the harm of others. The process of becoming aware of our feelings widens the area of consciousness, drawing material from the unconscious and this leads to growth.

We all feel comfortable with certain emotions and uncomfortable with others. We like to feel happy, joyful, cheerful, amused, enthusiastic, confident, etc. We can describe these as 'Agreeable' emotions. On the other hand we do not like feeling sad, disappointed, angry, ashamed, guilty, confused, embarrassed, etc. This second category is one which causes problems, and therefore is made subject of study in this book. Since generally no one seems to have a problem with the positive emotions, except perhaps the need to moderate them for the sake of something more important, the study here focuses mainly on how to deal with negative emotions.

ANGER[11]

I knew it had to be a virus I had on the computer. Certain programs couldn't open immediately. Others couldn't close. In general, the computer had become much slower than usual for no reason known to me. The telephone line had just been fixed by the technician that day after weeks of reporting, and waiting, and patience and impatience. That's 'normal' around here! Now it no longer broke down and one could stay on the internet long enough to execute a download. So, the first thought was to fix that virus thing, or worm, or Trojan horse, or whatever it was that made the computer behave in a strange way.

It had to be done after supper when I could have a longer uninterrupted time. I was already tired, but I wanted to put right my computer as soon as possible in order to go on with my work. It reminded me of childhood days when I used to walk barefoot. Occasionally I would get a jigger in the toe. If you have never got a jigger in the toe, then I can tell you with the authority of experience; a young jigger has to be removed on the day it enters your toe if you intend to have any sleep. So, I set up to remove the cyber jigger. First, I learnt about the recent worm: My Doom A, and My Doom B, and Doom juice. There were ways to diagnose and to remove those, free of charge, so I followed the steps. That took a solid one hour. Each second that passed was so much money more to pay to

---

[11] Cf. www.angermgmt.com and www.apa.org.

the internet server, and so much time less to sleep. The two put together resulted into a corresponding accumulation of anger. The only thing that would have caused the anger graph that was ascending more and more steeply to descend was a successful diagnosis and removal of the offending problem.

At the end of the long wait the program declared that there was no member of the doom family; neither A nor B, nor the juice itself. I don't know whether you have ever gone to a doctor with some physical complaint only to be told that there was nothing the matter with you; you were quite healthy! That is how I felt. There was no change at all in the symptoms that had made me look for a solution. The computer was still slow. I tried to run the anti-virus program I had in case it was some other virus. But that had to be updated first: more minutes, more money, less sleep, more anger. No virus, all clean, yet more anger. I went back to the original program: there was another doom uncle I had not seen before, called Blaster doom, so I set out to deal with that. After what I thought was considerable progress the program said that sorry, but you have first to have a certain update. So, I had to look for that. It was now 1.30 a.m. Eventually I found something that remotely resembled the update and started downloading it. The closer the bar showing the progress came to the end, the slower it became. The last three segments took 1800 painful seconds. When there was only one segment remaining, suddenly the connection to the internet broke! It was 2.30 a.m. I felt I badly needed to kick or tear something. But I had to unglue myself from the chair to go to bed. I had trouble unbuttoning my shirt, and in fact the next morning I found that the last button was missing…

We all know what anger is, and we've all felt it whether as a fleeting annoyance or as full-fledged rage. The causes and the situations differ of course, but the emotion is the same. Anger is an emotional state that varies in intensity from mild irritation to intense fury and rage. Many descriptions are used to express (or cover up) anger. People often say they feel worthless, depressed, bad, perturbed, uneasy, disturbed, unsure, wondering, bitter, irritated, puzzled, perplexed, victimized, annoyed, frustrated, etc., when actually they are angry.

Anger can be caused by both external and internal events. The slowing and crashing of the computer were external events. I was angry with the computer, as well as with the people who willfully create computer viruses for the 'joy' of doing harm to others. I was even angry at God, for at a certain stage, in an attempt to pray, all I could say was: "God, can you possibly be enjoying this? Was the fixing of the telephone line for which I thanked you intended to make me lose more money and time?" You could be angry at a specific person or event, or your anger could be caused by worrying or brooding about your personal problems. Memories of traumatic or enraging events can also trigger angry feelings.

The Value of Anger

Anger is a completely normal, usually healthy, human emotion. It is a natural, adaptive response to threats; it inspires powerful, often aggressive, feelings and behaviors, which allow us to fight and to defend ourselves when we are attacked, or to

Jesus then went into the Temple and drove out all those who were selling and buying there; he upset the tables of the money changers and the chairs of those who were selling pigeons... (Matthew 21:12)

protect those we love. One has only to watch animals or birds, especially those with young ones. They become particularly aggressive to whoever poses a threat to their little ones. A certain amount of anger, therefore, is necessary to our survival. On the other hand, we can't physically lash out at every person or object that irritates or annoys us; laws, social norms, and common-sense place limits on how far our anger can take us.

Since anger is part of our nature, and since every normal person is bound to experience anger in some form and at one time or another, the question is not how to stop getting angry, for that is neither realistic nor desirable. It is not realistic because any attempt to realize it would be futile: we cannot eliminate all the situations that make us feel angry, nor can we avoid all the people that antagonize us. It is not desirable because it would eliminate the useful role anger has to play in our lives. Rather, the question is how we should deal with our angry reactions: what is the best way to respond to the situations and people that make us angry. Today, there are different therapies and therapeutic techniques developed to deal with anger. One has only to insert the phrase "anger management" in any search engine on the World Wide Web, to see how many websites come up. Some of these offer very useful hints on anger management, although such hints present no magic cures, and there is no shortcut to the painful and slow process of genuine growth.

First, we examine some of the unhealthy and harmful ways of expression, or non-expression, of anger, and later we see the meaningful ways of dealing with our angry feelings.

70

Unhealthy expression of Anger

Anger may be expressed, suppressed or repressed. Below are examples for each of these forms of channeling anger.

Perhaps the crudest way of expression of anger is violence. Violence which results in physical harm to the object of one's anger is frequent in non-functional families. Often the victims of this violence are the wife and the children. We also see violence among street gangs, on football fields, in terrorist activities, and on a wider and more organized scale in form of wars. The consequences of violence are numerous including pain, physical injury, anguish, fear and in certain instances even terror. Violence usually also evokes strong feelings of reciprocal anger and desire for revenge.

In the perpetrator of the violence, it may cause emotions of remorse, deprivation of love from close ones, low self-esteem, hardening of heart, fear of retaliation from one's victims, which may in turn lead to further violence in order to stifle such retaliation. Many violent people in fact are very fearful deep inside. Anger may also be expressed through verbal abuse. Although this causes no physical injury it can be no less hurtful than actual violence.

Unlike directly expressed anger, suppressed anger comes out in indirect ways. A subtle form of expression of anger is through passive aggression. Passive aggression is action that is hurtful to another person and that is motivated by suppressed anger. The anger is then expressed indirectly. Often passive aggressive individuals are not even aware that their actions are motivated by anger.

Passive aggression takes on so many forms. It could be just a look, a sarcastic remark, avoidance of someone in order to hurt that person, stubbornness, embarrassment of another person, saying of nasty things, forgetting appointments, and coming late for functions. Passive aggressive individuals can be continually cynical or hostile, often with the result that they do not

But the synagogue official was indignant because Jesus had healed on the Sabbath, and he addressed the people present. 'There are six days' he said 'when work is to be done. Come and be healed on one of those days and not on the Sabbath.' Luke 13:14

make many friends, or lose those that they already have.

Even though it is indirect, passive aggression usually finds its mark: it is hurtful to the one on whom it is directed. It can be even more cutting than direct anger because it comes with the pretense of being innocent. When the synagogue official addressed his congregation telling them that there were six days in which they could be healed and that they could come on any of these days and not on the Sabbath, it was not difficult for anyone around to understand that this criticism was not intended for those who sought healing but on the healer. It would have been much less wounding if the official had confronted Jesus directly, accusing him of breaking the law by healing on the Sabbath.

Anger, like any other emotion, can also be repressed. But again, like any other emotion, it is not destroyed by repression. It can resurface in all sorts of psychosomatic disorders such as high blood pressure, stomach ulcers, pains in the shoulders or neck, or even heart attack or stroke.

Healthy ways of Dealing with Anger

SELF-ANALYSIS

The acknowledgement that one has an anger problem and the wish to deal with this problem effectively is the first and indispensable step towards anger management. There are times when it is obvious, even to ourselves, that we are angry. Sometimes, however, we may not know or may not want to know that we are angry. Or we may mistake our angry feelings for something else. Many behaviors and inner feelings, apparently unrelated to anger, may in fact be manifestations of it. Consider the following questions, for example, taken from a typical test designed to gauge a person's level of anger. Answers in the positive point to a certain amount of anger in the interviewee:

I worry about financial matters ☐ T ☐ F
I have been disillusioned with love ☐ T ☐ F
I often have felt inferior to others ☐ T ☐ F
I have had trouble controlling my sexual urges ☐ T ☐ F
I have known moments of great tension and stress ☐ T ☐ F
I find myself having many bodily aches and pains ☐ T ☐ F
I have had sleep patterns that do not seem normal ☐ T ☐ F
At times I seem to have an unusual amount of guilt ☐ T ☐ F
I find myself preoccupied with my personal goals for success ☐ T ☐ F
My conscience bothers me about things I have done in the past ☐ T ☐ F
I consider myself to be possessive in my personal relationship ☐ T ☐ F

It seems that I wind up helping others more than they help me ☐ *T* ☐ *F*
Many of the nice things I do are done out of a sense of obligation ☐ *T* ☐ *F*
I am hesitant for people to give me suggestions, even if they are positive ☐ *T* ☐ *F*
I am a fairly strict person, liking things to be done in a predictable way ☐ *T* ☐ *F*
It is not unusual for me to forget someone's name after I have just met him ☐ *T* ☐ *F*
Sometimes I have difficulty controlling my weight, whether gaining or losing ☐ *T* ☐ *F*
It is difficult for me to motivate myself to do things that don't have to be done ☐ *T* ☐ *F*

Looking at these questions one realizes that our anger often overlies other feelings and attitudes such as worries, rejection, inferiority, sexual inhibitions, stress, guilt, unfulfilled ambitions, remorse, jealousy, resentment, social obligations, pride, unrealistically high personal standards, depression. It is sometimes manifested by insomnia, bodily pains, weight control or forgetfulness. The questions further show that it is often not enough to deal with our angry feelings, once identified, but that we need to go deeper and find what other feelings underlie the anger. For if our anger is only a symptom, we need to identify the cause and deal with it in order to remove the symptom.

The following are suggested steps for analysis of one's anger:

- How do you describe your unpleasant feeling? Is it obvious anger or something you simply suspect to be anger? What physiological indications can you identify? Rising of your voice? Quickening of breath? Destructive mood? Clenching of your fists? Grinding of teeth? Cursing aloud or within yourself? Stammering in your speech? Are any of these usual indications of your angry state? Try to observe yourself like an outsider to yourself. That very fact may reduce your anger a little.

- Identify the object of your anger. What are you angry at? What happened to make you angry? Is it a person? Are they circumstances? Is it yourself? Were you simply reminded of something about which you were enraged in the past? Is it residual or transferential anger? Or is it a mixture of several things building on one another? Is it something you cannot put your finger on?

- At times in the midst of a strong emotion your very ability to reason is temporarily impaired. However, reason is one of your strong tools for anger management. Try to consciously and willfully bring it in your feelings. As soon as you can reason make an effort to do so. Is your reaction justified? Is there some reasonable way you can deal with the situation? What are the possible consequences if you followed the direction of your feelings?

- What are the underlying emotions to your anger? Sickness? Frustration and inability to do anything about a situation? Sadness? Bereavement? Shame? Fatigue? What can you do to realistically address this underlying emotion or situation? Is there any way you can work towards reversing the situation that gave rise to your anger? Or does the solution require accepting and living with it? One who can reach this stage has already gone a long way in dealing with one's anger.

CALMING

Another way of dealing with anger is that of trying to cool down and relax. This is particularly called for in cases of anger that is explosive. Often this is even prior to self-analysis. Usually, people with explosive anger think only after they have reacted, and by then it is regret, contrition or remorse that they feel and not anger. But it is important to remind ourselves often that our emotions influence but not control us unless we let them, and that if we desire hard enough to control them, we can. At a certain stage while your anger is rising you may become conscious of what is happening to you. This is the moment to act.

Simple relaxation tools, such as deep breathing can help calm down angry feelings. There are books and courses that can teach relaxation techniques, and once learnt these techniques can be called upon in any situation ("Centering Prayer" on page 153, and "Meditation with the Lectionary" on page 155).

Below are some simple steps you can try:

- o Breathe deeply, from your diaphragm; breathing from your chest won't relax you. Picture your breath coming up from your "gut."

- o Slowly repeat a calm word or phrase such as "relax," "take it easy." Repeat it to yourself while breathing deeply.

- o Alternatively, you can try some non-strenuous slow exercise, such as taking a walk.

MANUAL WORK

Some people may be helped to calm down by engaging in some strenuous exercise, such as splitting fire wood, gardening, jogging, or some other physical exercise. The rationale behind is that anger is energy, and like all energy, it can be transformed into some other form of energy. Therapists often use such techniques as requiring the client to hit a pillow, wring a towel or throw stones in a lake, thus venting out pent-up anger in a safe environment.

Sometimes circumstances do not permit one to immerse oneself into physical work. You may be enraged in an office or on a journey or in a meeting. You cannot get out and mow the lawn or split firewood. But when circumstances permit, it is a good practice for an angry person to put your energy and mind to some hard work, and keep at it until you are quite exhausted. The likelihood is that you will find yourself in better position to deal with the enraging situation more reasonably. At the same time, you have the bonus of work accomplished. If you can avoid it, in a state of enragement keep away from work that require intensive mental activity. Often you might end up messing things and increasing your frustration at the same time.

Manual work doesn't always have to be such as creates perspiration and brings blisters. You can put your office in order, file the papers or wash handkerchiefs. An untidy work environment itself is enough to increase if not generate anger. You are more likely to look for and fail to find things you need.

It is to be noted that calming and relaxation techniques may offer some temporary means of dealing with anger in order to bring it to manageable proportions. They are not a substitute to dealing with the issues which are the cause of one's anger. If a lazy student is angry at self for neglecting work that has to be done, no amount of wringing a towel or breathing technique will take away the cause for the anger. The situation has to be confronted squarely.

DOING SOMETHING ELSE IN THE MEANTIME

One of the frequent causes of frustration is waiting: waiting for your turn in a queue, waiting in public offices, waiting for someone with whom you made an appointment and who is late. The more you wait the more the frustration. But an easy anecdote to waiting is to do something useful in the meantime. Usually there is something that can be done to profit. If you are going to wait in a place away from your work environment you might choose to take a book. People place magazines and newspapers in waiting rooms, but you do not have to have them provided for you. You might have more nourishing literature than what is provided for the general public. When you do something useful in the meantime, time passes without you knowing it.

COMMUNICATION WITH ANOTHER PERSON

Another way of dealing with anger is talking to someone about it. This is more helpful to some people than to others, depending on temperament. If you are the type that finds this helpful, find someone preferably a friend and talk about the situation that angers you. Good friends might even have to absorb some of the anger in order to help their mates. To act like such a friend, you need to bear in mind that you are not the object of your friend's anger, even though it seems to be directed towards you, but a help to get out that anger.

COMMUNICATION WITH THE PERSON CONCERNED

One of the most effective ways of dealing with anger in situations involving relation with other people is communication in the appropriate way. Relations are broken, families divided and associations dissolved due to poor or no communication. Either people do not communicate all together, or they do not do so properly. Angry people tend to jump to, and act on, conclusions, and some of those conclusions can be very inaccurate. A key factor in effective communication is understanding of the other's view point and conveying the fact that one has understood. (More will be said with regard to the skills necessary for effective communication in the chapter on *Counselling Skills*, and particularly the skill of "Listening" on page 179).

- Try not to respond when you are under the influence of strong anger. If it is a letter you have to respond to, wait until you have calmed down. And if it is in the context of a dialogue, consider postponing the matter until a more opportune moment when you have regained your cool.

- It may be the best thing for some people to move away for some time from the person towards whom they are angry, particularly if this person continues to provoke them into saying something.

- Sometimes it is necessary or helpful to have a third party to mediate between two angry people, one who can guide the dialogue without taking sides or being emotionally involved.

- Before you respond make sure that you have understood what the other person has said. Listen to the whole message and not only to that part which is particularly irksome to you. Try also to listen to what is not said. Fights and quarrels among people who love each other, for instance, may be indications of frustrated love and feeling neglected, even though people may feel too proud to admit that.

- Respond also to the positive in what your adversary is saying. Take your time to answer. Think through your responses.

PROBLEM SOLVING

Sometimes our anger and frustration are caused by very real and inescapable problems in our lives. Not all anger is misplaced, and often it is a healthy, natural response to these difficulties. Tautological as it might sound, the healthiest way of confronting a problem that is within your power to solve and that is making you angry is to solve it.

It may be that even though a problem is within your power to solve, it is someone else's responsibility to deal with. Then the wiser course of action might be to be assertive without being aggressive, and make others take on their own responsibility. Otherwise, you might turn yourself into a doormat on which others wipe their feet. But it is equally important not to insist too much on your rights, or what you conceive to be your rights. Sometimes you can edify others by action more than by words; that is, by taking on what they ought to do and have neglected.

Where the problem is actually yours to solve, make a plan and check your progress along the way. Resolve to give it your best, but also not to punish yourself if an answer doesn't come right away. Have the good sense to postpone a problem to which you cannot find an immediate solution. You may be too tired or angry or both. There may be other issues equally urgent and requiring your attention. Avoid the temptation to lose patience and fall in an all-or-nothing thinking. You may end up ruining even the good that you have achieved.

Certain problems require you to admit failure, find help or look for alternative solutions. Know when a particular problem is beyond you and learn to live with the limitation.

FEAR

Anyone who has watched documentaries of the jungle will have seen the endless "drama" between the animals that subsist by eating others and those that survive by escaping from being eaten. One of the tools for escape of the latter is fear. They live constantly alert, wary of the enemy. When one spots a predator usually it utters a cry most likely motivated by fear, which cry in turn drives fear in the others causing them to scamper for shelter. If they did not experience fear, they would be easy prey unless they were strong enough to defend themselves physically. For humans too, fear serves to motivate us to escape from perceived danger of all sorts.

We fear so many things. We fear failure, rejection, death, bereavement, authority, abandonment, intimacy, animals, the unknown, strangers, exposure, war, the opposite sex, conflict, God, our weaknesses, the devil, making mistakes, etc. Everyone can make a private list of the things they are afraid of. Each has their way of coping with their fears, whether these ways are healthy or not.

What is important is not lack of fear, for we all experience fear. What is important is to relate to our fears in a healthy way. There are two possible ways of relating to fear. One goes into pain and then into helplessness and depression. Depression in turn leads into paralysis. Another possibility is that fear gets us into power which in turn leads to choice, to excitement and into action. Fear of overcoming a bodily weakness may sometimes lead one into remorse, into helplessness, into discouragement. But at times it can lead one into acknowledgement of the power of temptation, and one's own limitations, of one's need of the help of God and of his forgiveness and into dedication to meaningful activity.

It is important to understand that we cannot always remain in the position of power with regard to our fears. We vacillate between power and helplessness. What is important is to strengthen the side of power and to minimize that of helplessness by degrees.

The language we use betrays our attitude towards our fear. We can move from pain to power also in the change of our language. We put ourselves down if we say "I can't". By this we put into our subconscious the message that we are weak. We can change that. Instead of saying "I can't come to dinner" you might say: "I am not coming to dinner because I am choosing to do something else which for me is a greater priority". Being polite to others is no excuse for diminishing our own power. There has to be a way of saying the truth without putting ourselves down. Otherwise, we condition ourselves into a position of incapacity.

Pilate then said to him, 'Are you refusing to speak to me? Surely you know I have power to release you and I have power to crucify you?' 'You would have no power over me' replied Jesus 'if it had not been given you from above…' John 19: 10-11. "No one takes [my life] from me; I lay it down of my own free will, and as it is in my power to lay it down, so it is in my power to take it up again…" John 10:18.

We overcome fear by taking responsibility over our lives. We need to confront many things we fear with the same statement. They put us down to the extent that we allow them to, and they would not have power over us if we had not given it to them. People feel heartbroken because they are jilted and blame those who have turned them down. But they would not feel so if they did not allow themselves to feel so. Even when someone is bound by obedience, one can freely choose to obey and see that as the will of God, while at the same time inwardly one asserts one's own freedom. That is the kind of obedience Jesus exercised in regard to his father as he confronted the cross.

Below are a number of steps for overcoming fear, say of speaking in public:

Activity 6: Dealing with Fear

1. *Identify exactly what you are most fearful of.*

2. *Write down everything that could go wrong.*

3. *Take your greatest fear and develop a plan step by step. And outline specific ways to overcome your fear.*

4. *Verbalize aloud your feelings of fear.*

5. *Visualize yourself doing what you are afraid to do.*

6. *Practice aloud beforehand what you have prepared. Don't expose yourself before preparation.*

7. *Experience the whole process by breaking your fear into manageable parts.*

Activity 7: Drawing on past strengths against fear

Think of the greatest fear you have overcome in your life.

Think of the steps which helped you to overcome it.

Write down how you overcame the fear.

What feelings did you have after you had overcome that fear?

REGRET

Description

Regret is an emotion we experience after an action, omission or experience. With regret comes the feeling: "I should have acted differently" or simply "I should have acted". Some of the things we regret cannot be undone. A mother I know once suffocated her baby inadvertently. In her sleep she lay on the nose of the little infant and it was too feeble to make any significant struggle to wake her up. God only knows how much regret and remorse she experienced. In such a case she must have thought of the number of things she could have done and she did not do. However, other actions we regret are different in the sense that even though we cannot undo what is already done, we can at least do something to repair the damage. Whether the cause of regret is irreversible or not, we can always learn from our mistakes. The function of the emotion of regret is to remind me that I have violated my standards. It is an invitation to do something about that realization. It is important for us to remind ourselves that since our salvation was wrought, there is no situation that can be called hopeless as long as we live. Acting upon our regret and guilt helps us to keep our behavior in line with our standards.

There are different ways people react to regret in ordinary life. Many wallow in the emotion and never learn from their mistakes. They repeat the same mistake over and over again, and experience the same painful emotion over and over again. Sometimes the emotion even becomes more and more intensified while their hope of overcoming the weakness becomes correspondingly diminished. But others have the courage and the wisdom to learn from their mistakes. For them the very mistake, though regrettable, becomes an opportunity to acquire new wisdom.

Value of Guilt and Regret

Because guilt is a negative and undesirable emotion, and because there are many psychological illnesses connected with inappropriate guilt, it is sometimes not easy to appreciate the value of appropriate guilt. Today many psychologists attribute the accumulation of inappropriate guilt and consequent neuroses to the teaching and practice of the Church, particularly the Catholic Church. On the other hand, many are convinced that misunderstanding and misuse of psychology has led to an erosion of appropriate guilt. People burdened by guilt blame their past, their parents, their religion for their own mistake, or go for long and expensive, sometimes ineffective, therapy when probably what they really need is a good confession. There is a lot of truth in either side of looking at guilt. We need to assess the real value of guilt and how to deal with it, as well as how to deal with inappropriate guilt.

Guilt is to the psyche what physical pain is to the body. When we have pain in the stomach, it is a symptom that something is wrong. The pain signals us to take care of ourselves. If there were no pain, we could die. Healthy guilt warns us that something is wrong and invites us to atonement or change. In that sense it is a help towards growth.

How We Can Learn to Use Regret Fruitfully

Even when we find ourselves among those people who frequently do the same mistakes and who do not seem to learn from them, we can always change the situation and begin to learn from our regret. The following are some of the possible steps we can take to learn from our mistakes:

Activity 8: Exploiting the emotion of regret

1) Think of the situation that causes you to regret. Describe it to yourself as fully as possible. Allow yourself to experience the painful emotion of regret. It is part of the healing process not to avoid the pain. Think of the things you missed because of your mistake, think of the harm and pain you caused to yourself and to others, the time and energy you wasted, the opportunities you wasted; whatever the case may be. It might be useful to articulate your reflection better through writing it down. But often it is the case that we do not want others to know the things we are ashamed of or we regret having done. So, in order not to expose yourself it might be better afterwards to destroy your reflections. To write them in such a way that you want to preserve them is a good idea, but on the other hand it might impede you from expressing the situation as accurately as possible for fear that what you have written might be exposed to the wrong eyes. In that case you might decide not to keep a record, at least not of everything.

2) Revisit your standards. Sometimes we harbor regret or remorse because we have failed to achieve things which in the first place are too high for us to achieve. This is because we have set higher standards than we can meet. On other occasions our very standards are false. Still if we are convinced of them, we are likely to feel guilty for their violation. A fundamentalist might blame himself for having lost an opportunity to kill a person who does not belong to his religion, or to commit suicide for his convictions. A certain priest once narrated the story of his boyhood. For a long time, he had confession whenever he had seen the knee of a woman, simply because his grandmother used to scold his sisters if they put on a dress that exposed their knees. Our very standards may need to be revised to match reality.

3) Think of the circumstances and all the actions that led to the mistake. Usually, the tendency is to focus on the central action itself and to ignore the series of actions that slowly by slowly led to the final stage. And yet it is precisely the small, apparently insignificant mistakes which lead to the big one, that need to be dealt with for significant healing. Also, it might be easier to work with the small mistakes than with the big issue. Think of the circumstance that led to the failure.

4) Think of how you could have done the situation differently. Make a virtual reconstruction of the situation; how would life have been different if you had done the right thing, if you had not missed the opportunities that you missed, if you had obeyed the prior warnings? You might also think of other occasions in the past when you were faced with a similar situation and made the decision to do the right thing. How did you manage in those cases?

'Yahweh says this: Put yourselves on the ways of long ago and enquire about the ancient paths: which was the good way? Take it then, and you shall find rest' (Jeremiah 6:16).

5) What excuses do you have for having done the mistakes? In situations in which we feel remorse, regret or guilt we have the tendency to take on board more guilt than we actually deserve. Many of us have the tendency to harbor neurotic guilt; to blame ourselves more than is due, and to find it difficult to forgive ourselves. If you are one of these people, it might be useful for you also to reflect on the things that mitigate your guilt. What were the circumstances? What are your prior failures and habits in the same area? To what extent did these impinge on the action then? What were the external factors that put pressure on you? This is not to excuse or justify yourself but to help you not have an overwhelming sense of guilt. The important thing is not to feel the pain of guilt but to overcome the mistake and to prevent it from happening in the future. "I do not condemn you either; go and *do not sin any more*" (John 8: 1-11).

6) What can you do to repair the damage to whoever was hurt by the regrettable event? This applies only in the cases where it is possible to repair the damage. A person who has wronged another can make apology. The repair is just that: a repair. Things that are repaired are not quite the same as those that are not repaired. If I panel-beat my car after an accident it can look as good as it was before. But I also know that it is weaker and more susceptible to damage than it was before. Nonetheless the repaired car is much better than one which has not been repaired at all. In fact, certain repairs can be stronger than the original parts. In the same way a relation re-established through reconciliation may have the added advantage of humility on the part of the one who regretted the mistake and sensitivity from both sides.

7) What are you going to do to prevent to a repetition of the same mistake? In this case it is useful to revisit all the things that led you into the mistake, and to see the effective and realistic ways of preventing the same mistakes from being repeated.

8) What can you do to build resistance against the same fault? Failure is like a sickness. Even after it is cured it leaves the body weak and vulnerable. In order to withstand the same sickness in the future it is good if the body builds its strength anew. It is, therefore, profitable to think according to one's situation, about those things that can help one build resistance against the things that made one fail.

9) What external help is available to you? Certain weaknesses are best dealt with, with the help of others. A believer realizes that the help of God in prayer is indispensable. All of us do well to mobilize whatever help of others is available to us, such as a friend, support groups, a growth facilitator or a spiritual director.

10) What action plan have you got to carry out your resolutions? When do you start? With what? How do you gauge that your resolutions are being carried out? The earlier one starts with the action plan the better.

ANXIETY

"Most things we worry about never happen" (author unknown).

While the emotion of regret regards events and actions that have already happened in the past, that of anxiety regards events and actions that still lie in the future. Anxiety tells me that there is something in the future for which I have to prepare. Like other emotions there is healthy anxiety, but there can also be unhealthy as well as unnecessary anxiety. Again, there are people who nurse anxiety by not facing the necessary preparation to which the anxiety is pointing.

…Set your hearts on God's kingdom first, and on his righteousness, and all these other things will be given you as well. So do not worry about tomorrow: tomorrow will take care of itself. Each day has enough trouble of its own. Matthew 6:33-34.

The more they approach the event about which they feel anxious, the more intense the anxiety grows, sometimes turning into panic or even hysteria. But there are those who have the courage to face the anxiety by taking the necessary preparation. Usually this is also a way of getting rid of the unhealthy and undeserved anxiety. When I have done all that is in my power to do, then I do not blame myself for not having done something I could not have done. But unless I have actually applied myself to do what is required, I am unlikely to know that not all the anxiety I feel is due to my failure, or that I am holding myself responsible for something that was beyond my power.

Another way to deal with anxiety, particularly anxiety that comes from accumulation of work, meeting of schedules, deadlines, etc., is by confronting our duties well in time. Quite often we pile up duties through procrastination, and eventually these become a cause of anxiety when their execution is urgent and the time too little. The classical example is the student who prepares for the exam only at the last minute and then is caught up in panic. If the same student did a little each time, he or she might go to the examination with confidence and perform better.

The future is in God's hands, the present he has entrusted to ours. The trouble begins when we abandon the present and meddle with the future. We take time to work out how we shall manage future problems, time which should be used to deal with present ones.

NEGATIVE EMOTIONS RELATED TO LOVE AND SEXUALITY

Apart from the emotions seen above we also consider more briefly some other emotions related to love and sexuality.

Fear of Rejection

A variety of negative feelings comes with rejection: inadequacy, not being wanted, unworthiness, loneliness, not belonging, anger, disturbance, humiliation, feeling useless to self and to others.

The fear of rejection is the fear of becoming unacceptable to somebody or institution that we appreciate and that is important to us. We do not feel rejected if we are repulsed by one who is not important to us. The fear of rejection can be experienced when perceived needs are not met by parents or significant others. However, some expectations are not met because they are not expressed. It occurs often enough that one feels rejected simply because those from whom one desires acceptance do not know it and this because the person has never expressed it. This implies that one way of dealing with rejection is the acquisition of the courage to express our needs in a meaningful way.

Sometimes we forestall rejection by rejecting first, as a form of defensive mechanism. The fear of rejection can drive people to suppress their own needs and interests in order not to be rejected. What we want most is to be accepted and because of our fear of losing that we fit in with the real or perceived needs of the other at the expense of our own needs.

The intensity of the fear of rejection corresponds to how little we love and appraise ourselves. For people who have a low self-esteem this rejection is more devastating than for those who have a higher sense of self-esteem. One of the ways of countering the intensity of the pain of rejection is by building up self-esteem. In given situations it is helpful to communicate our pain of rejection to the subject.

Fear of Loneliness

People trained to rescue those that are drowning know the dangers of the operation. A drowning person grasps desperately on whatever they can get hold of and won't let go what they perceive to be their last chance of survival. The rescuer who is not careful may be rendered unable to detach himself from the clasp of despair in order to swim to safety with the person being rescued. A loving relationship is not meant to be like a rescue operation of a drowning person. But the fear of loneliness sometimes makes one of the partners approach it as such.

What matters to him or her most is not the other but his or her own loneliness and so he/she uses both the relationship and the other to ensure that he/she will not be lonely again, thus suffocating the relationship.

Mistrust

Our deep-seated sense of inadequacy means that we cannot really believe that we are lovable, and we may enter into a destructive game whereby we keep forcing the other to prove they love us. Finally, they can bear it no longer and they leave us, once again confirming our worst fear that we are unlovable.

Demanding too much

A partner's need for love, reassurance, sex, support; one's desire to fulfill every need of the companion; one's desire for them to fulfill one's own desires; one's wish that there is no-one else in the life of the companion… etc., all this can be overwhelming to the mate or friend. Instead of taking responsibility for the nudging behavior ourselves we demand that the other deal with it and this can become too great a burden, thus wrecking the relationship.

One can destroy friendship or love by becoming dependent upon the other to an impossible extent so that the love becomes an intolerable burden – even to the extent of wanting the other to take responsibility for most elements of the relationship.

Possessiveness

We can want the other too much – want to know everything about them, want their attention, want their undivided love, want them to spend all their time with us; it can stifle love and create huge resentment and wreck the very love it craves for.

Withholding of Self

We can quite deliberately (or unconsciously) withhold parts of ourselves so that the giving is punishing at times – it is almost a trading off of self for something one wants from the other.

Irresponsibility

We cannot be bothered with responsibility within the relationship so when it becomes boring or difficult or the other becomes in some way a problem for us, we opt out of the relationship. We are usually good at dressing up so that it looks noble.

Inability or Refusal to Communicate

At times we can refuse or not be bothered to communicate with the other and choose to 'live alongside' rather than with the other. We argue to ourselves that the other should know that what they do or fail to do hurts us, not knowing that actually often they do not know. Or even when we feel that it is necessary to communicate pride and self-righteousness holds us back. We wait for them to make the first move.

Fear of Intimacy

This is the fear of being fully open and transparent to others. It is a self-protection against being hurt. When we share completely with others, we make ourselves vulnerable. But unless we are willing to undergo a certain amount of vulnerability, we may not be able to understand others and ourselves. When we live behind defenses, we fail to understand ourselves. The dilemma is that we both long for intimacy and at the same time we back away from it. We want intimacy but we do not want to be hurt. This fear is even greater among those who have been hurt before in the process of being intimate. Betrayal in families is a great source of the fear of intimacy.

Sometimes when the fear of intimacy is not consciously acknowledged, it may take on some form of projection. Because I am not aware of my fear I fabricate reasons why this relationship will not work. I may project onto the other person and say that they are afraid of me. Or I may reason and say that the relationship is too demanding, or that it is shallow. We can argue that the other person is immature. Or we may say to ourselves: "I want this year for myself, and I don't want to enter into a relation. I have too many problems to sort out and I do not want to enter into others." Any of these reasons may be true, or it may be a defense mechanism. In relationships of intimacy often people tend to control their partners, keeping them at bay in order to put a safe distance between the partner and themselves, playing it safe.

How do we get out of the fear of intimacy? First of all, we need to decide whether or not it is the best thing for us to get intimate with this particular person. Some relations are best not developed. We need to acknowledge the fear of intimacy. By sharing it we make this fear work for us. This fear can also be shared with the person with whom we want intimacy. I can say to them: "I want to be intimate with you, but at the same time I am afraid of being hurt". That person will understand why at times you come close and then on other occasions seem to withdraw. That way the other person understands that they are not being rejected.

Another way of dealing with this fear is not to rush into relationships. Being too hasty may spoil an otherwise growing and positive relationship. Or indeed one may suffer the very thing they fear in entering intimacy: rejection. If someone is not psychologically ready to deal with that rejection it may be damaging.

Jealousy

One's insecurity can dominate a relationship so that one becomes obsessed by a quite unreal fear of losing the partner's love or of being less important to the partner than others. Jealousy is fueled not by too much love but by too little trust (often of oneself rather than the beloved). The way to deal with jealousy is to look at self rather than at the other.

Often jealousy is linked with low self-concept: people seek exclusive attention from the beloved because of their low self-esteem. Jealousy is what we feel watching someone from whom we expect to have attention, give that attention or part of it to someone or something else. Or it may be that someone gives attention to someone we feel we should have the prerogative of giving attention to. Jealousy is caused by a perceived scarcity of love.

It is not easy to see the value of jealousy, and yet it too has its positive function. The value of the emotion of jealousy is for us to defend our own. We feel jealous when there is a rival who threatens our well-being. As with other emotions the healthy way to deal with this feeling is to allow it to be there and consider the appropriate way to act. Learn from this feeling of jealousy by developing different relational skills.

CONCLUSION

The above brief discussion of different emotion is far from exhaustive, but it helps us to draw a number of useful conclusions in general:

- Emotions are very much part of us and must be integrated in the effort to grow. Whether with regard to our own growth or the growth of others we are helping, we need to pay particular attention to emotions and feelings.

- From a moral point of view emotions in themselves are neither good nor bad. Even though they incline us towards certain choices, they do not actually determine us. It is what we do with them that determines the morality of our actions.

- Every emotion, even one that is disagreeable, has some useful purpose. In learning to integrate them we need to appreciate what is positive about them.

- In the process of integration of emotions, it is important to get in touch with them: to identify them for what they are, to allow ourselves to feel them. Part of what distinguishes a mature personality is how developed their emotional intelligence is, how much they are in touch with their feelings as well as the feelings of others.

DEFENSIVE MECHANISMS

Another area that is worth paying attention to in that complex reality that is our being is that of defensive mechanisms. These are cognitive distortions which form in the course of a person's struggle to cope with reality.

Like emotions defensive or defense mechanisms are not bad. They are tricks of the mind that keep us from seeing what we don't want to see. However, a lot of energy is spent in keeping defenses in place, and this can sometimes lead to psychopathological behavior. Defense mechanisms operate outside our awareness. However, self-reflection can help us to get in touch with our defenses. Removing all the defenses all at once can be dangerous. One can fall apart. It is better to dismantle them layer by layer, especially those that do not help us in our relationships. The following are some of the defenses.

PROJECTION

Projection, succinctly put, is seeing in others what I don't acknowledge in myself. A projection is a trait, attitude, feeling, or bit of behavior which actually belongs to a person's own personality but is not experienced as such; instead, it is attributed to objects or persons in the environment and then experienced as directed toward self by them instead of the other way round. The projector, unaware, for instance, that she is rejecting others, believes that they are rejecting her; or, unaware of his own desire to make sexual advances towards others, feels that they make sexual approaches towards him. Projection is the unconscious attribution of one's ideas, feelings and attitudes onto others especially those ideas, feelings and attitudes that are disagreeable to self.

Projection, although a fairly normal condition, can lead to paranoid behavior when carried to the extreme. It can be both individual and collective, although the collective form may sometimes more properly be termed prejudice rather than projection. Often projection is negative. We attribute something bad and unacceptable within us onto another. When we find something painful or conflictual within us, we may first deny it, and then attempt to expel it, as it were, by attributing it to another. In the case of paranoia, for example, one's own hateful or suspicious feelings about others may impalpably contradict one's self-image; they may then be projected so that others are perceived as harboring hate and mistrust towards oneself. The colloquial term 'dumping' is often used synonymously with projection.[12]

> "Our projections transform the world around us into a mirror that shows us our own faces, although we do not recognize them as our own. These projections so form our attitude towards others that eventually we bring about what we project. If we project negative intentions onto others, we will react to them with anger and defensiveness. Others will experience our unprovoked hostility, and this will arouse their defensiveness and negative shadow projections, which in turn will make us more defensive, and thus bad feelings escalate. Only when we begin to recognize and integrate the shadow/projection will such an impasse end."[13]

Projection can also be positive when we attribute something good on to others. People who fall in love often project the good qualities to be found in themselves on to the beloved. But whether positive or negative, projections are a barrier to knowing the truth, and to the extent that they hinder us from perceiving reality as it is they impede our growth. In order to work on our projections, we need first to identify them.

How Can I Recognize My Own Projections?

From a purely physical point of view, we cannot see ourselves in exactly the same way that others see us. They can observe in us what we cannot see ourselves: our back, our gait, our face, and our unconscious habitual gestures. When we look in a mirror, we can then see our physical image as others see us, but even then, we only see the view that is facing the mirror. As long as we are in our physical body, as it were, we cannot observe it like an outsider. But we can get a fairly good idea of how we appear to others through indirect ways: looking into the mirror, looking at our photographs, hearing our voice on tape, watching a video image of ourselves, etc. If we are not used to observing ourselves as an outsider, we may even be surprised by our own appearance or habitual behaviors when we observe them.

---

[12] Feltham and Dryden, *Dictionary of Counselling.*
[13] Au and Cannon, *Urgings of the Heart: A Spirituality of Integration.*

What is true on the physical level is even truer on the psychological. As a rule, it is not easy to recognize in ourselves what operates outside of awareness, for then it would no longer be unconscious. Observing our defenses is particularly hard because by their nature they hide reality from us. It requires us to take a distance from ourselves, to observe ourselves as an outsider, to be willing to be surprised at our own selves, to dismantle the illusion that we know ourselves best. In the same way that we can indirectly but accurately get to know our physical appearance and behavior, so too can we see through our defenses if we make the required effort.

What indirect ways are there for observing our defenses? One of them is our reactions and responses. The intensity of my emotional responses to others is a fair indication that I may be projecting a part of myself onto them. For example, people whom I single out for special criticism, who irritate and upset me and whom I cannot tolerate may be carrying aspects of myself that I dislike and disown. Similarly, people whom I greatly admire may share positive qualities with me, qualities that I do not recognize in myself. The difference between perception – i.e., responding to a trait that really exists in another – and projection, lies in the intensity of the response. However, it is important to point out that this is only a rough guide; it does not mean that each time you perceive in another something that evokes strong feelings in you, this is a projection.

The observation of our projections is an invitation to have a closer look at ourselves, to call the projections home. If what we are projecting is some good quality in us, we can then appreciate those good qualities in ourselves and strive to enhance them. If the projection is something we dislike in ourselves, we can then focus on the best way for dealing with them. The realization that our intense and negative reactions to particular individuals are caused by our own projections would then mitigate our feelings and reactions towards them.

PREJUDICE

Prejudice is a cognitive distortion that colors our way of thinking and makes us perceive others in absolute terms. We can make conclusions on a race, a nation, a tribe, a congregation, on the basis of a few individuals that we have met. Prejudice is the fallacy of generalization. A man hurts a woman and she concludes that all men are like that, or the other way round. The conclusions we make about others without hearing them are not about these people but about us: they do not reveal reality about the object of our prejudice, rather they reveal the distortion in our own cognition.

Prejudice is often a deficiency in our understanding of a person or an issue. It is deceptive to go by appearances. Many people of Jesus' time thought that he was less austere than John the Baptist, just because he did not wear camels' skins or feed on locusts and wild honey or live alone in the desert. But was he really? Even well-intentioned disciples of John the Baptist once came to Jesus, disturbed that his disciples did not fast the way those of the Pharisees and they themselves fasted (Matthew 9:14-17). And perhaps they were only polite, but actually wondered whether he himself ever fasted. The likelihood is that these men had an idea of self-discipline – namely, through fasting and self-abnegation – and considered a person who did not match this idea as lacking in self-discipline. But there was even a higher form of self-discipline than voluntary fasting and abnegation, namely the unwavering submission of one's will to the will of God. Moreover, if Jesus ever fasted, he would never let it be known, for that is what he himself taught to his disciples (Matthew 6: 16-18). There is a hymn by Luke Connaughton that says: "love is his word, love is his way, feasting with men, fasting alone..."[14] When we have molds of what should be right, or good or proper, we are bound to judge whatever does not fit our molds as not right or bad or improper, which may not be the case. The only way to get to the truth then is to try and put aside or even dismantle these molds if necessary, and be open to the possibility that there are other molds.

When one understands why people behave in a certain way then it becomes easier to be tolerant towards such people. It is important to try and understand what is behind the negative behavior of people.

Activity 9: Reducing Prejudice

Recall occasions when you began to accept people better because you learnt to understand them more.

The anecdote to prejudice is rigorous dedication to reality. A famous saying of St. Francis of Assisi is that "Our first task in approaching another people, another culture, and another religion, is to take off our shoes for the place we are approaching is holy. Else we may find ourselves treading on another's dream. More serious still, we may

---

[14] McCrimmon Publishing Co Ltd.

forget... that God was there before our arrival." In other words, we try to lay aside our pre-conceived ideas about them, try to understand them as they understand themselves, have a feeling of what they feel about themselves. To know people – or culture, or religion – as they know themselves is still not the full truth, for each one's knowledge of self has limitations as well. But this kind of knowledge is a long way from prejudicial knowledge, and is in the direction of knowing people as they truly are, that is, as God knows them; knowledge which can't but generate love. In conclusion, below are a few practical considerations in overcoming our prejudice:

- *Listen!*
- *Seek to be informed.*
- *Seek clarification when you are not sure.*
- *Presume people good until they contradict it.*
- *Do not go by hearsay, particularly when it is negative.*
- *Draw conclusions from the given facts and do not go beyond them.*
- *When contradicted by facts, admit. Do not adamantly stick to your guns.*
- *Be aware that people that love a person, a culture, a religion, etc., are more likely to give you truer information about it than those who do not.*

THE 'DESTRUCTIVE CRITIC'

The "Destructive Critic" is the inner tendency in us to blame ourselves in a manner that is more exaggerated than the actual reason for self-blame when things go wrong. It pulls us down leading us to discouragement and depression. It takes on many different forms. Sometimes it is the comparison of oneself with others and conclusion that "I am no good." It may also be that we set very high standards of perfection for ourselves, and each time we fail we put ourselves down. Although the intention of setting high standards seems to be noble, in fact when they are beyond our capacity for achievement, they become a source of harm to ourselves and to others. It may result among religious in a neurotic frequenting of the sacrament of confession to quell the sense of guilt. It may be a result of words and attitudes of others towards us which we accept without questioning in our childhood: "I am ugly", "I am stupid", "I am weak"; "I never finish things on time", "I always fail in relationships, etc." and which are not all together true. It is so woven in the fabric of our thinking that we hardly ever notice the devastating effect it has on us. Because it appears to aim at our good it seems justified and reasonable.

One way of looking at the destructive critic is from the perspective of scripts taken from Transaction Analysis. The words "always", "until", "after," "never", "almost" often relate to negative scripts in our life. "Why does this *always* happen to me?" "I can't really enjoy myself, *until* I have accomplished this or that", "I could enjoy myself now, but *after* wards I will feel bad about it", "I have forgotten his name again, I *never* remember people's names".

The destructive critic consumes and wastes much of our energy, keeping our lives in unnecessary misery. We need to dismantle it in order to grow. This does not mean getting rid of a sense of reasonable guilt and remorse which are healthy, but it means striving to strike a balance.

Dismantling the Destructive Critic

o Face and listen to your destructive critic but critically and with a filtering mind. There are moments when it is most active. These are moments of failure, of discouragement; moments when things go wrong. Accept that which is true in the self-criticism and reject what is not. One way to catch it is in statements of generalization. "You never get it right", "you always say the wrong thing". Challenge those statements with an inner dialogue. Consider the many other occasions that disprove them; occasions when you got things right or said good things. Often these by far outnumber the times you got them wrong.

o Sometimes, when the destructive critic pulls you down on a minor negative occurrence in a day, it is helpful to sit down and write the good things that you have done well in that day.

o Celebrate the moments of success, however little. Count your blessings. Thank God for them.

o Learn to accept the appraisal of others and positive strokes.

o Learn to use power language.[15]

---

[15] "Healthy ways of Dealing with Anger" on page 75.

o Learn from your mistakes. See them as an opportunity for learning. The biggest mistake is to cling to our past mistakes and fail to learn from them. Learn to forgive yourself.

o Affirm yourself. You do not have to wait always to be affirmed. Self-affirmation is part of self-love.

o Learn to accept that it is all right to be less than perfect. Imperfections are part of our nature as finite beings.

o By all means set for yourself high standards. But set down intermediary manageable goals by which to attain the high standards. If what you are aiming at is something that takes a year to work on for instance, focus on the daily manageable portions. Watch yourself particularly when you aim at gaining too much too soon. Do not forget to celebrate the little victories achieved. If you realize that the small goals are still too big, revise them still and break them further into more manageable portions.

o The goals one sets for oneself need to be stated in the positive, i.e. something I can move towards. They need to be well within our control. They ought to be as specific as possible. This includes foreseeing what the situation will be when you achieve your goal. One should have the resources to initiate and to maintain the goals. Goals should be in harmony with one's principles, as well as with one's whole wellbeing and that of others. They should not be attained at the expense of others.

OTHER DEFENSIVE MECHANISMS[16]

Compensation Covering up weakness by emphasizing desirable traits. A misunderstanding of the saying that love covers over a multitude of sins is a form of compensation. Compensation can also mean making up for frustration in one area by gratification in another. Often people who are frustrated may try to compensate by drinking, taking to drugs, over-eating, etc. The compensation only offers temporary relief, in the long run it only compounds one's problems.

---

[16] Zimbardo 396 (slightly adapted).

Displacement	Discharging pent-up feelings, usually of hostility, on objects less dangerous than those which initially aroused the emotion. A person who in therapy throws stones in a lake, hits a pillow or wrings a rope in order to get explosive anger out of the system is actually making use of displacement. This too is a temporary relief. More often angry people may be seen to kick objects, throw things about or hit the table.
Emotional Insulation	Withdrawing into passivity to protect self from being emotionally hurt. It is not uncommon to hear people in a malfunctioning family relationship say that they no longer care about the hurting things their partners do to them. Emotional insulation does not help the other to overcome the annoying behavior. Sometimes indifference may even cause further harm, because it is perceived as withdrawal of love.
Identification	Increasing feelings of worth by identifying self with another person or institution, often of illustrious standing. The snob who likes to be identified with those that are higher than self uses identification as a defensive mechanism. Usually all that is earned from those who can see through the snobbery is the very opposite of what is desired; namely, disdain and not admiration.
Rationalization	Attempting to prove that one's behavior is "rational" and justifiable and thus worthy of the approval of self and others. Instead of admitting an obvious mistake a person may go at great length to argue in defense of the mistake, convincing no one. Political propaganda often uses rationalization to justify mistakes. It may persuade some but not all.
Regression	Retreating to an earlier developmental level involving more childish responses and usually a lower level of aspiration. What was said about rubber bands is one form of manifestation of the defense of regression (see page 55). A person suddenly caught up in an intensely embarrassing situation may all of a sudden

cover the face with the hands or bite the thumb and/or the index finger, like a child.

Repression Pushing painful or dangerous thoughts out of consciousness, keeping them unconscious; this is considered to be the most basic of the defense mechanisms. Eventually they find a way of manifesting themselves, often in a manner that is unhealthy to the personality.

Sublimation Gratifying or working off frustrated sexual desires in substitutive nonsexual, socially acceptable activities such as work, art, exercise. Sublimation is not just an unconscious defense mechanism; it is a useful tool to develop as a help towards growth.

POST-TRAUMATIC STRESS DISORDERS

Meaning.. 102
Causes 102
Immediate and Short-term Effects 103
Long-term Effects 104
Personal Coping with Trauma.. 106
Helping others cope.. 107
Expert Treatment 109

The sound of a car engine often acts like a lullaby for me, if I am not the one behind the wheel. It very quickly sets me dozing. On this particular occasion I was in a minibus, back home traveling from Kampala to Jinja. And true to habit, this early afternoon of a fine day I was dosing off when I had a sudden loud noise of metal rubbing against tarmac. I realized that the car was swerving from one side of the road to the other. That lasted only a few moments, even though it is still very vivid even as I write about it. A sudden fear gripped me. The next thing I realized was that the car had overturned, but it was still moving, on its back or one of its sides or whatever. It was now all dark around me. I was 'sitting' on my head with a lot of pressure of what felt like a heap of other people on top of me. I felt a lot of pain on my chest and I also felt the chilling realization that I am dying. I don't remember that I prayed. It all lasted a few seconds.

Then next I realized that there was a bright white-bluish light below me. I felt that I was falling in a very wide expanse of this white bay. I tried desperately to grasp something in order to stop the falling. I held on to what felt like grass, but it could not hold me from falling. Then slowly I began to focus and started seeing tree leaves as well. I realized that I was not falling from above but that I was lying on my back looking at the bright sky. Somehow, I had been catapulted out of the car onto the side of the road, fortunately on the soft grass. It did not feel as if there had been an interval between the accident and waking up on my back. But what made me realize that I must have fainted for some time was the crowd of people around the scene of accident. In the forest reserve where the accident had occurred there was a long stretch from the nearest human settlement, and only a considerable time interval would have allowed people to gather as they had.

Apart from the stunning realization of what had happened I did not seem to have suffered much physical injury. I had a bruised hand and shoulder and I had lost my glasses and one shoe, but for the rest I felt fit, so fit that I could even help lift those who had been less fortunate into the cars that had stopped to help. I didn't get to know the exact number of casualties, except that at least two died on the way to hospital. One woman who had been sitting beside me had a piece of her hand hanging. Another who had occupied the seat in front of me with three lovely children was crying frantically holding one of them with its face covered in blood and looking for another she could not find. The conductor of the minibus had his back literally skinned; presumably he had been dragged on the bare tarmac as the vehicle rolled on its side leaving the door behind.

As we were taken to hospital together with those who had been more seriously injured, I wondered to myself whether I should not have taken another vehicle simply to go home, since I felt well enough to do so. But on the way I felt a sudden nausea and restlessness, and had to ask people to create space so I could lie down. Then I knew that perhaps I was more affected than I thought.

Time passed and I recovered from my minor bruises. But for a long time, the memories of what happened during that accident always came back whenever I traveled in a car, I was not driving myself. They came back especially when the engine made a particular kind of sound which I can only describe to myself, the sound it made on that occasion waking me rudely from my snooze. They came back whenever I passed the spot where the accident had happened. This came close to a traumatic experience in my conscious memory.

Many of those caught up in that car accident were much more affected than I: some incurred more severe wounds, broken limbs and perhaps even brain damage: others, like the poor mother, may have suffered the loss or injury of a loved one besides themselves. For others, especially the young children, the experience might have been much more frightening and with more intense psychological effects.

There are so many more stressing situations than what happened even to the most affected in that car accident. There are accidents in which entire families are wiped out leaving only a single member to recall the experience. Those caught up in a war situation suffer for a much longer extended period than in an accident which lasted only a few seconds. A fellow attendant at a course once narrated how he once fell in the hands of rebels during a civil war in southern Sudan. They tied him to a tree, and then gave a gun to his niece and ordered her to shoot him. When she refused, they raped her, beat her and finally killed her in his presence. He said that when he recalled this incident, he found it extremely difficult to forgive.

MEANING

Trauma is any emotional shock following a stressful event and leading to long term neurosis. It is an event or context which overwhelms an individual's capacity to cope. The events mentioned above would be called traumatic if their effects persisted afterwards. The central nervous system has a limited capacity to cope with shock. If trauma is overwhelming, the central nervous system breaks down and then you have post- traumatic stress disorders.

Post-traumatic stress disorder (PTSD) is a collection of distressing symptoms that sometimes occurs following a frightening event. This trauma, called the stressor, is any situation in which the person actually has experienced bodily injury, has been threatened with death or bodily injury, or has witnessed the death or injury of someone else. By definition, the trauma must cause a strong subjective experience of intense fear, horror or helplessness.

CAUSES

The causes of trauma are manifold. They include: serious motor vehicle accidents, plane crashes and boating accidents, war, both for those who fight and those who are caught in it; rape, incest and child abuse, natural disasters (tornadoes, hurricanes, volcanic eruptions, earthquakes, famine, epidemics, floods, etc.); industrial accidents, terrorism, hostage situations and kidnappings, refugee situations in which people lose among other things: dignity, identity, homeland; situations of kidnap, robberies, imprisonment in concentration camps, torture victims (even those who torture are affected), street violence, family violence, work conditions of emergency personnel, etc.

IMMEDIATE AND SHORT-TERM EFFECTS[17]

Shock and denial are typical responses to disaster and other kinds of trauma, especially shortly after the event. Both shock and denial are normal protective reactions. Shock is a sudden and often intense disturbance of your emotional state that may leave you feeling stunned or dazed. Denial involves your refusal to acknowledge that something very stressful has happened, or not experiencing fully the intensity of the event. You may temporarily numb or disconnect from life. As the initial shock subsides, reactions vary from person to person. The following, however, are normal responses to a traumatic event:

o   Feelings become intense and sometimes are unpredictable. You may become more irritable than usual, and your moods may change back and forth dramatically. You might be especially anxious or nervous, or even become depressed.

o   Thoughts and behavior patterns are affected by the trauma. You might have repeated and vivid memories of the event. These flashbacks may occur for no apparent reason and may lead to physical reactions such as rapid heartbeat or sweating. You may find it difficult to concentrate or make decisions, or become more easily confused. Sleep and eating patterns also may be disrupted.

o   Recurring emotional reactions are common. Anniversaries of the event, such as one month or one year, as well as reminders such as aftershocks from earthquakes or the sounds of sirens, gunfire or even fireworks, can trigger upsetting memories of the traumatic experience. These "triggers" may be accompanied by fears that the stressful event will be repeated.

---

[17]   Cf. *Warning Signs of Trauma Related Stress (Symptoms)* at http://www:apa.org/practice/ptsd.html and Managing Traumatic Stress... At http://helping/apa.org/daily/traumaticstress:html

o Interpersonal relationships often become strained. Greater conflict such as more frequent arguments with family members and co-workers is common. On the other hand, you might become withdrawn and isolated and avoid your usual activities.

o Physical symptoms may accompany the extreme stress. For example, headaches, nausea and chest pain may result and may require medical attention. Other signs of anxiety and distress like shortness of breath, palpitations, sweating may be felt when exposed to persons, objects or situations that trigger memories of the trauma. Pre-existing medical conditions may worsen due to the stress.

o The intense anxiety and fear that often follow a disaster or other traumatic event can be especially troubling for children. Some may regress and demonstrate younger behaviors such as thumb sucking or bed wetting. Children may be more prone to nightmares and fear of sleeping alone. Performance in school may suffer. Other changes in behavior patterns may include throwing tantrums more frequently, or withdrawing and becoming more solitary.

o Other effects of trauma include: aggressive outbursts, exaggerated sense of guilt, startle response, nightmares which may be recurrent, avoiding places and people that trigger memories of the event; being unable to remember important details about the trauma, believing that one's life will be shorter than originally expected, losing interest in activities that were once enjoyable, avoiding discussions of the trauma; showing signs of increased arousal or vigilance, as if expecting danger, re-enacting the trauma again and again (e.g. when those abused expose themselves to situations in which they may be abused, or those who were traumatized as soldiers seek to fight again), those abused becoming abusers (as an unconscious desire to master their helplessness), avoidance of intimate relationships or finding it difficult to build alliance.

LONG-TERM EFFECTS

It is important to realize that there is not one "standard" pattern of reaction to the extreme stress of traumatic experiences. Some people respond immediately, while others have delayed reactions - sometimes months or even years later. Some have adverse effects for long periods of time, while others recover rather quickly. There are those who have exceptional ability to transcend trauma and become very creative, e.g. Nelson Mandela. Outwardly normal people may have a serious fixation in their life. Moreover, reactions can change over time. Some who have suffered from trauma are energized initially by the event to help them with the challenge of coping, only to later become discouraged or depressed.

Those who have been traumatized say in child abuse or incest may tend to idealize people they consider good; thus, setting themselves for disappointment. Or they may hate intensely. It is common for them to make the same mistake again and again. Those who transcend the fixation may arrive at integration of the traumatic event; they acquire the ability to learn from their trauma, and go on in life. Others may develop a dissociative identity disorder: they perceive themselves as two different persons in their life.

Most people who are exposed to terrible trauma do not develop PTSD, and doctors have not yet determined why this is so. In addition, contrary to what one might think, the severity of the stressor does not predict the severity of symptoms. Although the person is often aware of a connection between the stress and the symptoms, it still is not clear what makes some people more vulnerable to stress than others. A number of factors tend to affect the length of time required for recovery, including:

- o The degree of intensity and loss. Events that last longer and pose a greater threat, and where loss of life or substantial loss of property is involved, often take longer to resolve.

- o A person's genetic pre-disposition and general ability to cope with emotionally challenging situations. Individuals who have handled other difficult, stressful circumstances may well find it easier to cope with the trauma.

- o Other stressful events preceding the traumatic experience. Individuals faced with other emotionally challenging situations, or who have suffered prior traumatization, such as serious health problems or family-related difficulties, may have more intense reactions to the new stressful event and need more time to recover.

o Developmental stage: how much one is affected will depend on whether he or she is an infant, a child an adult or whether they are in their old age.

o Social support system. Compare for instance the American Veterans of the War of Vietnam with all the support accessible to them, including websites set-up specifically for them; and the people traumatized in the genocide of Rwanda, many of whom do not even know that they are traumatized.

PERSONAL COPING WITH TRAUMA

There are a number of steps you can take to help restore emotional wellbeing and a sense of control following a disaster or other traumatic experience, including the following:

o Give yourself time to heal. Anticipate that this will be a difficult time in your life. Allow yourself to mourn the losses you have experienced. Try to be patient with changes in your emotional state.

o Ask for support from people who care about you and who will listen and empathize with your situation. But keep in mind that your typical support system may be weakened if those who are close to you also have experienced or witnessed the trauma. Communicate your experience in whatever ways feel comfortable to you - such as by talking with family or close friends or keeping a journal.

o Find out about local support groups if these are available such as for those who have suffered from natural disasters or civil war, or for women who are victims of rape. These can be especially helpful for people with limited personal support systems. Try to find groups led by appropriately trained and experienced professionals if you can afford it. Group discussion can help people realize that other individuals in the same circumstances often have similar reactions and emotions.

o Engage in healthy behaviors to enhance your ability to cope with excessive stress. Eat well-balanced meals and get plenty of rest. If you experience ongoing difficulties with sleep, you may be able to find some relief through relaxation techniques. Avoid alcohol or drugs.

o Establish or re-establish routines such as eating meals at regular times and following an exercise program. Take some time off the demands of daily life by pursuing hobbies or other enjoyable activities.

o Avoid major life decisions such as switching careers or jobs, if possible, because these activities tend to be highly stressful.

o Become knowledgeable about what to expect as a result of trauma.

o Grieve for the losses: get in touch with the losses. Name the losses. Take time. Do not blame, just name what you lost. What did it cost? The intensity of the feeling helps you to grieve. It does not matter whether you shed tears or not. Stay with the feeling. Other emotions may also well up: guilt, anger…, anger with yourself, with the environment, with others, with God. Work through each of these emotions that come up. You will know that you have grieved enough when the memory of the event brings no pain anymore, or when similar events do not bring you the pain or traumatic experience. Accept the pain that comes up as pain.

o Set your boundaries. Nobody is allowed to enter your emotional state unless you invite them in.

o If your particular trauma involves persons who have wronged you, to complete the healing process forgiveness has to come in.

HELPING OTHERS COPE

o Dealing with trauma requires in the first place that you stop the trauma if it is still continuous, and that you create a safe environment. Treating people traumatized in a war situation requires first that the war stops. Similarly, a person suffering from abuse in a family should first come out of the traumatizing environment. Obviously quite often the counselor is faced with the pain of powerlessness to stop the stressful situation.

o Dealing with post-traumatic disorders requires experts. Do not presume to handle traumatic issues if you do not have the necessary expertise, otherwise you might open up wounds you cannot handle, like a surgeon who opens up a patient without knowing how to sew them up. A surgeon might call up another doctor for consultation, but in a counselling relationship you may not have that possibility, for the client requires time to build trust, and will not allow you to mess them up further by bringing in a third party. All the same if in a helping relationship the person you are trying to help brings up issues that you judge to be the result of trauma, do not refuse to help them, particularly if there is no possibility of expert help. Do listen to them with empathy, for that in itself goes a long way to treat the trauma.

o Build trust in the client. Be very patient, deal with what the client brings. It is very difficult for clients who have suffered trauma to start. Sometimes they waver from wanting to trust and fearing to do so. Just be with them.

o Once rapport is built let the client re-live the whole trauma (if you are capable of handling the situation). Allow them to narrate. It is through this re-living that healing is attained.

With regard to children, there are several things that parents and others who care for children can do to help alleviate the emotional consequences of trauma, including the following:

o Spend more time with children and let then be more dependent on you during the months following the trauma - for example, allows your child to cling to you more often than usual. Physical affection is very comforting to children who have experienced trauma.

o Provide play experiences to help relieve tension. Younger children in particular may find it easier to share their ideas and feelings about the event through non-verbal activities such as drawing.

o Encourage older children to speak with you and with one another about their thoughts and feelings. This helps reduce their confusion and anxiety related to the trauma. Respond to questions in terms they can comprehend. Reassure them repeatedly that you care about them and that you understand their fears and concerns.

o Keep regular schedules for activities such as eating, playing and going to bed, to help restore a sense of security and normalcy.

EXPERT TREATMENT

Some people are able to cope effectively with the emotional and physical demands brought about by a natural disaster or other traumatic experience by using their own support systems. It is not unusual, however, to find that serious problems persist and continue to interfere with daily living. For example, some may feel overwhelming nervousness or lingering sadness that adversely affects job performance and interpersonal relationships.

Individuals with prolonged reactions that disrupt their daily functioning should consult with a trained and experienced mental health professional. Psychologists and other appropriate mental health providers help educate people about normal responses to extreme stress. These professionals work with individuals affected by trauma to help them find constructive ways of dealing with the emotional impact.

With children, continual and aggressive emotional outbursts, serious problems at school, preoccupation with the traumatic event, continued and extreme withdrawal, and other signs of intense anxiety or emotional difficulties all point to the need for professional assistance. A qualified mental health professional can help such children and their parents understand and deal with thoughts, feelings and behaviors that result from trauma.

Some of the most common types of psychotherapy used to treat PTSD are:

o   Anxiety management techniques – these include relaxation training, in which people with PTSD learn to control their symptoms by using imagination and muscle control; breath retraining, in which breath control is used to help alleviate PTSD symptoms; and thought stopping, in which a person with PTSD learns to halt distressing thoughts by saying (or thinking) the word, "Stop," and then performing a distracting action (for example, snapping the wrist with a rubber band).

o   Cognitive therapy – in this form of treatment, a therapist helps the patient to identify anxiety-provoking thoughts and memories, and to recognize that these patterns of thinking may not be consistent with the reality of current everyday life. The patient then learns to develop new thought patterns that are psychologically and emotionally healthier than the old ones.

o Exposure therapy – this treatment involves re-exposing the patient to people, situations and objects that trigger memories of the traumatic event. After repeated re-exposures, the patient's fear diminishes, and he or she gradually learns to control anxieties related to the trauma. The re-exposures can be done in actual real-life situations, or the patient may be asked only to imagine them.

o Play therapy – this treatment uses play to help children with PTSD to confront traumatic memories and deal with them.

o Education, supportive counselling and family therapy – these treatments help patients with PTSD and their families to learn about the origin and effects of the illness, and to cope with its effects.

Part III

INTRODUCTION

A fundamental attitude to have in the arduous struggle of human growth – whether this concerns one's own growth or one's duty in assisting the growth of others – involves three convictions: 1) Change is *difficult*. A realistic appraisal of this fact does not lead to discouragement. On the contrary it leads to perseverance, to patience, endurance, courage, and acceptance of occasional failure – all factors that accompany genuine growth. It helps us avoid the pitfall of looking for quick tangible results. Perseverance is a difficult but a most important virtue in the process of growth. It is relatively easy to do some good action for some time. That good action becomes habitual and therefore virtuous, only when it is done constantly.

2) Change is *important*. In fact, conversion and growth are not just important, they are fundamental to a life worth living. Striving towards our ideal self is the most important thing in our lives. Jesus told his disciples that all the wealth of the world was not worth battering for one's soul. *What then, will a man gain if he wins the whole world and ruins his life? Or what has a man to offer in exchange for his life? (Mark 8:36-37)* For that reason it is worth spending on it every ounce of strength in us. When we are convinced of this, then we are motivated to work for it. People can attain extra-ordinary results as long as they are convinced and motivated.

3) Change is *possible*. It is possible to improve, to be converted and to grow. When we have struggled to overcome one difficulty or another for years without visible success, we may get into the belief that it is hopeless to think of the possibility of overcoming the difficulties. Through habit we re-enact the same situation of failure over and over again. Our good resolutions have been frustrated over and over again by changing moods and loss of motivation. The destructive critic in us, feeding on past failures constantly pulls us down. We know by now too, that our unconscious influences our conscious thoughts and actions more than

we think. The network of human acquaintances also sometimes induces us to keep the status quo. But in spite of all this we can surmount the weak spot through a conscious choice to change. The good news about each one of us is that however much the beautiful image of God in us has been tarnished and disfigured, we have the possibility to have it restored to its original beauty.

There are four agents involved in the restoration of the tarnished image of God in us: we ourselves, other people, the circumstances of our life, and God. We look at these one at a time.

THE ROLE OF THE SELF

We are free to choose to be happy. We choose our own destiny. That is the wonderful gift of God who gave us a little bit of his own nature. God has created us free. That means that ultimately our happiness or lack of it is the result of personal choices. There are many other factors that affect our growth, as we are going to see in the following four chapters. However, the primary role is played by us. In order to play this role, the first condition is for us to want to change.

IT IS IMPORTANT TO WANT TO BE WELL AGAIN

"Do you want to be well again?" This is the question that Jesus asked the cripple at the pool of Bethzatha (John 5:1-18). It sounds to us an irrelevant question, considering the circumstances. The pool was known to be frequented by those who needed healing. The man's physical condition must have been visible to all. His proximity to the pool in the company of others who were also ailing left no doubt about whether or not the man wanted to be healed. Yet Jesus asked the man a most important question: "do you want to be healed?" As a matter of fact the man did not answer the question directly; he started explaining how the quicker cripples jumped in before him every time the water welled up But Jesus had gathered all he needed; the man wanted to be healed. It would have been different if the man had answered "no, thanks, I am just relaxing here, marveling at the wonders of nature."

Do *you* want to be healed? Do you feel there is room for improvement in your life, or do you feel like, "No thanks! I am as normal as anyone can be. I know that no one is perfect, and I am not about to try the impossible. I do my best to be a good husband or wife, a good boss or employee. I am a good citizen who never cheats on taxes. I say my prayers daily and go to Sunday Mass. I even give money to beggars and fast during Lent. I respect others and I expect them to respect me in return."

The desire to change, to improve, to grow, is crucial. Unless there is a certain amount of emptiness in us, we cannot be filled. The Pharisee who prayed thanking God for his own virtues was quite a good man (cf. Luke

18:9-14). Apart from keeping some of the commandments that prove the most difficult to many, he fasted twice a week and paid tithe on all that he earned. But he did not feel he needed any improvement. He was full of himself and there was no space for growth.

There is nothing wrong with feeling satisfied and at peace with oneself. Nor is it healthy to constantly accuse and bedevil oneself with guilt and remorse. What we need to do is to see ourselves, not in the light of the standards we set for ourselves, but in the light of truth. In order to know the truth which sets us free we need to perceive it. In order to perceive it we need to listen to it, to pay attention to the reality within and around us. The phrase in a song that says "look, listen and love" captures all that I am trying to say. In order to perceive truth, we need to look, listen and love.

LISTENING TO THE BODY: BURNOUT AND SELF-CARE

Burnout

Things that burn eventually burn out. That is the natural order. The reason why Moses found the burning bush strange was because it did not seem to burn out (Exodus 3:1-6). He very soon realized that he was in the presence of the supernatural; of the living God. In fact, this Theophany gives us a beautiful description of God: the fire that burns without ever burning out. The sun and the stars would seem to defy the natural rule of "burn and burn-out," but this is only because they have a much longer lifetime than us. We know now that they eventually burn out, even though it may take them several billion years. Charity organizations that gather enormous quantities of supplies which they then ration out to the needy know that they must continually receive in order to continuously give out. We eat and drink regularly because we constantly burn our energy that we gain from food and drink. If we do not replace spent energy we starve and die.

Similarly, when we spend our spiritual energy, when we give ourselves out in work, in charity, in benefiting others in various forms, we burn some form of energy and we eventually must suffer burn out, unless we have a way of replenishing our reserves.

We all have moments of energy, exuberance, zest and motivation. At such times we can delve into our work hand and foot, and accomplish a lot to our satisfaction and the satisfaction of others. We feel good about ourselves. We build reputations. We portray commitment. We earn gratitude and admiration. However, now and then we also experience moments of physical exhaustion, rejection, dejection, questioning, uncertainty, and discouragement. There are times when we question the value of our work or even our own worth. There are moments we feel we want to be left alone. Although unpleasant, these feelings are quite normal; they are indicators that we need rest, support or encouragement, solitude and reflection. It may be that we need to take it easy or to evaluate our standards. Such moments are not burnout if they are occasional, and if we take the necessary steps to redress the situation.

Our day-to-day occupations of looking for food, shelter or clothing, of searching for a job, of reading hard to pass an exam, of looking for capital, of trying to beat a deadline, of scheming to pay back, of family wrangles and squabbles, of sealing a business deal… can make us forget our bodily needs. The purpose of the institute for Ongoing Formation of Priests where I work at present is basically to help diocesan priests recuperate their energies both physical and spiritual, in a ministry that can quite often be stressful. However, frequently those who need such rest and renewal are the ones most reluctant to attend on the grounds that they are too busy.

Burnout results when we do not listen to the indicators over a long time. It may be that we are not aware of these indicators; that we do not pay much attention to our personal needs, absorbed as we may be in attending to the needs of others. It may be that we are aware of our physical needs but we find ourselves in a situation where we cannot do much about them, or we think we cannot do much about them. It may also be that we are aware of neglecting ourselves and the possible consequences, and that we are in position to do something about it, but we do not move ourselves to action due to our own laziness.

Whatever the case, constant neglect of our personal needs may result into habitual depression, apathy, cynicism, and negativity. Emotions are blunted; life does not seem worth living, there is a feeling of detachment and demoralization. This is Burnout.

Experts name two as the commonest forms of burnout: Workplace and Care-giving burnout. Workplace burnout can come from such causes as boredom resulting from doing repetitive and unchallenging work, working under what one perceives to be unreasonable pressure from superiors, routinely carrying out tasks that violate one's ideals, striving to meet standards that are beyond one's capability, whether these standards are self-imposed or set by others. Workplace burnout is also to be found among those that carry out high stress jobs like taxi drivers, teachers, law enforcers, and high technology professionals. Care-giving burnout on the other hand comes to those who are committed to the service of others, particularly when this service proves unrewarding. This form of burnout may sometimes also be described as "Compassion fatigue." Clergy, nurses, doctors, those who give out relief services, etc. are among the people more likely to suffer Care-giving burnout. Burnout of this kind is more likely to occur when the caregiver is met with ingratitude, scanty resources, unrealistic demands from the recipients, deception from beneficiaries, insensitivity by others to the needs of the caregiver, loss of faith in God, apparent lack of a definite end to the care-giving or lack of hope for a happy outcome. These are not the only forms or causes of burnout. In fact, no one is absolutely safe from it, not even those who tell others about it.

In the journey of faith burnout, which is a secular term, is comparable to, if not commensurate with, the "dark night of the soul." It is the gradual death of self-interest and a call to self-transcendence. It is a reminder that the fully mature person is not driven by enthusiasm alone, but especially by knowledge of and will to do what is right. It is better for us if we can avoid suffering burnout, but if we do or have suffered it and overcome it, the outcome is a more mature and seasoned personality.

Self-Care

Moses was a holy man. He attended to the many needs of God's people. But he was not a great one at attending to his own needs. It was his father-in-law that drew his attention to the fact that he too needed to take care of himself. We read the full story in the passage below:

Moses sat to judge the people, and the people stood about Moses from morning till evening. When Moses' father-in-law saw all that, he was doing for the people, he said, "What is this that you are doing for the people? Why do you sit alone, and all the people stand about you from morning till evening?" And Moses said to his father-in-law, "Because the people come to me to inquire of God; when they have a dispute, they come to me and I decide between a man and his neighbor, and I make them know the statutes of God and his decisions." Moses' father-in-law said to him, "What you are doing is not good. You and the people with you will wear yourselves out, for the thing is too heavy for you; you are not able to perform it alone. Listen now to my voice; I will give you counsel, and God be with you! You shall represent the people before God, and bring their cases to God; and you shall teach them the statutes and the decisions, and make them know the way in which they must walk and what they must do. Moreover choose able men from all the people, such as fear God, men who are trustworthy and who hate a bribe; and place such men over the people as rulers of thousands, of hundreds, of fifties, and of tens. And let them judge the people at all times; every great matter they shall bring to you, but any small matter they shall decide themselves; so it will be easier for you, and they will bear the burden with you. If you do this, and God so commands you, then you will be able to endure, and all this people also will go to their place in peace." So, Moses gave heed to the voice of his father-in-law and did all that he had said. Moses chose able men out of all Israel, and made them heads over the people, rulers of thousands, of hundreds, of fifties, and of tens. And they judged the people at all times; hard cases they brought to Moses, but any small matter they decided themselves (Exodus 18:13-27).

There are many fathers-in-law and mothers-in-law who would have regarded the behavior of Moses as one of admirable and heroic self-sacrifice in the service of God and his people, and who would have encouraged him to his death, and then who would have given wonderful eulogies at his burial. There are many people who wear themselves to death in the belief that they live out a kind of bloodless martyrdom. They even apply to themselves the example of Jesus who at times did not have time to take his meals. It is easy to forget that even Jesus invited his disciples to come aside for a while at take their rest. Moreover, although he himself took little rest he grabbed every opportunity he got to emerge himself in prayer, and this was a source of great solace and refreshment for his spirit. It is true that there are times when the demands of our work leaves no time to have a much needed rest. There are occasions when it is valiant and laudable for a person to die in the service of others. Nevertheless, willful neglect of oneself that results into self-harm is not a virtue, particularly when there is the possibility of continued rendering service to others even as a person takes reasonable care of self.

Like Moses, we too need to take good care of ourselves. We ought to include ourselves among the people we take care of. In the first part of this book the different ways we take care of our bodies were outlined briefly. (See "The Embodiment" on page 26 above). We now look at these ways in a more elaborate manner.

NOURISHMENT

The body needs nourishment to recuperate lost energy, to remain healthy and to replace worn-out cells or to grow. Usually, we do not need much persuasion to take care of the bodily need of food and drink. The body communicates this need in an unambiguous way through hunger and thirst. The enjoyment we draw from good food and drink motivates us to eat and drink, even when we do not feel very hungry or thirsty. For those who have nothing to eat, the nourishment of the body usually assumes the primary role overriding all other needs. Most people who can afford it have regular eating habits so that they do not need to worry much about feeding the body. This is not to say that we do not need to worry much about the feeding of the body.

In order to keep the body optimally healthy our feeding habits need to be regulated by our intellect and will. For those who can afford to eat whatever they like the challenge is that of not eating that which they like but which does harm to their bodies. The obese must reduce the quantity of food, and also avoid particular types. Diseases like ulcers, hypertension, and diabetes require the avoidance of certain foods. Pregnant mothers must take great care what they eat and drink. People who enjoy smoking and taking alcoholic drinks are required to give them up for health reasons. Strangely enough, it occurs frequently that the behaviorite foods are those that must be knocked off the menu due to health reasons. This implies that the care for the body means for some people a considerable amount of self-discipline.

Conversely nourishment of the body requires sometimes that a person must eat against their will. There are many diseases that lead to the loss of appetite. Here again a gap is created between what one feels like doing or not doing, and what one ought to do.

We have talked of those who have enough to eat and whose problem is not to eat what they like. However, there is the bigger majority of those who do not have enough to eat, even when they work very hard to earn what to eat: those caught up in areas of famine, of natural disasters, in areas of the world with scanty resources, or even those in areas where there is plenty to go around but who are too poor to earn what to eat. It is often amazing how little it takes for those with surplus to meet the basic needs of those without, and how much pain they would relieve by exercising a little generosity, and how much joy they would obtain for themselves with the act. This does not apply only to the relation between the developed and developing world, but also between the rich and the poor of the developing world. Of course, the practical and effective way of doing that would have to be worked out. It would be too much to expect that everyone has the generosity of heart to invite the poor neighbors to table or go out in the street dishing out food. But whoever has the will to help feed the hungry can find a way to do without depriving self and dependents. The generous understand very well the saying that it is more blessed to give than to receive. They know how fulfilling and rewarding acts of kindness to the needy can be.

MEDICATION

Today in Uganda one hears many announcements made by health organization through the media, offering people free testing as well as counselling for HIV and other sexually transmitted diseases. Such organizations also offer free or subsidized treatment of these diseases. This assistance is offered for the purpose of reducing the proliferation of these diseases. However, the primary beneficiary is the person who is infected. By responding to such invitation – or by going uninvited for any testing or treatment for that matter – a person does himself or herself a behavior in the first place.

The body suffers damage and needs repair or medical care. As in the case of its need of food, the body usually communicates its need of medical care through pain. However, more than in the case of food, in this case the body must be assisted by conscious choices of the mind. Motor repairs are expensive, and one hopes that when one takes a car to the garage, the mechanic will fix the broken part and report nothing else damaged. But quite often one receives the unpleasant surprise that there are other parts, sometimes more expensive, that need working on. Unless repaired in time the damaged parts can cause further damage to those parts that are good at the moment or lead to a motor accident. The same happens often with medical examinations. A routine check can reveal the initial development of a tumor. No one wants to hear that. But if it would be unwise to avoid ever going to the garage for fear that mechanics will discover damages that might cause you to incur unplanned-for expenses, it is much more imprudent when it comes to one's body, because body spare parts are not as available and as cheap as those of cars. Bodily pain not treated in time could lead to malignant cancer, a heart failure, a stroke or full-blown AIDS.

Our responsibility for the medical needs of our body includes reception of routine checks, submission to unpleasant but necessary treatment, and following medical advice regarding necessary health precautions.

LEISURE AND REST

There are too many people who rest when they should be working; people who make long phone calls to exchange gossip, people who chatter to each other or read the newspaper in a public office while others are kept waiting, people who attend overnight discos during week days and then sleep it off the next day, people who fake reasons to have a day off from their work. There are men who go to the garden from early morning until 10.00 am and then for the rest of the day sit at home to be fed by their wives and then go to join their drinking partners in the evening. In many cases it is more pleasant to indulge in leisure than to work, and it is tempting to seek the more pleasant activity. If you are the kind of person who tends to work less than you should, please skip what is said below and move over to the next topic. The following paragraphs might only serve as permission for further escape from honest work in order to indulge in unwarranted leisure and rest.

The body needs rest and recuperation. The harder it works the greater its need of rest. Those who do intense mental work do well to have rest that involve physical exercise. All need to have sufficient sleep. Lack of rest over a long time may lead the body to such malfunctions as physical and mental exhaustion, development of health complications, less productivity, sickness or even death. On the other hand, when work is interspersed with meaningful rest, it remains interesting and productive.

Rest takes on different forms, depending on the nature of work. It includes retirement for those who have worked for a certain number of years or who must give up work early due to some ailment, annual leave, retreats and recollections, monthly days off, Sunday rest, sufficient sleep during the night, moments of break during the day, and occasional pauses in the actual execution of work. Everyone needs to know their need of rest according to the nature of their work and their bodily constitution, as well as to utilize or create opportunities for leisure and rest. Again everyone needs to discover what kind of activities make them rested, for it is not always true that refrain from doing the usual activities brings about the needed rest.

PHYSICAL EXERCISE

In Africa it sometimes appears funny to locals when they see expatriates run, walk, ride bicycles or go out for mountains climbing, all for the joy of carrying out these activities. Natives do all this in their daily activities out of necessity, such that they are baffled at anyone who seems to find joy in hard toil for the sake of it. As a matter of fact, those whose daily activities involve a lot of physical exercise may need no extra exertion of their bodies as a form of self-care. However, people whose work is mainly intellectual and involves a lot of sitting definitely need some form of physical exercise.

Playing can be particularly valuable in restoring physical and mental health. It is fallacious to attribute play exclusively to children. The inner child in us needs every now and then to recapture the excitement and hilarity of play. One does not have to be a football star or tennis celebrity. Winning is a major motivation in many forms of play, but it is also possible to play for the sake of the merriment involved and not in order to win. Sometimes it is not as childish as some might think, for an adult to play with children.

The choice of physical activity or amusement takes into account such factors as the nature of a person's work, the time available, the age and physical condition of the person. Physical exercise includes such activities as gardening, jogging, different forms of sports, hiking, lawn mowing, swimming, etc.

RELATIONS

To be considered in the first place are a person's closest relations. These may be fellow priests in a presbytery or institution, fellow religious in a convent, family members, close friends, partners at work, etc. The nurturing of these relations is of great value in the process of self-care. Community life can at times be difficult, such that one's closest associates are also part of one's major source of stress or burnout. The easy way of escape is to find alternative relations outside while neglecting the closest community. However, this may only aggravate the problem. Sharing common meals, spending quality time together, talking about disagreements, celebrating moments of joy together, listening to each other's troubles, informing each other of one's whereabouts, making efforts towards reconciliation; all these are possible means of nurturing relations with one's closest relations.

Outside the close circle of associates one can also seek to relate with people doing the same kind of work. One may join a social, religious, or support group where one meets people of similar minds.

EXPERT ASSISTANCE

Although the focus in this book is on self-help, bearing in mind that the a big number (perhaps the majority) of its readers are people who have no access to or cannot afford expert help, still it is important to mention that, as in the case of addictions (see page 146), there are occasions when care for the self-demands seeking help from an expert. People may be at the stage of requiring professional assistance if they feel they cannot resume a normal routine, if they have frequent feelings of committing suicide or hurting others, if they find relief in dangerous alternatives like alcohol and drugs or sex, or simply if they feel extremely helpless.

CONCLUSION

There are many other elements that can be included in the care for our bodies. The clothes we wear, how much or how little time we spend on enhancing our physical appearance, our concern for hygiene; all these features under Self-care. Underlying all this is the element of true love for self. This love implies choosing to do that which promotes one's wellbeing. At times love of self means taking it easy with oneself, but at other times it means discipline. Proper love and care for the body requires us to give to it what it needs. However, this is not the same as giving the body *all* that it *wants*. Self-care demands that sometimes the body must be denied what it craves for and that sometimes it must be given what it would have preferred not to have. The wellbeing of the body and of the entire person demands frequent discipline of the body in the light of reason.

SELF KNOWLEDGE THROUGH THE INTENSIVE JOURNAL

From the care for the body, which is in the realm of the conscious, we move on to the care of our unconscious self. How can I stoop and peer into that aspect of me that I am not immediately conscious of and that, as we have seen, plays a big role in my wellbeing? There are different ways. One of these is that has been extensively examined by Professor Ira Progoff is that of the *Intensive Journal*.[18]

---

[18] The ideas presented here are partly based on, partly inspired by, Ira Progoff's book *At a Journal workshop: The basic text and guide for using the Intensive Journal Process*, New York: Dialogue House Library, 1975. See also website at www.intensivejournal.org

Many people have the practice of keeping a diary. Some write in their diaries events that have transpired in their lives for each particular day. Others use a diary merely to keep schedules and appointments. The use of a diary to record the chronological flow of one's life is remotely comparable to one aspect of the *Intensive Journal*. People have used diaries of famous people to write their biographies or to write history. The intensive journal is kept for the present: for growth of the owner.

Intensive Journal is a method of spirituality that has no religious bias: it can be used by a secular culture, for those searching for God, as well as people already established in different creeds and denominations. The method is called 'intensive' because it requires much work and reflection. But the fruits make it worth the trouble.

In working in the *Intensive Journal* method, we need to be sensitive to spontaneous stirrings of emotion. Those stirrings guide us to the contents of life that have something to say to us. It is immaterial whether the emotions be positive or negative; what is important is that they be freely given to us and that we accept them and follow their lead.

The first time I got acquainted with the *Intensive Journal* method was at a summer counselling course. It was introduced in this intensive program as one of the many instruments of growth. That time, for some reason, I was not terribly impressed by the theory. After three years, I became acquainted anew with *Intensive Journal* and this time it took root. Even then, I did not write all the journals proposed to us in the way that they were given. Rather, I wrote only what appealed to me and in my own style; but even that paid off. In fact, it was insights gained from the journal method that inspired the writing of this book, and some of the ideas have actually been gleaned from the journals written at that course. The reader is advised to refer to the actual sources already indicated for a fuller understanding of *Intensive Journal* as a theory of growth. Here there is space only for a rudimentary presentation of the method in the light of personal experience, intended to rouse one's interest in the method.

Briefly the method consists of two categories. The first category is that of the recording of events of one's life, and more importantly, the inner movements accompanying those events. This category consists of five sections: "the *Period Log*, the *Daily Log*, the *Dream Log*, the *Twilight Imagery Log* and the *Life History Log*. In each of these we record the facts of our inner experience from a particular vantage point, always without judging, censoring, embellishing, criticizing, justifying, or interpreting the facts."[19] Even as we write these Logs and read them to ourselves, we receive what Progoff refers to as experiential feedback: we capture meaning that might have escaped us during the events, we are surprised at how much we recall, we see connections between events. This observation of the processes that take place in us is what generates energy for our growth. The second category is that of Feedback proper where "we carry out the active exercises that generate the energy and bring about the transformations of awareness in the Journal work."[20] The feedback section is also called the dialogue phase. We dialogue with persons, with works, with our body, with events, situations and circumstances, with our dreams, with society; and we eventually come to an inner wisdom dialogue.

Data Collection about Self in the Logs

The starting point of journaling is the present, the Now. This is the *Period Log*. The participant sits in a meditative posture and observes the feelings about one's present; where one is in one's life now. We then realize that our now is not a fixed moment, but that it is elastic stretching back into the past, and into the future. Right now, I have a cold, and as I reflect, I can feel the pain in my chest, the burning in my eyes, the constant need to sneeze. I know that I started sensing this cold two days ago, while playing table tennis. I know that probably I got it earlier at table from a colleague who has been suffering from it. I remember that even as I sat next to him, I felt a bit of apprehension knowing that I might get the flu, but couldn't politely avoid him. I know that after realizing that I had got it from him I felt a little resentful towards him, even on the conscious level I told myself that the poor man did not desire it for himself either, and did not wish to pass it on. I can recall the disturbance in my sleep last night because of it. I can stretch it into the future, and consider how long it is likely to stay, what I am going to do about it. I can observe the present feelings it is evoking. That is one aspect of my "now".

I am aware too that I am writing about the period log. I know that it is three years since I first got acquainted with it. I can recall that first acquaintance, on a warm afternoon, while the lecturer tried to guide us into the meditation and how I felt both bored and sleepy. I can recall my

---

[19] Progoff, (1975), 38.
[20] Progoff, 38.

experience with the method since then. That is another aspect of my now. I can go on and on, depending on what images go through my mind as I sit, feeling my now. When eventually I am ready, I start writing in my Period Log what has gone on in my mind. No matter when you want to start, there is always a new now, and you can be sure that something new will come up.

A second Log, one that I have personally used more intensively, is the *Daily Log*. I had never really got adjusted to the daily examination of conscience which I learnt early in my seminary training, as a necessary part of one's prayer life. There were times in my life when I made an effort to be faithful to it; and there were times when it proved particularly difficult. Perhaps the difficulty lay in the fact that I rightly or wrongly understood it to be the recalling of the sins one has committed and the sins of omission. Recalling my faulty commissions and omissions has always been difficult at any one time and much more difficult just before bed when I was tired and sleepy. But the Daily Log offered me something new and refreshing.

Progoff describes it as having "the function of gathering into one accessible place a running record of the subjective experiences of all kinds that move through a person's mind and emotions in the course of a day and a night."[21] Because it involved the whole of one's life and not just the omissions and the wrong doings it was more fun to write.

My preferred time for writing was in the night after retiring to my room. After a moment of reflection, I would capture the first event of the day that came to mind, however insignificant. Usually in the course of writing down this, another came to mind. Soon I would be struggling to keep pace with the flow of memories. The use of a computer is particularly helpful, for then one has the ease of later rearranging what one has written in a more chronological order. Progoff insists, however, that you do not edit or embellish, if these written experiences are to have growth value.

In writing the Daily Log one should understand that the more important element is the process and not the content. One should, therefore, write only enough content necessary for understanding the dynamics of one's actions and reactions. Emphasis should be placed on one's subjective reactions and feelings. However, in the course of writing it often happens

---

[21] Ibid, 86.

that a person is energized to write on and on. This too is useful and should not be hindered. Later on, the extensive material can be transferred to the appropriate section of the Intensive Journal where it may be exceedingly important.

There is also the *Twilight Imagery Log*, in which we try to capture the pearls of inspiration that occur to us mainly between the time of sleeping and waking up. While I personally found it somewhat difficult to work with this particular log, I was nonetheless inspired by the idea, to capture inspirations that occur at other times of my day apart from the twilight period.

It happens often that in the course of looking for something we find something else we were not looking for but whose discovery is important. Sometimes the desire not to be distracted from our set purpose may drive us to ignore what we have found but were not looking for. But then it may occur that on another occasion we actually need what we ignored, and we may spend more time looking for it as well. While it is good to be focused and not to be distracted by everything that attracts our attention, it is equally important to value the unsought discoveries. The trick lies in striking a balance. We might for instance place in a safe place the thing we found accidentally to come to it later.

A similar experience occurs in the field of study or research. In the course of thinking over or reading about a particular subject an idea may 'drop' in the mind about something else, not sought for at the moment but nonetheless valuable. If we do not capture it at the moment, we may lose it forever. It is a useful practice to jot down such discoveries or inspirations. Thanks to the computer age, it is possible to work on several documents at the same time without being too much scattered. When you get such fortuitous ideas, you simply slot them where they belong. That way knowledge 'grows' almost organically even if perhaps more slowly and less orderly as one may have wanted.

We often stumble on insights, intuitions as well as ideas that border between the conscious and the unconscious. Inspiration may occur anywhere and anytime: it may be in bed when we take a prolonged sleep; on a jogging field, in the bathroom, etc. Unless we capture this inspiration usually it escapes us. On the other hand, when we capture it and expand it, it usually brings out further inspiration. We can increase our awareness and extend the possibilities for our growth by dragging back what is slipping into the unconscious.

There are people who have experiences that border on the normal and extra-ordinary; experiences which they are hesitant to share with others for fear that they may be misunderstood or taken to be abnormal, visionaries, paranoid, etc. But this happens only because those to whom they happen to tell their experience have never had the same experience. The fact that others have not had this experience does not make those who have them abnormal. These experiences may be very rich areas to investigate; they may even be extra-ordinary gifts we have received for our own good and the good of others. The tendency, however, might be to suppress them and even forget about them, just to appear 'normal' like other people. This is another area to register and to look at more closely. Writing down the event helps towards articulation of one's thoughts in the event of seeking assistance from another person.

Yet another way of recalling and recording the significant events and inner movements of our life is the *Life History Log*. The Life History Log is in a way compared to the writing of one's autobiography with the purpose of psychological growth. As with other Logs, the procedure suggested is to sit down comfortably in a reflective mood and let the events of one's life flow spontaneously. A key term in this log is 'Stepping Stones'; those significant moments of our life, either as we perceived them internally or as they occurred externally, or both. Externally, the day of birth, the first day at school, the death of a close relative, the change of jobs are all stepping stones.

We know that the templates from which we act today are largely laid down in our childhood. We also know that often we act in very definite patterns without realizing it, unless we take time to map out our lives and try to discern these patterns. Writing out the Life History Log can help us to recognize the scripts from which we act, as well as to work on the negative scripts that require changing.

In effect the exercise of writing the life history for me yielded the following results:

o It came as a pleasant surprise that I could recall so much of my life history.

o It revealed patterns, links and connections in what I would have thought to be totally unconnected.

o Looking through what I had written revealed a certain kind of motif in the stories where I was more prolific. This revealed to me certain things that were of greater significance in my life.

o A detailed description of certain people in my life who had evoked strong emotions in me, whether positive or negative, allowed me to see them in a different light. It led to greater understanding of these people's actions in my regard.

o The exercise made me to discover a potential for writing.

o It also persuaded me more about the power of meditation. If one puts one's mind to it, and if one gives it time, meditation is bound to yield results.

o It helped me appreciate more the value of the present moment. Many of the things that had seemed unimportant as they happened turned to be valuable moments when I recalled them. Situations that had been painful turned out to be particularly valuable, depending on the way I responded to them. I came to see that in the same way things that are happening now will one day turn out to be important memories, depending on how I have responded to them.

This then is a subjective description of writing of using the journal. The invitation is that the reader gets to the actual source if that is accessible; that is, the more authoritative writings on the Intensive Journal. If one can follow the method exactly as it is suggested, well and good. But if one cannot, there is no reason to be discouraged. Take what appeals to you and use it in the way that appeals to you. See what benefits it brings in the process of your own growth.

Dialogue Logs

The Dialogue Log section of the *Intensive Journal* as 'growth data' accumulated in the previous section is processed to provide meaningful material for growth. In a normal dialogue two people communicate: one speaks and the other listens. Then the listener responds and the one who spoke before listens. We can apply the same procedure on ourselves as a means of getting to know ourselves more. We can dialogue with works, another person (not physically present), our body, etc. The difference from an actual dialogue is that in this case we think, feel and speak for ourselves as well as for the other party in the dialogue. We express our side of the issue and as we do so we listen on behalf of the other party, and similarly as we express the other side, we do the listening on our own behalf.

The concept of 'works has a special meaning in the context of the *Intensive Journal*. It does not refer simply to a job that you have to do or a task that is placed as a burden upon you. Having a work implies a strong and warm caring, a special interest and concern in a particular activity. It means to be engaged in an activity which you value as something meaningful in your life, and which you are seeking to enlarge or strengthen. A work is a special project which emerges as an outer activity drawn from an inner source in the person's life. Writing this book can qualify as a work. It is important to me if I have given it so much time, so much energy and resources. The process, like any serious work goes through moments of enthusiasm, of discouragement, of impasse, of frustration, of doubts, of fatigue. Dialogue with it can yield new energy to go on.

The first dialogue I carried out in the course of the workshop was with a person. After the preliminaries of sitting comfortably and recollecting ourselves we were prompted to write names of people on a piece of paper, as they came to our minds, whether these people were dead or alive. Five names came to my mind. When we were asked to choose one for the dialogue, I decided to choose a name whose appearance in my mind had been a surprise, for I had long forgotten the person. It was a grandmother who had died over twenty years before, and whom I had not particularly liked. At the end of the exercise, I was amazed with the discovery. During the course of the dialogue, I had gone through the reasons why I had not liked her and was surprised to see how few, insignificant and prejudicial they were. More important, I had recalled the many likeable things about her and they struck me strongly for the first time. I even felt a certain amount of guilt for having resented this woman in spite of her goodness, and for having thought little of her in her last days, even though I was just a teenager. From that moment I started thinking of her more tenderly, and in fact I made it a point to pray for her in the next Mass I celebrated.

That exercise had persuaded me about the value of a dialogue. I decided to try it on a living person, one with whom I had had a slight misunderstanding. Again, I was surprised about how things got clarified in my mind, and how much of the positive side that had been obfuscated in my indignation became illuminated. This gave me energy to initiate an actual live dialogue and to reconcile. We became friends once again and the slight tension was removed.

What might sound a bit strange at first is dialogue with one's body. But here we need to bear in mind that while the meaningful contents of our lives are *expressed* in our emotions, our aspirations, and our deep inner experiences, they are all *carried* by our body. Our personal existence is dependent on our body. Also, we make contact with the world of nature, with music, with the physical arts of dance and sports, sexuality and the realm of the senses, all by means of our body. A dialogue with one's body is prepared for by calling to mind the different memories of one's body: hot and cold, pain and sensuality, a warm bath. My five senses: seeing, hearing, smelling, touching. Shame, guilt, pleasure, thrill, too many feelings, fear, darkness, violence, exposure. Dentist, a mountain, getting old. Fasting, cuddling a baby, being massaged. Childbirth, nose bleeding, tickled, fainted in church, smells, excited feelings in my stomach. A blow to my face, cold water on my naked body, a music concert, strum of the guitar, learning to drive, woods and leaves, lakes, rivers. Cycling. Birds singing, steam train, puffing. Cooking food, hunger, eating. Fatigue, stomach-ache, headache, pain of a wound, a sprain, eyes. Feelings of jealousy, infatuation, anger, longing, loneliness, worry. Peace in the presence of a friend. Saying farewell.

The list above is only an example to refresh one's memory with regard to personal experience. Once one has gathered several memories then one chooses one to dialogue with. The purpose is to learn to accept ourselves better. But the results of the dialogue are not prescribed. One has to make one's own discoveries.

LISTENING TO THE UNCONCIOUS: SELF KNOWLEDGE VIA DREAMS

In ordinary language we often think of dreams as regarding things that are unattainable. Somebody holding onto plans that are impossible to accomplish is said to be dreaming, to be a dreamer. We say of something we would like to achieve but which still seems remote as something which is only a dream. I recall nights when for some reason or other I slept hungry, and then woke up in the middle of a dream in which I was just about to partake of a sumptuous meal. I could not make myself go back to sleep and finish the meal, however much I wanted to. It was only a dream. There were other occasions when I dreamed being caught up in a situation in which I was in serious trouble, unable to extricate myself. And then all of a sudden, I woke up and said, thank God it was only a dream. People in similar difficulties out of which they do not see how to come can sometimes wish it was only a dream, something unreal. We may then think of all dreams like that: just dreams far removed from reality. And yet dreams can be in a certain sense more real than many other things that go on in our consciousness, for they reflect something of our true self.

It is probably not erroneous to say that the majority of us do not make much of our dreams. We might tell somebody about a dream that was so vivid. We may sometimes think about the dreams that have made a deep impression on us. But most dreams we do not remember, others we remember only vaguely. And yet dreams are an important tool for giving us a glimpse into our unconscious, if we know how to listen to them. This is precisely because they spring from our unconscious.

The Bible is full of episodes of dreams. The underlying motif is that God can speak to us through dreams. Genesis 28:12 describes Jacob's dream.

God speaks first in one way, and then in another, but no one notices. He speaks by dreams, and visions that come in the night, when slumber comes on mankind, and men are all asleep in bed…. (Job 33: 14-15).

In the New Testament Joseph had made up his mind to divorce Mary informally in order to spare her publicity, when the angel of the Lord appeared to him in a dream and said, 'Joseph, son of David, do not be afraid to take Mary home as your wife, because she has conceived what is in her by the Holy Spirit…" (Matthew 1: 20). However, the Bible also indicates that dreams can be falsely construed to be messages from God. "I have a quarrel with the prophets who make prophecies out of lying dreams – it is Yahweh who speaks – who recount them, and lead my people astray with their lies and their pretensions. I certainly never sent them or commissioned them, and they serve no good purpose for this people – it is Yahweh who speaks." (Jeremiah 23:30-32).

Throughout history there have been people with extraordinary powers in the realm of dreams. There are those who dream something and find that a few days later, or even at the same time, what they dream happens almost exactly as dreamt. There are people who are so sure of the accuracy of their dreams that a dream about something tragic really puts them down, convinced that it is bound to happen. There are those whose dreams are strongly prophetic. Yet others have a capacity to understand other people's dreams without applying much analysis.[22] This is not the kind of dream-work considered here. We can also be deceived by our dreams if we interpret them erroneously, particularly if we read in them what we want to convince ourselves of. They can be a form of wishful thinking. For that reason, it is important to know how to draw meaning out of a dream without making our own interpretation.

The analysis technique below concerns very ordinary and everyday dreams. These too have a message, and it is this message we try to decipher using this technique. Our ordinary dreams do not speak in plain terms. It is not uncommon to dream of places you do not recall ever having visited, to dream of dead people speaking to you as though they are back to life, to have the same character in the dream changing identity, or to have situations which in ordinary life could never be connected. This is perhaps one reason why many times we decide to disregard our dreams; they sound so unreal and weird. But dreams speak to us through a symbolic language, and we need to take time to understand these symbols.

The first step in dream work is to try to recall our dreams. We all dream whenever we fall asleep, often several times in a night. Sometimes our dreams are so vivid that we are able to remember them in detail the next day or even long after that. But more often our memory of dreams is very vague. Quite often we do not remember at all what we dreamt, and some are heard saying that they never dream at all, whereas the truth is that they very seldom remember their dreams. If we want to process our

---

[22] For example, Joseph's interpretation of Pharaoh's dream in Genesis 41:1-36.

dreams as a means towards self-knowledge, we need to put in some conscious effort to recall our dreams. It is even possible to influence our minds to choose what to dream about.

Our attitudes towards dreams affect our ability to remember our dreams or even to dream. Not being capable of remembering one's own dreams may be an unconscious fear of what to do with our dreams.

We can use our dreams to connect with God, with ourselves and with others through dream work. Dream work is a conscious intentional response to a dream.

Activity 10: Dream work

o *Start by thinking of any dream at all that you remember. Write whatever you remember of that dream. Almost invariably, when you start writing you will find out that you recall more than you thought. If other dreams come to mind record them as well. If you can recall them in their order of succession place them in that order.*

o *Have next to your bed a switch bulb, as well as recording material. As soon as you awake, write down the dream, without censoring or editing. You may divide the paper in two parts leaving a margin about one third of the paper for later comments. In your record include images, actions, reactions, thoughts, attitudes, feelings, conversations, choices, character descriptions; anything that you can recall.*

o *Describe things in sensory details: what you see, hear, smell, taste, observe moving, etc. Write quickly; don't worry about grammar or spelling.*

o *When you have finished writing the dream, go back to sleep. Let dream work not deprive you more than necessary of the sleep you need. Sometimes for the sake of your sleep it is enough just to jot down the main features of a dream and then go back to sleep. These few notes may help you in the morning to recall the rest of the dream.*

o *Next to the dream, on the margin that you left aside, have comments. What are your thoughts and feelings that immediately come to you as you write? Do this in a separate column. Do not analyses. Simply record your mood, questions, associations, images that come. This may help to clarify the meaning of the dream. All this is the first step.*

o *Try not to stop with the recording of one dream. Record them in a series. The more you get into the habit of writing down your dreams the more you will be able to recall them. Moreover, serial dreams are more likely to give a more authentic message uncorrupted with your own interpretation than a single dream.*

o *When you have accumulated a considerable number of dreams, sit quietly and put yourself in a meditative mood. Let memories of your dreams come to you. Note which first or most strongly. Go back to it and read it within the chronological context in your file. See whether any new insights come to your mind or not. Jot down any insights that come to you. Try to refrain from reading meaning in a dream. Pay greater attention to your intuition than your reason.*

o *Dialogue with this strong memory, for instance, a person that figures most prominently in the dream – record briefly any felt experiences that occur. Can you use colored pens to put an impression or picture on paper? What is your deeper psyche saying to you in the dream? What impressions are you left with at the end of the dialogue?*

o *The result of your dream work must be your own discovery. To suggest what you might discover is to bias your results. If you do not gain anything from the exercise, try another way of gaining self-knowledge that is more helpful to you. Important is not to force meaning, and much less to direct your actions guided by your own self-deception. Usually, we intuitively can tell a real discovery from what we are only imagining to be such.*

LISTENING TO THE HIGHER FACULTIES: THE VOICE OF CONSCIENCE

Whether people believe in God or not; whether they profess a certain set of moral values or not, at times there are things they do and feel they should not have done. There are also things they don't do and they feel they should have done. We have a "should' voice in us; we have a conscience.

We also know how we feel when we refuse to listen to this voice in us. It is not a pleasant feeling. Depending on what we have done or omitted, we do not feel peace of mind until we have done something to pacify the voice of conscience: an apology, a change of behavior, a confession, compensation; according as the situation may be.

Although often perceived as an enemy, a nudging voice, a nuisance, conscience is actually a friend. It is a guide to our authentic self. We sense this friendship when we take courage to listen to it and to obey it, regardless of how hard or unpleasant the required task may be. In Jesus last words "it is accomplished" (John 19:30) we sense the ultimate triumph of conscience in this life, in spite of how much the accomplishment of his mission cost him.

Conscience is a sort of nerve for our spiritual nature. Nerves protect the physical body from harm. If we did not have them, we would suffer injury without feeling it, and that would not be for our good in the wrong run. Nerves tell us not to touch fire nor to rub our bare eyes nor to stick pins in our bare feet. Therefore, nerves are friends not enemies, although it is through them that we perceive pain, and no one wants to feel pain. The same can be said of conscience.

Conscience is our higher faculty of intellect at work in matters of what is perceived as right and wrong. Every act of conscience is in fact a full-fledged syllogism, although the process is not perceived as such. If my conscience bothers me over having been rude to a friend, there is behind this feeling a three-step perfect syllogism: 1) It is not right to be rude to friends 2) I have been rude to a friend 3) Therefore, I have done what is not right to do to a friend. Every act of conscience can be analyzed in this form. One can then see that in each case the first or major premise is a kind of moral principle the subject is convinced of.

It is not possible to placate conscience just by rationalizing or trying to reformulate my moral principles. The conviction that is the basis of these principles involves not only a rational judgment but feelings as well. While I can play around with the rational judgment I cannot create or remove a feeling at will. Yet convictions can be changed.

To change my conviction, I must come to the realization that what I considered to correspond to truth before actually does not. In the film entitled *Speed* one of the main actors driving a bus is very much troubled realizing that she has run over a baby stroller pushed by a mother. She believes she had crushed the baby, and I think she would have had no peace through any amount of rationalizing, to the effect that it was an accident or something like that. But she calms down by the discovery that the buggy contained foodstuffs and not a baby. We can be bothered by a conscience based on false moral values, and it is within our interest to form our conscience correctly by seeking to know the truth.

In brief we can identity five ways of applying for our own good this God-given voice in us we call conscience

1) Continually form or reform your conscience. Read what you know to nourish your soul. In this regard Scripture claims first place. Read what your faith teaches on moral questions. Read good literature. Listen to and seek advice of good people.

2) Listen to the voice of conscience. Pay attention to that nudging feeling; do not strive to suppress it. Take a moment if necessary to reflect and bring it to full consciousness.

3) Obey your conscience. Follow what you believe to be the right course of action, even when this is unpleasant. Obey conscience also in what seems to be insignificant: making your bed, washing the dishes, saying "thank you" or "sorry" when your pride feels wounded by the gesture.

4) Make amends as far as you can for the times you are conscious of having disobeyed your conscience. Apologize, work harder, pay a debt; whatever the case may be.

5) Pray for the strength of will to choose rightly and carry your choices through, no matter the challenges. When we feel strong it is very easy to forget how weak we can very quickly become in moments of trials and temptations. The classical example is that of Peter who thought he was ready to die for his Master, even when he was warned and advised to pray for strength, and who discovered the hard way how weak he was (Luke 22:31-34; 54-62). Pray to God who knows how weak we are, and who provides help for the asking.

MANAGING MONEY STRESS

You might wonder what financial management has to do in a book on personal growth and counselling. However, you might also nod in approval, recalling how much anxiety, misery, fear, hard work, humiliation, anger, have been caused by the shortage or lack of money in your life at one stage or another, as well as how much relief, comfort, peace of mind, enthusiasm have been caused by possession of money. My mother used to say of my father, that once you see him become irritable and quarrelsome, then you know he is broke.

Money may be the deciding factor whether or not you are able to read what I have written. There are those who cannot afford to buy this book. There are others who never had the money to acquire an education that would enable them to understand what is written here. There are yet others who are so bent on having to earn their daily bread, that reading a book for personal nourishment or relaxation is a luxury they cannot afford to have.

Money is largely responsible for the difference of the northern and southern hemispheres, for the gap between the life style of the poor and the rich within any country, for so many crimes and so much misery in the world; the same money is the lifeline of all organizations engaged in the relief of misery and all sorts of humanitarian activities. Money can make some people debase themselves or maltreat others beyond imagination; it can also help others do so much good that they could not do in any other way.

Jesus warned his followers about the danger of money. He said in Matthew 6:24: *"No one can be the slave of two masters: he will either hate the first and love the second, or treat the first with respect and the second with scorn. You cannot be the slave both of God and of money."* Everything depends on how money is acquired and how it is spent; whether it is acquired through dishonesty, or unfair rivalry, whether its acquisition causes many others to suffer want, whether its acquisition makes the owner lose sight of much higher values, or whether it is acquired through hard work or some other honest means. Money can also be spent selfishly, wastefully, vindictively, or it may not be used at all, when its use would relieve so much suffering of those around; but it can also be spent for the reasonable well-being of the owner as well as for the good of others. Because money can also be put to good use for the benefit of those who have less, Jesus also advised his followers: *"...sell your possessions and give alms. Get yourselves purses that do not wear out, treasure that will not fail you, in heaven where no thief can reach it and no moth destroy it. For where your treasure is, there will your heart be also"* (Luke 12: 33-34). Since money affects our lives, whether we want to admit it or not, and since the we way we acquire and spend it has a lot to say about what kind of people we are, the change in our attitude to money and the way we obtain and expend it might be a necessary factor in our personal growth.

Let us take an example of a calling I know best. Catholic priests in Africa are rarely to be counted among the poor who do not know where their next meal will come from. In comparison to many people, they are better fed by their flock or by the institution, and they hardly ever go about dressed in tatters. Many of them have some means of transport: a bicycle, a motorcycle or even a car to carry out their pastoral work, but also for their other needs. It would come as a surprise to many people, to learn that even priests can be quite often stressed over money. After all, they have no families to feed. If they assist families, it is out of a desire to help, and not out of a sense of obligation.

Precisely because they look to be or are actually financially better off, and because they are helpers by profession and vocation, they receive so many people in need, not so much of sacraments or spiritual advice as of financial help. Since almost always these priests do not have enough money to meet all the needs, genuine or false, of those who come to them. Unless they are careful, they can fall in one of two extremes. Either they grow hardened against human need in order to protect themselves, or they get stressed up trying to help so many.

As a priest I have had my own share of this financial stress too. When I was in secondary school my father retired from his job in a tsetse control department. Soon the retirement package expired, and there was not enough money to keep me and my siblings in school. It was a Catholic priest, chaplain of the school where I was studying that pushed me on through secondary school. Fr. Benedict Kizza was not a very rich man. Apart from the meager pay from the school and some allowance from the diocese he earned his money through taking photographs at Church functions and printing them in his crowded black and white studio, as well as raring ducks. With that paltry income he continued assisting me and other boys through the seminary. Three of these became priests as well, and others made it into meaningful careers.

Reflecting on my own history, and not being spared the invasion of need that every priest faces, I decided to help a few children who were too poor to pay their fees. Over the years I have learnt that although schools require the payment of their fees in a very regular fashion, the income of a priest – of mine at least – is very sporadic and unreliable. At one time I get quite a lump sum from the many good people I meet who understand what amount of good a priest is in position to do, yet for long stretches of time that income peters out. Therein is the source of stress.

The education of a child in school is a kind of personal commitment, once one starts one needs to go the whole way; stopping before the child has acquired some skill or career for self-sustenance is almost like throwing away all that one had paid before. There have been times when I have tussled with God, asking him: if he sent so many people in need to me why did he not also send me the corresponding means to help them. I have even wondered how realistic the teaching of the Lord is: *"do not worry about tomorrow, tomorrow will take care of itself..."* (Matthew 6:25-34). I said to myself, how can I not worry about tomorrow, knowing that tomorrow schools reopen? This I must concede, help has often come when least expected, or even in answer to prayer. But during the waiting I could not quite help worrying.

It would be presumptuous to think that the stress people experience as a result of financial worries can be eradicated by reading a few paragraphs. Yet this stress can be reduced, or at least spread out more evenly, by the following simple hints summing up the principle: *Live within your income.*

1) Make a record of your income and expenditure. For many people this is as needless as advising them to brush their teeth in the morning; it is part of the routine of their daily life. Others are meticulous about making financial records of monies they must account for, but they are careless about their own money for which they do not have to make account to anyone. Yet the strict recording of one's own income and expenditure increases the sense of carefulness about money, particularly for those who are spendy. Record keeping is the basis of any meaningful financial planning.

2) Budget your expenditure. The idea of budgeting is easy enough for one who receives a regular income. It is much harder when the income is patchy. However, even in this case it is possible to budget. The trick is to budget not basing on what one will get but on what one has. If I chose to budget for one year, and, to make the mathematics easier, if I had 365 shillings at the beginning of my financial year, then I would say that I permit myself to spend on average one shilling a day, nothing more. My weekly budget then would be 7 shillings. If I got another 365, I would double my weekly budget to 14 shillings. If some need required me to spend much more than my weekly budget at a time, then I would divide the remaining figure with the remaining part of the year, and I would know that I have to reduce my weekly expenditure accordingly.

Within one's budget, whether lean or otherwise, one can include a percentage for helping the needy. There is no obligation to help beyond one's income. On this point St. Paul gives us sound advice: *"As long as the readiness is there, a man is acceptable with whatever he can afford; never mind what is beyond his means. This does not mean that to give relief to others you ought to make things difficult for yourselves: it is a question of balancing what happens to be your surplus now against their present need…"* (2 Corinthians 3:13-14).

3) Avoid borrowing as far as possible. There are acute situations in which the only possible course of action is borrowing. But having to pay debts is usually a greater stressor than lack of money. Even when one has the money to pay the debt with, the likelihood is that other needs have come up in the meantime. For some people the temptation to ignore the debt can be very strong, thus postponing one's troubles. It is wise, therefore, to avoid taking debts, unless you really have to.

4) Pay debts as early as possible. Some creditors lend with an interest. It is obvious in those cases that the earlier the debt is paid the better for the debtor. But even when there is no interest expected on a loan, the earlier payment is effected the better. Clearance of debts brings peace of mind, preserves friendships, and maintains trust. It is also a sign of consideration to the lender. It is sensible to make it a principle to clear debts before making any expenditure that can be postponed. If you borrowed money, pay back money, not explanations. However good an explanation is, it is not good enough. Your creditor cannot carry out business transactions with explanations, and certainly not with yours.

5) Spend within your income. A popular song narrates the story of a young man who, preparing for marriage, collected a large sum of money from friends. Some was given to him, some he had to pay back. He then made a sumptuous wedding at the home of one of his friends who had a decent house, since he himself was renting a tiny cabin. On his return to his "home" with the bride he met the landlord waiting for him at the door to claim all the rent he had not paid for months. The landlord had concluded from observing the lavish wedding that his tenant was actually very rich, but simply did not want to pay. Not having anywhere to get the money or to stay with his bride, the wretched groom begged the landlord that he might at least keep the bride in the rented house while the groom went off to look for the money.

The singer concludes that this is how he hit a dog with a potato… It is not uncommon especially among the young – but not exclusively – to want to show off a lifestyle higher than their actual income. This cannot last long, and almost always there is a price to pay.

Failure to live within one's income manifests itself quite often in a "beggar mentality;" a mentality of living off the assistance of others, without having to work for it, even when one is quite capable of working. Africa and other parts of the developing world where extreme poverty is rampart attract the generosity of so many charitable people and organizations in the developed world. While there are millions of beneficiaries who deserve all the assistance they can get, there are also many who could exert themselves to better their condition but do not make the necessary effort. They forget or don't know that the help they receive quite often comes from the sacrifice and hard work of people who often enough are not even very rich.

One who has learnt to live within one's income can say with St. Paul: "I know how to be rich and how to be poor." It is wisdom to learn to accept want when this is inevitable, and to learn to use wealth for the *real* good of self and of others.

10

THE ROLE OF OTHERS

In the first part we saw how our social nature requires that certain things we cannot do without the help of other human beings (see page 31). In the same way we cannot grow to wholeness entirely independent of the help of others. This means that if we are to direct our own growth, sometimes we shall have to ask for the help of others. On other occasions we shall need the humility to accept other's help where our pride would want us to reject it. And at all times we do well to show gratitude for the help we receive from others.

All this is fairly easy to see. What may not be too obvious is the fact that we enhance our own growth through facilitating the growth of others. By truly loving others we are fulfilled, not just because they may love us back – which happens often enough and which is a bonus when it does – but even when they don't love us back our hearts are expanded, as it were. If I find so much that is good and lovable in others in spite of their mistakes, the likelihood is that they in turn find me an amiable person. If on the other hand I complain all the time about others, there is a big possibility that they too complain about me. A superior who constantly finds fault with the work of a subordinate and never seems to find anything laudable might be pleasantly surprised if he or she one day decided to change attitude and approach towards the inferior. By deliberately deciding to observe every praiseworthy detail, however minimal, and kindly pointing it out, the superior makes the inferior feel valued and motivated. This in turn may bring within the inferior a desire to please and to pay attention to what pleases the superior. While the work may improve and the atmosphere of work becomes more pleasant, something higher is achieved in addition, that is, the mutual esteem, and even love between the two.

The good we do to others comes back to us. As the Lord said, the measure we dish out is the measure we get. More could be said on this subject. However, since the next Part (on page 168) is about how we enhance the growth of others, here we concentrate on how others more directly facilitate our growth, and we isolate one particular area: how can others help me if I am enslaved by some form of addiction?

OVERCOMING ADDICTIVE BEHAVIOR

It is common in my culture for adults to name a particular object, animal or person as a scare for naughty children. Whether that is good for the children or not is another matter. Mad people and drunkards are among the typical scares used for children who misbehave. I grew up under the frequent threat that if I cried without a good cause, or if I refused to carry out an errand, or if I was naughty in one war or other, adults would call a small man with one ear called Kiberu, who was almost perpetually drunk, and this would eat me. I was so afraid of the man that if chanced to meet him on the way I would run back desperately yelling for help. I must even have had nightmares in which Kiberu threatened to eat me. On the rare occasions when I met Kiberu sober he would attempt to be friendly, and I was convinced he was enticing me in order to catch and eat me. In my adult life I came to the realization that apart from the loss of all esteem and being the laughing stock of the village, Kiberu who could have no wife or children of his own due to his drunken and desolate condition, suffered for being the scarecrow of children whom he seemed to like very much. I have met other people who are overpowered by alcohol in a similar fashion that they are eventually driven to death by it, either directly or indirectly. I am sure you can name a few you have encountered in your own life as well.

Nature of Addiction

Alcoholism and drugs are two of the more common and noticeable forms of addiction. In reality, however, addictions can be to many other things including gambling, smoking, sex, work, computers, money, pornography, books, slander, etc. It has been said that whatever action rewards us in some way is capable of creating an obsessive and compulsive dependence or addicting.

The consequences of addiction depend very much on what one is addicted to. Addictions to alcohol or to sex can have very devastating consequences on self, close relatives and friends and on society at large, while addiction to books may even seem useful to a certain extent. Another observation to point out is that there are degrees in addiction. Some would restrict the use of the word "addiction" to a condition where the victim is no longer capable of extricating self without expert assistance. Here the term is used more loosely to cover all strong and compulsive habits that are extremely difficult but not impossible to break without the assistance of others, experts or otherwise.

There is a tendency for the addict to feel in moments of failure and remorse, that there is nothing he or she can do to overcome the enslavement. This discouragement then becomes part of the problem. In actual fact, however, as long as there is some amount of knowledge and will left, there is no addictive condition that cannot be overcome.

Whereas all addictions reduce a person's freedom of choice and therefore are harmful, the degree of harm depends on the nature and extent of the addiction, as well as the strength of will of the victim.

Whether mild or severe, whether advanced or not, addictions need to be dealt with if we are to grow into the freedom for which we were created. This growth usually requires the assistance of others. The addicted needs to open up to some other person who is knowledgeable about the addiction and how it can be dealt with, and who is non-judgmental towards the victim. The admission to having a problem and needing the help of another is usually a humbling and painful decision, yet it is crucial to the beginning of the journey of recovery.

Half cures or relapses into addictions reduce or may even prevent the journey to total recovery. We are reminded of what Jesus once told his disciples, that *"When an unclean spirit goes out of a man it wanders through waterless country looking for a place to rest, and cannot find one. Then it says, 'I will return to the home I came from'. But on arrival, finding it unoccupied, swept and tidied, it then goes off and collects seven other spirits more evil than itself, and they go in and set up house there, so that the man ends up by being worse than he was before."* (Matthew 12:43-45). In the process of healing of some compulsive behavior there are bound to come moments of melancholy, of wishing to go back to Egypt (cf. Exodus 16:3), of reminiscing over the comfort that the addiction used to give. With the recently acquired strength it is possible to fight back at this stage, but if the person gives in, the process of gliding down the well-known path gathers momentum until there is no possibility of return. If, however, the person courageously acknowledges the longing without attempting to ignore or suppress it and owns the loss while at the same time accepting the pain, boredom, or craving as the price of growth, progress is made. A deliberate decision to undertake an undesirable but important task and sticking with it until it bears fruit can make the progress exponential. This is because addictions often are a form of defensive mechanism that help the victim avoid legitimate but unwelcome pain.

Positive Results of Overcoming and Addiction

Every painful experience can bear wonderful fruits of victory if we are willing to persevere through the painful price of healing. The overcoming of an addiction can give the healed victim the following results:

1) New strength and energy to delve into fruitful activity: Quite often people who indulge into some addictive behaviors are otherwise very talented and efficient in some field. The most effective facilitators of growth from addiction of alcoholic addicts are those that have suffered and overcome the dependence themselves. As long as the addiction lasts, energy is used to feed the compulsive behavior as well as to cope with all the painful consequences that the addiction creates. When all this energy is reverted into useful activity it blossoms into creative action.

2) Humility: one who has suffered an addiction has also learnt the limits of human strength and the power of temptation. Such knowledge yields humility.

3) Compassion and the capacity to help others who suffer the same or a similar addiction. There is no person who understand an addict better than one who has suffered it and overcome it. This person understands, not only the pain the addiction causes, but also the painful struggle to overcome the addiction, the frequent failures and need to start again.

4) Caution and precaution not to fall again. One who has known the snares of an addiction also knows how easy it is to fall and how much harder it is to rise again. The former addict knows the importance of avoiding the "danger of sin."

5) Gratitude: The ex-addict who has been helped by friends to overcome the enslavement experiences a deep gratitude to the helper, having experienced the common tendency among many other people including close acquaintances of judging, shunning, slandering, or condemning the one with a problem.

Suggestions for Healing

How does one overcome an obsessive-compulsive disorder? The best and more effective way is to find an expert. In fact, at a certain stage of addiction this is the only way. So much so, that this topic has been placed within the chapter: *The Role of Others* in our growth. Where a person follows a program of healing directed by an expert, all that the individual needs to do is submission to the guidance of the expert, so we need not say much about that here. However, since for many people it is not possible to find professional help, either due to the unavailability of experts or to lack of funds to pay for expert service or to both, here are a few suggestions for self-help.

1) Admit to yourself that you have a problem. Courageously look at the cycle of compulsive behavior in your life

2) Have the sincere desire and determination to overcome the problem

3) Have God as your companion in the fight. Follow what your faith says on how to get out such a problem. Let prayer have a definite place in your life, even in moments when you feel very low. A sincere examination of one's prayer pattern along with one's failure will often reveal that the inclination to failure is in direct proportion to the decline in prayer. Pray even when you do not feel like it. Just continue praying. Pray with the words of Jesus: "Father, why have you forsaken me?" (Matthew 27:46); "Father, into your hands I commend my spirit" (Luke 23:46). Pray to forgive your enemies: "Father, forgive them (Luke 23:34).

More needs to be said about the role of God in overcoming addictions, because it is very important. Addictions are a form of worship of a false God. The heart of a human being that was created for God is restless until it rests in God. We need God in our life, and if we do not have God, something or someone else replaces that need. Those who become "addicted" to God receive a feeling of coming home because addiction to God is the singular addiction that is healthy, while addiction to anything or anyone else to the exclusion of God makes a person always feel that there is something missing. Addiction is like eating pigs' feed given to you grudgingly (Luke 15:16), or spending money on what is not bread and wages on what fails to satisfy (Isaiah

55:2). True freedom is found when a person finds God. Fortunately in the search for God we do not have to do the entire return journey by ourselves. God who loves us more than we can imagine is looking out to see any signs of our return, like the father of the prodigal son he sees us a long way off and comes running to meet us.

4) Face reality. Deal with painful activities in life as the situation demands, without trying to evade them in any way. Usually, the pattern of addictive behavior begins as a desire to cope with some painful situation in life. By facing reality squarely, you reduce the need to find a substitute. The facing of reality often means accepting unavoidable pain and not trying to evade it.

5) Be dedicated to your duties. Look at duty also as a therapy against the obsessive behavior.

6) Avoid the occasions in which the addictive pattern begins, even when you feel confident enough to withstand the temptation. The pattern of behavior never begins with something big, but with the cumulative effect of small, seemingly insignificant things. Don't keep alcohol in your room, if it is alcohol you are addicted to. Avoid smoking rooms if it is smoking you are addicted to and if you can do this. Running away from trouble is sometimes considered a cowardly thing, but at times it is the best option.

7) Cultivate the activities that give you joy and that are useful or at least harmless in your life. Indulge your hobbies during your free time.

8) Mourn your losses. In moments when you tend to look at the addictive behavior as totally negative have the courage also to see its good side. It is not by denying what attracts you to it that you overcome the addictive behavior. Recognize the attractive side, and then choose freely to overcome, having considered also the painful consequences of the attraction.

9) During moments of temptation strive to see the negative consequences. One of the "tricks" of the addiction is to screen off the negative consequences at the moment of temptation. The passion tends to overpower reason. Make an effort not to lose reason or reality.

10) Count and celebrate your victories, however small. These give you strength to go on. Thank God for every little progress made.

11

THE ROLE OF THE ENVIRONMENT

You must be familiar with people who seem to live forever in the past. They reminisce constantly about the glorious days of their youth. They are forever complaining about young people of this generation, the bad weather, the rising prices of domestic products, the inconsiderate neighbors, the traffic jams, the shortage of money, the corrupt politicians. At times it can be tiresome to live with these people.

You have also met those who seem to live in the future. These are the dreamers. They are always thinking of what they will do if… what they will become when... They have a good reason why things are not working out well in the present. It is because they did not have a good science teacher, or they had a toothache at the time. They complain about any appointment they get. They make resolutions that remain on paper. They constantly work out elaborate action plans which they never follow. They are constantly stressed about what will happen. Or they may be eaten by envy of those who seem to do better than themselves. These too are tiresome to live with.

What is more tiresome to live with, however, is to have these characteristics within ourselves: to mismanage the present simply because we live too often in the past or in the future or both. The antidote is to capture the grace of the present moment.

We already made reference to the text where Jesus advised his hearers not to worry about tomorrow, for tomorrow would take care of itself (Matthew 6:25-34). Today has enough troubles of itself. He himself lived and operated in the present. He said that as long as his hour had not come he would keep on doing his work (Cf. Luke 13:31-33). He could not have accomplished anything if he kept worrying about his future, gruesome as it was. Although always unwavering, he was ever ready to adjust plans due to a sudden turn of events. On his way to any place, he would be interrupted by people who wanted favors of physical healing, and he would attend to them. Poor Jairus must have been consumed with anxiety and perhaps also a little bit of resentment when the Lord was distracted by the woman who had stolen a healing. "If she has been unwell for twelve years, couldn't she have held on to the disease for another hour and given a chance to a dying little child?" he might have wondered (Cf. Matthew 9:18-26). But the Lord sensed his anxiety and encouraged him to have faith. As he resolutely took the road to Jerusalem to face his final battle, the Samaritans would not allow him to cross their territory (Luke 9:51-56). His disciples showed more frustration than him, suggesting that they call down fire from heaven to rid the earth of the stubborn and stupid Samaritans, but he was willing to make a detour.

The amount of energy we can dispense of at any one point is limited. If we spend it on worries about the past or the future, there is not enough left for today. And yet we can neither change the past nor the future, but the present. And once the present turns into past, this means it will remain unchanged forever, for it will never come back to the present. To live in the present is to consider NOW as the most important moment of my life. I can only act in the present, and not in the past nor in the future. The Chinese have a saying, that "the best time to plant a tree was 20 years ago. The second-best time is now."

I need to stop seeing problems and start seeing challenges that must be confronted with the resources I have at hand, and be dealt with as best as I can. There is an appropriate response to every human encounter I make today. The present situation might require that I ignore the insolent, that I endure with patience the unwelcome, that I listen to the troubled, that I pay attention to a child, that I enjoy the company of a friend, that I write to the lonely, that I admonish the one going astray or that I pay the debt of the creditor. These are the concrete situations in which the law of love is exercised. My changing moods are a call to take it easy and relax if I am overworking or to overcome lethargy if I am idle; to calm down if I am angry; or to show appreciation if I am pleased; to seek solitude or to play a social role, according to the situation.

Living in the present means tackling problems rather than complaining about them. Whenever I have seen slums habited by healthy young men, some quite well fed, capable of putting up better structures if they applied themselves, I have thought to myself that it is because nature has been too kind to us in Uganda. If it happened that in a certain year we experienced winter, many people would die for lack of adequate shelter. But then if winter continued year after year, the next year people would be better prepared. The Bakiga of South-Western Uganda are renowned for their strength because of the mountainous terrain on which they have to spend strenuous work. They have learnt to harness the difficult terrain and not to complain about it.

150

Strange as it might sound at first, one of the factors that makes us fail to live in the present is urgency. What I consider urgent may make me miss out on what in fact is much more important. Struggling to meet deadlines I may fail to respond to the cry of someone who needs my attention vitally. Dedication to work can damage relations in a family.

To stress the importance of the present moment is not to underplay that of the past. For this again we have no better teacher than the Lord himself. More than anybody else Jesus was aware of a mission given by his Father. His joy and driving force were to fulfill this mission foretold by the Prophets. He constantly explained the scriptures and their meaning. He continually drew lessons from Israel's history, About Abraham, Elijah, Moses, the Prophets in general. He came not to destroy the Law and the Prophets but to bring them to completion (Matthew 5:17). For us too, the past is always to serve as a lesson for the present. The past may consist of a mission to be accomplished, a promise to be fulfilled, a plan of action to be executed or even an error to serve as a lesson. It is a great mistake not to learn by our mistakes of the past, for then we condemn ourselves to suffer them again and again, as long as it takes to learn from them.

Living in the present does not imply ignoring the future either. Nor did Jesus ever ignore the future. On the contrary, his whole mission was in view of the future. His first words during the public life were a call to repentance because the kingdom of God was close at hand. He was never absorbed in the present in such a way that he would forget the future. If he ate with sinners, it was to call them to repentance (Luke 5:32). After he had fed the hungry the next time, they looked for free bread he advised them to look for bread that endures unto eternal life (John 6:27). He warned his followers not to strive to win the whole world at the price of their soul (Mark 8:36-37).

The art of capturing the grace of the present moment is listening: listening to all that lies in the past, present and future, and of acting in the present.

THE ROLE OF GOD

PRIVATE PRAYER

For a believer authentic human growth must take into account an essential factor which is God. If we are made in his own image, then a rediscovery of our true self is at the same time a rediscovery of the one in whose image we are made. This journey of discovery is prayer.

Strange as it may sound, our self-discovery or self-fulfillment is not the end of the journey of growth, but the discovery of God is. Or expressed differently, we do not attain fulfillment until we find it in God. From our standpoint the ultimate goal is not discovery of self but self-transcendence. A text that demonstrates what is being described here is St. Paul's description of himself:

"I was born of the race of Israel and of the tribe of Benjamin, a Hebrew born of Hebrew parents, and I was circumcised when I was eight days old. As for the Law, I was a Pharisee; as for working for religion, I was a persecutor of the Church; as far as the Law can make you perfect, I was faultless. But because of Christ, I have come to consider all these advantages that I had as disadvantages. Not only that, but I believe nothing can happen that will outweigh the supreme advantage of knowing Christ Jesus my Lord. For him I have accepted the loss of everything, and I look on everything as so much rubbish if only I can have Christ and be given a place in him. I am no longer trying for perfection by my own efforts, the perfection that comes from the Law, but I want only the perfection that comes through faith in Christ, and is from God and based on faith. All I want is to know Christ and the power of his resurrection and to share his sufferings by reproducing the pattern of his death. That is the way I can hope to take my place in the resurrection of the dead. Not that I have become perfect yet: I have not yet won, but I am still running, trying to capture the prize for which Christ Jesus captured me." (Philippians 3: 5-12).

Before Paul was converted, he believed without a doubt that he was a pious man, a man of God, spending all his life for God. He was convinced that one could attain perfection by one's efforts. There are many of us who are in that phase of life: people who were born in good Christian families, who may have undergone long religious training, who are given some job in the Church which we accomplish with all our efforts, who have been keeping the rules with an impeccable reputation and who in spite of all this have never been converted, for we have never really known Christ the way Paul came to know him. There are two fundamental rules of conversion which we draw from Paul's experience. 1) When he really got to know Christ, he considered him as the supreme value in comparison with whom all that he had held dear before counted as 'rubbish'. 2) When he became converted, he also discovered that perfection cannot be attained by one's own efforts. At the same time, paradoxically, he did not think that he no longer needed to make any effort to attain it. On the contrary he could say: "…: I have not yet won, but I am still running, trying to capture the prize…"

Authentic spiritual life is not attained by our own efforts. And yet it does not exclude our effort. In our struggle towards growth, we cannot do without God's help. Jesus compared himself to a vine and his followers to branches; just as the branches cannot grow and bear fruits without the mother plant, so too the disciples cannot bear fruit cut off from the vine.

There are so many different forms of prayer. Each authentic form of prayer brings us closer to God. But we cannot discuss them all. Only three forms associated with meditation are expounded below. The reader can find among these three one which is agreeable to self, or can even find a completely different form. The most important thing about prayer is not to hear about the experience of others of what it is like, but to learn to pray and to develop our own experience of prayer. And the only way to learn how to pray is to begin and continue praying.

O taste and see that the Lord is good: blessed is the man that trusts in him. Psalm 34:8

Centering Prayer[23]

The saying that "Action speaks louder than words" was lived out in a lecture given to us by Professor Franz Strieder on Centring Prayer. He spoke for about 25 minutes about the basics of the prayer method and then invited us to go to the chapel and try it out with him. We did that at regular times of 20 minutes each day until I got enamoured of the method. Earlier courses on meditation in the seminary had had little or no effect on me.

Professor Strieder invited us to assume comfortable postures. Some sat with legs stretched ahead of them, hands in their laps, leaning against the

---

23 Cf. www.centeringprayer.com *"The Method"*

wall. Some sat on the carpet cross-legged with hands on their knees, either facing upwards or cupping the knees; a typical prayer posture of the oriental world. They looked to me so calm and composed that I decided to try out that posture myself. But then my second leg could simply not fold under the other. When it did and I tried to sit straight I simply toppled over, to the amusement of those around. So, I gave up this sitting position. Like many others less schooled in meditative prayer I chose to sit on a low chair with a straight back, with one hand cupped in the other on my lap. After all, even the old prof. himself stat in this fashion.

We closed our eyes, following his slow, deliberate promptings. We were told to relax, to listen to the noises around us, within us; to listen with every sense in us. We were told to breathe regularly, normally, easily. Whatever came into our consciousness we were to be aware of and let go gently, without fighting it or holding on to it.

After calming down each was to introduce in the silence of the self the self-chosen "mantra" or sacred word; a kind of anchor of thought that was used as a tool for further calming. I could not think of a better one than the words Jesus Christ; "Jeeesus" with every inhaling and "Christ" with every exhaling. We were instructed that if distractions came and for a moment made us forget the sacred word, on becoming aware of this, we would have to gently and without being disturbed return to the sacred word. As a way of Christianizing the prayer method, at the end of the agreed period the leader slowly intoned the "Our Father," and we recited it together. After a few moments of further silence, we left. The prayer session was over.

During the meditation period everyone was to strive at least to refrain from any external voluntary actions like shifting posture, coughing, sneezing; not even scratching the itching part. Funny, that immediately you are told not to scratch yourself, all of a sudden you become aware of an itch that demands to be scratched. But with a firm decision to let go of every voluntary action, even the itch disappears. In a crowded room one could "hear" the silence and absence of noise from others.

The professor warned us not to expect tangible and quick results. And I did not get any. However, he emphasized that the effectiveness of this and any other form of meditation lay in constant dedication to the practice. But then, we asked, what is the point of undertaking the exercise every day? We learnt that strictly speaking Centering Prayer is not prayer in itself, but a method of calming that makes a person to be aware of the presence of God; a most import ingredient of meditation. Along with other prayer forms and particularly carried out alongside regular reading of scripture in a meditative way or *Lectio Divina*, the method can become a powerful form of Christian meditation.

As long as we practiced Centering Prayer in a group thing went very well, although a few people dropped out, the prayer exercise being as it was, completely voluntary. I was among those who persisted. However, when the group was dispersed and each had to continue on their own, then it became a little harder for me to maintain a regular timetable. This made me realize that, at least for the beginning, the prayer method works best in the context of a group. Through the assistance of the group individuals are helped to overcome the temptation to give up the exercise.

I am not very sure whether this method made a significant difference to my prayer life. One thing I am sure of, it made me more conscious of the world around me. Moreover, it taught me how to remain still for a considerable period – never mind the pandemonium within – so much so that one day, a seminarian having observed the "outside" during the communal meditation before morning prayer, asked me to teach him how to pray! I thought the best think was to give him what I had learnt and let him make his own discoveries. That is how we started another small group of Centering Prayer with a few others who were interested. After some time, some seminarians spoke of having been greatly helped by the method. I have no way of knowing whether they were sincere, or whether they said that to please me. All I know is that I have come to appreciate and use this method, for what it is worth. To be frank, I use the method in a way that appeals to me, not exactly as you might find in the official books on Centering Prayer.

Meditation is an important element of private prayer. I am not aware of any one way of doing this. If you find this method of meditation appealing to you, you are welcome to try it out. There is a lot of literature in bookstores and on the internet about Centering Prayer.

Meditation with the Lectionary

Another form of meditation is that which involves the liturgical readings for each day. When you think about it, it is in fact a modified form of Centering Prayer within which the liturgical readings of the day are inserted.

Many if not most Christian denominations make use of a lectionary or order of readings which sets out biblical passages for each day throughout the liturgical year. Many people by the nature of their work or by choice cannot attend daily services or Mass. Even those who do may be affected by the routine of the services so that the message of the readings does not strike them as strongly as it should. It is possible to integrate the daily message of the word of God into one's meditation.

There is something to be said about using lectionary readings instead of readings personally selected from the bible. When we choose our own passages we are more likely to choose those which we are already familiar with and which we like. We can of course draw growth from them, but perhaps not as much as from those which have an element of surprise because they have been chosen and arranged by another. Besides, incorporating the readings of the lectionary in one's meditation helps a person to find the celebration of the liturgy more meaningful. Moreover, the lectionary has been carefully arranged so that it provides a panoramic picture of the history of our salvation, it harmonizes with the liturgical seasons which in turn reflect that history of salvation, and it offers the best passages from scripture from a pastoral point of view.

Meditation using the lectionary rather than drawing passages directly from the bible takes into account the ecclesial dimension of our growth. There is the old saying that two heads are better than one; one could also add that many heads are better than two. In many areas of human progress we observe that success is achieved through cooperation, through unified action. We cannot go it alone. To use the readings from the lectionary is to be sure that millions more are reflecting on these same readings for this particular day. It is as if we were united somehow in prayer at a distance. Moreover, one who uses lectionary readings has a liturgical bonus to reap. For this person the nourishment by the daily word of God does not depend on the effectiveness or deficiency of the pastor. If the preacher is good, well and good, but if the preacher's expounding of the word of God is nothing to write home about then one need not be bothered by that. And if the person who meditates on the lectionary happens to be one whose duty it is to comment on the day's message for others, that person's commentary will all the more be enriched by the daily reflection. The practice may even encourage someone to go to church more often than before. For that person no service is mere routine, for each has a different set of readings which do not return after at least a year for weekdays, and at least three years for

Sundays and feast days. Every day is an opportunity to discover further the inexhaustible reaches of God's word.

For a person whose scriptural knowledge is rudimentary a good biblical commentary that is more pastoral than academic may be of some use with regard to passages that may be particularly difficult to understand. The best that comes to my mind is William Barclay's *Daily Study Bible*[24] which covers the entire New Testament. There is the more comprehensive and more technical *Interpreter's Bible*[25] that covers the entire bible, but this is more costly and more academic. It must be emphasized, however, that use of such commentaries is only for particularly difficult passages. Even one who has them might do well for much of the time to ignore them, at least for this exercise of meditation, for the point of focus is personal growth, and the more important subject matter is the self.

Since the point of focus in this case is meditation and not liturgy, it is useful to reduce the passages for reflection to one instead of two or three offered each day, not counting the responsorial psalm. And when one cuts them down to one the most obvious choice becomes that of the gospel reading.[26]

This form of meditation includes the silence of Centering Prayer, the traditional Examination of Conscience, and the reflection on the passage of choice. It is useful in this case as in the case of Centering Prayer, to have a fixed place and set time of day dedicated to this prayer, a time when a person is unlikely to be interrupted and when one is fully alert.

The main stages of this meditation are four: awareness of God's presence in 1) the perceptible and the imperceptible, 2) the day's events, 3) reflecting on God's Word, 4) talking to him.

Before you begin the meditation have next to you the gospel reading of the day.

THE PERCEPTIBLE AND IMPERCEPTIBLE

---

[24] William Barclay, *The Daily Study Bible*, (17 volumes including an index), Bangalore, Theological Publications in India, 1975.
[25] George Arthur Buttrick and others eds., *The Interpreter's Bible* (in 12 volumes), Nashville, Abingdon Press, 1992.
[26] The Jesuits offer online something similar to what is described here. See their website at www.jesuit.ie

1. Sit still and relaxed. Become aware of all that is within the range of your perception: what you can hear, what you can feel, what you are touching, what you can smell. For instance, as I write this I can hear the constant burr sound of the computer hum as well as the broken purr of the hard drive. I can hear the sound the fingers make at the key board. At the same time, I can hear the sound of different birds outside, of some crickets, of the hammering of some builder in a distance.

2. Be aware of what these things are in themselves. I make a conscious effort to be aware of the intricate process going on in the computer. I know that if I opened it all I would see would be still chips and wires, apart from a few lit diodes and the turning fan, but I know there is complex activity in the deceptive quiet. I also know that even if the only sign of electrical power is the lit button on the monitor, the constant flow of electric current is what makes the computer work. I think of the birds outside chirping away. They do not do so aimlessly. Each one chirps to its own kind. They are in search of food, or communicating danger, or companionship or some other 'bird sentiment' I am not aware of. They may be busy building nests or marking territory or calling to a mate. I take more time to dwell on the perceptible.

3. Become aware of what you can perceive within yourself. I can perceive the slightly cold feet in my shoes, of the pressure of my elbows on the office chair as I type, of the slight pain in my neck. I am aware of my breathing, of the pressure of my bottom on the chair. But I am also aware of what is not perceptible: of my effort to think what to write next, of the fact that my brain is working, my heart is pumping, my veins transporting blood, and all internal organs active, each with its respective duty, all in harmony.

4. Be aware that among the imperceptible is God's presence. More silent than the current through the electrical wire, busier than the activity in the computer and in my brain, he is here controlling all the things I mentioned and by far the many other things I have not mentioned. He is here aware of me, loving me.

THE EVENTS OF THE DAY

Be aware of the events of the day as if you were preparing to write your day's journal. Try to go mentally through what you have experienced and done. Do not be selective but pause at each and draw meaning. Dwell on how you felt. Try to go through the day with God whose presence you are aware of, like a person showing a friend through your house, proud of this, a little ashamed of that, asking for advice on that other. Thank him for the good things that happened to you. Thank him for what you did well, for anything that you are grateful for. Ask him to forgive you for anything that you feel ashamed or regretful about. Ask him to help you realize that which is yet to be accomplished. Talk to him about the day's events as you feel disposed. Conversations are not prescribed or dictated. You say what you spontaneously feel you want to say.

GOD'S WORD

Now read the gospel of the day from the Lectionary. For instance, on Monday, 18th week in Ordinary Time, Year I: from Matthew 14: 13-21

> Now when Jesus heard this, he withdrew from there in a boat to a deserted place by himself. But when the crowds heard it, they followed him on foot from the towns. When he went ashore, he saw a great crowd, and he had compassion for them and cured their sick. When it was evening, the disciples came to him and said, "This is a deserted place, and the hour is now late; send the crowds away so that they may go into the villages and buy food for themselves." Jesus said to them, "They need not go away; you give them something to eat." They replied, "We have nothing here but five loaves and two fish." And he said, "Bring them here to me." Then he ordered the crowds to sit down on the grass. Taking the five loaves and the two fish, he looked up to heaven, and blessed and broke the loaves, and gave them to the disciples, and the disciples gave them to the crowds. And all ate and were filled; and they took up what was left over of the broken pieces, twelve baskets full. And those who ate were about five thousand men, besides women and children.

Imagine the scene of the gospel as it might have been. Try to capture the feelings: Jesus withdrew to be by himself after he heard something, in this case the death of John the Baptist. What feelings would he have had? Then the crowds went to his hide-out before him, what would you have felt if you were him? What did he feel? How did the crowd feel looking for him? What motivated them to do so? You can also picture Jesus telling you the story, how would he tell it? Imagine another person telling the story: one of those cured, or some Pharisee who came out of skepticism or a doubting disciple told by the master "you give them something to eat yourselves" what would he say? Imagine yourself as this disciple, told to make the people sit in groups on the grass and not sure what Jesus was really going to do… Ask Jesus what he is saying to you today in your own circumstances. Do not force the message; just listen. If nothing particular comes out at the moment, do not mind, go on. God speaks in his own time and in his own way. Maybe now the seed has been planted and you will see the shoot days later. Just try to be disposed to whatever God has in plan for you.

CONVERSATION

Focus on Jesus' presence again. He is still here, imperceptible but present and active. Imagining that Jesus is the one who has been telling you what happened on that day, about the feelings he had that were expressed in the passage and those you have deduced with your imagination, now say back something to him. Normally when a person tells us a story of their life we say something back and we listen to their response. Listen to him saying something back with regard to your own story of today. Ask him a question and imagine what he would respond. Hear him respond.

Conclude by thanking him. Use some scripture reading or prayer. Glory be to the Father or the Our Father.

Switching Narrators

In a retreat I once received a gifted preacher mentioned in one of the seven sessions he gave, that sometimes a familiar biblical story gains new meaning if told in a way different from the one we are used to. One way to do this is to choose one of the characters in the familiar story, even an insignificant one, and to retell the story as if this character was the one narrating it. In fact, a number of biblical epic stories and movies use this method to create an altogether absorbing story, even though presenting what we are already familiar with from scripture. The retreat preacher demonstrated the truth of what he said by narrating to us in this fashion the story of Jacob's marriage to Rachael, of the Samaritan woman, and that of the Prodigal Son. He pointed out that such retelling is made with the understanding that the teller is not giving the listeners gospel truth. If they want that they can always read the bible for themselves. With that understanding one is free to use imagination without being accused of falsifying scripture. Fr. Denis McBride in fact uses this style in one of his books entitled *Impressions of Jesus*.[27]

There are obvious dangers to that, of course. This preacher was a biblical expert. Besides he was a very gifted person and storytelling came rather naturally to him. Not all people who might want to employ his method on enlivening the familiar are equally trained or gifted. Someone else's having a go at the technique might end up presenting the inspired word in a banal fashion. However, even if this might not be a method suitable for all who have the duty to explain the scriptures to others, I found it meaningful and harmless if one uses it as an alternative manner of making the scriptures meaningful to self. It could be adapted as an alternative method of meditation. One simply takes a story from scripture, and, having gone through the usual preliminaries for meditation one tries to view this story through the eyes of some chosen character within the story. I did, and the result was the story below.

REFLECTIONS OF A PHARISEE

I was particularly bitter about the man called Jesus. Like my fellow Pharisees, I referred to him as an impostor; a carpenter from Galilee where prophets do not come from, who had never belonged to any formal school of Rabbis and who

---

[27] Denis McBride, *Impressions of Jesus*, Redemptorist Publications: 1992.

gave himself off for a Rabbi. In fact, he claimed much more than that. He did not respect the Law, well at least not the whole of it. He worked on the Sabbath and defended his disciples when they did the same. He allowed them to eat with ritually unclean hands and had all sorts of justification for his misunderstanding of the honorable customs. His disciples were undisciplined and never fasted like our disciples or even those of John the Baptist. John himself was questionable but at least he and his disciples were disciplined. This one went as far as eating with sinners, being hosted in houses of famous tax collectors like Zacchaeus and Matthew. In fact, he accepted Matthew among his ranks of disciples. Just think of that! A tax collector for a disciple! Yes, I had forgotten, he had a former Zealot as well. His name was Simon. The rest were crude fishermen from the fishing villages of Galilee, at least many of them. I am told he collected a whole bunch from there, without scrutiny calling them to follow him from where they were working. And would you believe it? They left their work there and followed him! Two left their father and his working men in his boat mending nets. Another left a wife! Such was his bunch. And if you are not yet shocked enough hear this as well: the fellow associated with prostitutes, and was impudent enough to include some of them among his disciples. Such was the case for instance with respect to that infamous sister of Lazarus of Bethany who had made a name for herself in Magdala.

This man seemed to have set out to deliberately discredit us as well as the Scribes. He openly criticized us even in our presence. Can you imagine that he once described us as white-washed graves which are clean on the outside but with putrid flesh inside? That was more insulting than the affront of John who called us a brood of vipers. I tell you, the kind of insults we have suffered! If you invited him to your house, you did so at your own risk. He would not hesitate to humiliate you even as your guest. Simon the Pharisee learnt a lesson he would never forget when he invited him to his house, and when this Jesus compared him with an infamous woman who came in uninvited and rubbed his feet with her hair in public. *In public!*

Recently he had become a real danger to the nation. When he raised the body of his friend Lazarus back to life, the crowds saw in him a king and shouted hosannas to him. When we tried to warn him of the possible consequences of such an act, he impudently and proudly told us that if the people stopped even stones would sing his praises. Can you imagine that? He could not see the real danger that the Romans could see in this a rebellion, a desire to usurp the imperial power of Rome, and thus destroy the nation. And so, we decided that this man should die, to save the nation. We also agreed that he should die such a death that would prevent any of his followers to even think of reviving his movement: he would die on the infamous shameful and painful death on a cross hang in a public place around the celebration of Pascha when all the pilgrims had come to Jerusalem.

It must be admitted however, that there were certain things that the man said and did which were upsetting and disquieting. Take for example the miracles he performed. You might explain some away that they were simple tricks on simple people. For instance, the child of Jairus whom the crowds claimed he had raised might actually not have been dead, but was in a comma or even just sleeping. But some of the miracles were undeniable. The last one already referred to was such. Lazarus had been buried for four days. His body had been embalmed and there was no question of his being dead. We sent people to Lazarus' home under the pretext of paying condolences but in fact to find out whether he would come and raise him. We were glad that he did not turn up for days. Here was clear evidence; for one who had saved others could not save his own friend. When we saw him weep, we really felt a wave of triumph. At last, it was going to be clear that his "power" was nothing but deception. Yet the fellow brought him back to life. Some of the Pharisees said that he did this through the power of Beelzebub the king of devils.

His magic was not only in miracles. Even when he talked, he was indeed captivating and you had to be careful not to be carried off by his language. The simple people of course did not have the power to resist such a sweet tongue. They would say that no man had ever spoken like him. That is all right and congruent with their low education, but it did no good to our reputation, for the rabble kept comparing us with this rascal. Still there were other things that were disquieting. For one thing no one had ever managed to get the upper hand over him in an argument. He always merged as winner. Even when some daring Pharisees used underhand tricks like bringing to him a woman caught in adultery or trying to put him between Caesar and fidelity to the Law. He always had a smart way of getting himself out. Anyway, we decided to do away with the man, for the harm he caused outweighed the good.

The night we got him was totally a sleepless one for us. We were gathered in the house of our leader the High Priest waiting for those who had gone to arrest him. We had a long debate regarding him. Everything went according to plan and the next day he was executed. At last, we had got him. Even the people who had sung hosannas to him were "persuaded" to shout "crucify him". With the proper price you can get anything you want!

Now, I was at the scene of the crucifixion, and here is where my misgivings began. The sorrow in his mother's eyes was upsetting and I tried not to focus too much on her for she weakened my resolve. After the long laborious climb to the top of the hill which was admittedly arduous also for one without a cross, the crucifixion finally took place. It was not until we saw the man finally hanging on the cross in obvious pain that we got sure that we had him at last. You could never tell what he would do. But we were sufficiently sure of having literally nailed him down at last that we could permit ourselves the luxury of jeering at him to save himself as he had saved others. But then there was something about the man's face that was disturbing. There was utter absence of bitterness in that face. In fact, there was even serenity in it. What kind of person was this? He had lashed people out of the temple in a rage but now he did not show any of that rage at all. Then there were things he said while on that cross. In spite of his pain, he could think of the sorrow of his mother. He entrusted her to one of his disciples who had dared to come as far as the scene of the crucifixion. The others were nowhere to be found. Actually, this ability to think of others even amidst his own sorrow had shown itself already on the ascent to the hill of crucifixion. He had told the women of Jerusalem not to weep for him but for their children, whatever that meant. He said other things to them which I did not quite understand: something to do with green wood. But that is not all! You won't believe this, but while they were crucifying him, he actually said "forgive them Father, for they do not know what they are doing." Those were his own words, and I remember them clearly. Tell me what kind of a person can say that in the middle of his own crucifixion? At the moment I was still so incensed that all I thought of was that there he goes again blaspheming and calling God his Father. The words of forgiveness of his enemies did not strike me so forcefully then as they did later.

As I said before, there was something unexplainable about that man's face in the midst of pain. It was already swollen with the blows it had already suffered. It was crusted with dry blood as well as wet with the fresh blood coming from the thorns which the soldiers had put on his head in the form of a mock crown. But in spite of the torture from the wounds and the nails which held the whole weight of his body, that face was serene. I will never forget that face. Never!

We wanted to be sure the man was really dead before we left the place, so we waited. And I tell you it was a long wait; nearly three hours. Towards the end of that waiting he appeared to have entered a new phase of his torture. He became more restless than before and actually he raised his face as best as he could and said: "my God, my God, why have you deserted me?" Now this sounded closer to reality. It sounded as if he was finally coming to the realization of his mistake. A little too late you might say. One of our party misheard and thought that he was calling on Elijah to save him. Anyway, neither God nor Elijah came to his rescue. Shortly afterwards I could see that his end was not far. And in fact, I was not mistaken. He drew a long breath and said in a weak voice "It is accomplished." Those were his last words. That is another part of the scene that I can never forget. What was accomplished? I kept asking myself. These did not sound like words of despair. On the contrary they sounded like words of victory. "It is accomplished!"

A few things happened around this time that made me for a moment forget the rapid succession of events. All of a sudden, the weather changed and it looked as though a heavy storm was coming down. Besides, evening was coming soon and the Sabbath rest was due to come. Everyone was in a rush to get to their homes. As I too rushed home, I could not quite place a name to my feelings. I should have felt triumph after having eventually got the upper hand over the enemy who had troubled us for nearly three years, upsetting the whole social order. But it was not quite triumph I felt. There was no time to think. All the same that face kept returning again, as well as the words "It is accomplished." Eventually I got home. I did not realize how tired I was until now. Only now did I remember that it had been a long day and a long night. But strangely enough, in spite of all the fatigue and loss of sleep, when I went to bed, I could not fall asleep. I kept turning and rolling in the bed and no sleep came. "It is accomplished!" what was it that was accomplished? Other phrases and scenes kept now popping up into the mind. I remembered what one of the executioners, the centurion in fact, had said at the death of the man. He had described him as truly being the son of God. At the time I thought to myself disdainfully that what did this son of a gentile know about sons of God? But you dare not say that openly to a centurion! But now I was no longer sure. Could this gentile have seen what we had failed to see? But then I remembered his cry of despair: "my God, why have you deserted me…" At this time, he did not even call him Father anymore…

"…but wait," I said to myself, "those words ring a bell. Where have I heard them in the Scriptures?" I remembered that they are drawn from a psalm. Eventually I was so intrigued with them that I went for my roles and looked up the psalm. It was not difficult for me to locate the psalm, for I am not ignorant in the scriptures! I am a Pharisee, remember! And then I got the shock. It suddenly occurred to me that what I had taken for a cry of despair was in fact the recitation of a psalm. And the more I read the psalm the more I realized how so graphically it depicted the scene on that hill. Listen to the words yourself:

"My God, my God, why hast thou forsaken me? Why art thou so far from helping me, and from the words of my roaring? O my God, I cry in the day time, but thou hearest not; and in the night season, and am not silent. But thou art holy, O thou that inhabitest the praises of Israel. Our fathers trusted in thee: they trusted, and thou didst deliver them. They cried unto thee, and were delivered: they trusted in thee, and were not confounded. But I am a worm, and no man; a reproach of men, and despised of the people. All they that see me laugh me to scorn: they shoot out the lip, they shake the head, saying, He trusted on the LORD that he would deliver him: let him deliver him, seeing he delighted in him. (These are the words some of us literally said beneath the cross!) *But thou art he that took me out of the womb: thou didst make me hope when I was upon my mother's breasts. I was cast upon thee from the womb: thou art my God from my mother's belly. Be not far from me; for trouble is near; for there is none to help. Many bulls have compassed me: strong bulls of Bashan have beset me round. They gaped upon me with their mouths, as a ravening and a roaring lion. I am poured out like water, and all my bones are out of joint: my heart is like wax; it is melted in the midst of my bowels. My strength is dried up like a potsherd; and my tongue cleaveth to my jaws; and thou hast brought me into the dust of death. For dogs have compassed me: the assembly of the wicked have enclosed me: they pierced my hands and my feet. I may tell all my bones: they look and stare upon me. They part my garments among them, and cast lots upon my vesture. But be not thou far from me, O LORD: O my strength, haste thee to help me. Deliver my soul*

from the sword; my darling from the power of the dog. Save me from the lion's mouth: for thou hast heard me from the horns of the unicorns. I will declare thy name unto my brethren: in the midst of the congregation will I praise thee. Ye that fear the LORD, praise him; all ye the seed of Jacob, glorify him; and fear him, all ye the seed of Israel. For he hath not despised nor abhorred the affliction of the afflicted; neither hath he hid his face from him; but when he cried unto him, he heard."

I read the entire psalm to the end, occasionally pausing to wipe the sweat from my brow, even though it was already the cool of the night.

What was so painful to see was not so much that I knew too well who the person in the psalm was that cried to God in anguish; but that I could clearly see what role we were playing. We exactly used the very words in the scriptures to jeer at the Holy One. I don't know whether you noticed some words which factually described things that happened to him that afternoon. Just hear these words once more: *"they pierced my hands and my feet. I may tell all my bones: they look and stare upon me. They part my garments among them, and cast lots upon my vesture."* Oh God! I groaned. How could we have been so blind to the scriptures; we whose life and ministry were these scriptures? The more I reflected in my misery the more texts from Scripture came to my mind with their cruel and starkly accusing clarity. I also remembered the words which Jesus had once said that "When you have lifted up the Son of Man, then you will know that I am He."

I also recalled the story of the Bronze Serpent in the desert which Moses hang on the standard for the healing of the people who had displeased God and incurred his punishment through the fiery serpents. Was it possible that I too could have forgiveness from his Messiah after all that I had done to him? Was such a crime as ours ever forgivable? Did I dare hope to be included among those for whom he had prayed because they did not know what they were doing? Could he forgive me as he readily forgave the tax collectors and prostitutes whom in my blindness and pride I despised? I could not possibly hope to get forgiveness from any man, I thought in despair, not after all I had done in spite of the glaring evidence to the truth. The Romans did not know what they were doing when they crucified him. But I could not possibly say the same. But then I remembered my newly-discovered insight. This was no ordinary man. This was what he had claimed to be all along and what we had denied. This was the Son of God as the centurion had said. This was He Who Is. What he had said was absolute truth. "When you have lifted up the Son of Man, then you will know that I am He."

LITURGICAL PRAYER

So far in this book we have seen how we human beings strive to re-assume the beautiful image of God in which we were created, whether by ourselves or with the assistance of God who created us. However, the wonderful surprise for those who do not know it already, is that long before we existed God had his own plan of recreating us in his own image. This plan has been elaborated throughout the centuries and all we need to do is to respond to it. Very briefly outlined it runs like this.

God who made the human being in his own image chose to assume the nature of a human being in order to give back what humanity had lost through disobedience. This he accomplished in three ways:

1) By *showing* us how to live as we were meant to live, in spite of all the human limitations that we experience: in love of God, of neighbor, and of self. This kind of life precludes all that is against authentic love, and that is sin.

2) By *teaching* us all that we needed to know in order to attain the purpose for which we were created.

3) By *giving* us all the aid we need in order to overcome our limitations through his suffering, death and resurrection. The merits of his sacrifice he entrusted to the Church which dispenses them by means of visible signs or sacraments. And so, God recreates us through Baptism and the reception of his Holy Spirit in Confirmation. He feeds with his word and with himself in the Eucharist, he forgives our failures in the sacrament of Reconciliation, he strengthens those who are sick with Holy Anointing, he propagates the human family with his blessing in the sacrament of love, that is, Matrimony, and he continually gives to the Church ministers through the sacrament of Holy Orders.

The liturgy, and in particular the Eucharist, is a complete plan of renewal of humanity in the image of God if we play our role of response and cooperation. We respond in three ways:

1) By *faith* in the mystery of God's plan that has been revealed

2) By *celebrating* this mystery as a community of believers in the liturgy

3) By *living* according to what we believe and celebrate.

In the book *If You Only Knew the Gift of God* which is a follow-up of this one, God's plan of recreating us through the Eucharist is elaborated.

Part IV

RE-CREATING IN THE IMAGE OF GOD: HELPING AN INDIVIDUAL

Up to this point the focus has been on personal growth; how I was meant to be, how I have turned out to be, and how I can recuperate my true beauty and dignity. With this and the next part the stress shifts to the role I am called to play in the growth of others, whether individuals or groups.

Helping in the growth of an individual can be viewed from two perspectives. There is the helping in ordinary life, of the colleague you complement or gently correct, of a friend who asks for your advice or whom you advise because you judge that it is appropriate to do so, of the child you direct, reprove or whose conduct you approve. This is the subject matter of chapter 13. However, there is also the help that is given in a more professional context of counselling. This presupposes that the one who needs help comes to you, and that you have some kind of arrangement or working agreement. This is the focus of chapter 14.

While it is necessary to separate the previous part from the present due to the limitations of human communication, in reality helping in the growth of others is inseparable from personal growth. In the process of helping, others heal, become mature, and learn to manage problems. By helping another, the helper heals, matures and learns to deal with personal problems.

EVERY HUMAN ENCOUNTER COUNTS

When a lawyer asked Jesus "who is my neighbor" Jesus narrated to him the famous parable of the Good Samaritan (Luke 10:29-37), and made him draw the conclusion to his own question. However, by asking the man "Which of these three, do you think, proved neighbor to the man who fell among the robbers?" Jesus ingeniously turned the lawyer's question from "who is my neighbor" to "whom am I neighbor to." His conclusion "go and do likewise" seals the change of the question.

Love is the greatest commandment because love is the primary activity that makes us reflect the image of God. Love of neighbor need not be imagined in some lofty activities of benevolence. It is exercised in the day-to-day human encounters. In the parable the Samaritan did not set out on the journey looking for victims of robbery to exercise his acts of mercy on. He was on his way going about his own business. He had to interrupt his program just as the Levite and the Priest would have had to do if they had stopped by the unfortunate victim of robbery. His oil was not intended for wounds of strangers; the money he gave to the inn keeper was not part of his budget. But he shelved his own plans for a moment and let that human encounter count. We enrich others and ourselves when we let every human encounter count, not just those encounters that are budgeted for.

The first category consists of people we meet every day; those that are closest to us: members of our families, as well as close acquaintances. Our closest acquaintances need us as much as we need them (See "Relations" on page 121). It is not uncommon to find people who have a wonderful social reputation but who are quite insensitive to those closest to them. Making an effort to be present and in time for meals and other common activities, informing others in anticipation of one's absence, saying "I am sorry for mistakes made," responding when asked a question or talked to, giving complements when these are due, listening to the joys and sorrows of those closest to us; all these are important ways of loving and helping others grow. One doesn't need to make an elaborate program of how to love; one only needs to be attentive in order to capture every opportunity of love as it comes.

Then there are those who ask our help. We are not in position to meet all the needs of all those who approach us for assistance. However, the way we respond can be supportive or devastating. And when we are in position to help but then we withhold our assistance, then we diminish our human worth as well.

There is also the category of those who need help but who cannot ask for it: vagabonds in streets, orphans, victims of war and of all sorts of injustice, abandoned children, the unborn, etc. There is nothing as sweet to these as getting relief from their misery, when they least expect it.

Yet another category is of those who are indifferent to help though they need it. Some may even be downright aggressive to the one who helps them. It takes much greater courage to help these.

But the hardest and perhaps the noblest manifestation of Christian love is the love of one's enemies. It is easy to preach about if you have not had a person who hurt you really bad. I know a priest who in a war situation was tied to a tree and badly beaten. His torturers then gave a gun to his niece to shoot him. When she refused, they raped her in his presence and later killed her while he watched. Asking a person like that to forgive is not an easy thing. Yet having the courage to forgive in such or worse circumstances has great healing power, both for the forgiven and the forgiver.

HELPING USING COUNSELLING SKILLS

Chapter 14 focuses on the counselling skills necessary in the course of one person helping another in the growth process. The main focus is the context of one-to-one: the helper and the client, but obviously the skills can also be used in group work, as well as in the improvement of ordinary relationships outside of counselling or spiritual direction. (Experts usually make a distinction between a therapist, a counselor and a growth facilitator, in descending degree of expertise. This work is written mainly as a tool for a growth facilitator, even though the same skills can, of course, be used by a counselor or a therapist. The person helped is referred to here as the "client," to cover a range of people including a client proper, a therapeutic patient, a friend, one receiving spiritual direction, etc. Here the term 'counselor', 'growth facilitator', and 'helper' are used interchangeably, even though the emphasis is on the non-professional helper.) The following is the outline of the chapter.

Counselling in General.. *173*
Working Alliance... *174*
Time Management *176*
Prayer in Counselling... *177*
Attending *178*
Listening.. *179*
Advanced Empathy *184*
Feed back *187*
Paraphrasing... *190*
Exploration.. *191*
Reluctance and Resistance *196*
Immediacy *200*
Self Disclosure... *201*
Decision Making and Problem Solving... *202*
Helping Others Solve their Problems... *208*

A word of caution needs to be given to non-professionals involved in the work of facilitating the growth of another person. "…non-professional helpers should always focus on the current conscious life situation of the individual seeking help. They should avoid psychological archaeological expeditions that lead to levels beneath the everyday consciousness of the troubled person. Non-professionals should help those who come to them to keep their discussions on the level of what they can, with relative ease, draw out of their consciousness…" [28]

---

[28] Eugene Kennedy and Sara C. Charles, *On Becoming a Counsellor*, Dublin: Newleaf, 1977, p. 13.

COUNSELLING IN GENERAL

Probably it is true to say that all of us have on various occasions counseled someone else. And it is equally true that we have been the beneficiaries of counselling on many occasions. If we have friends, if we are concerned about the well-being of others, if we are aware of our own limitations and value listening to others, then we are constantly involved in counselling both as agents and as recipients. All the counselling skills we are about to see are exercised in ordinary life by ordinary individuals even without being able to name them, depending on how sensitive they are. Studying these skills merely makes us aware of them, value them, consciously develop and apply them.

From a technical point of view, counselling is a relationship between a trained helper and an individual seeking help. It is explicitly contracted and the boundaries of the relationship are clearly identified. The counselling process is designed to facilitate the exploration and understanding of experiences, feelings and behavior and to enable the client to learn new ways of thinking and behaving. The growth facilitator brings to this task certain attributes or personal qualities, such as empathy, genuineness, respect, as well as a range of communication skills and an understanding of the causes of human distress and how to facilitate change and foster growth.

The overall aim of counselling is to provide an opportunity for the client to work towards living in a more satisfying and resourceful way. Counselling may be concerned with personal developmental issues, (for example, sexual development and how it gets blocked, fixations, "perpetual teen-agers"; adults who are rebellious against authority); addressing and resolving specific problems, (conflicts, effects of traumas, malfunctioning relationships), making decisions, coping with crisis, (such as those regarding identity, relationships, vocation, illness, mid-life), developing personal insight and knowledge, (exploring which direction to go, overcoming one's phobias, becoming aware of one's strengths and limitations), working through feelings of inner conflict (such as the ability to say NO and YES).

The growth facilitator's role is to facilitate the client's growth in ways which respect the client's values. This puts on the helper the responsibility to try to understand these values. That is done through exploring with regard to such areas as the client's background, culture, education, formation, religion, commitments, convictions, etc.

Counselling needs to be distinguished from spiritual direction. The main purpose of spiritual direction is to help people grow in the life of the Spirit. Spiritual directors and directresses try to help directees understand more fully their relationship with God and how God is working in their lives. While in counselling there may not be reference to God when God happens not to be within the value system of the client, spiritual direction necessarily involves relating to God.

Nonetheless counselling can be integrated with spiritual direction especially for a priest or nun involved in formation – that is: where both the counselor and counselees share the same value system. In this context the spiritual counselling relationship is a relationship of three: the counselor, the counselee and the Holy Spirit. This awareness of the triad helps the growth facilitator to have the kind of respect and acceptance needed for a growth producing relationship. Moreover, the Holy Spirit helps in exploring the unique personhood and spirituality to which the counselee is called. There may be appropriate times when you pray with, for and over the counselee.[29]

Effective assistance in the growth of another requires that the helper really cares about the person being assisted. "Caring about people in trouble – and even actually liking them – is vital to helping them deal more effectively with themselves and with life."[30] Often people distance themselves for fear of getting involved emotionally and of the consequent pain in the process of helping another. But doing that may, in fact, drain our helping potential of its most significant component.

A mere reading of the skills below may not turn one into a qualified counselor; usually one requires substantive training for that. But at least they can make a person more effective in relating to others.

WORKING ALLIANCE

People who are going to compete in a match or game must not only be aware of the rules of the game, but also be agreed that they know the same rules, otherwise chaos and misunderstanding might ensue afterwards. Similarly, in a counselling relation it is important to synchronies expectations right from the beginning.

---

[29] See "Prayer" on page 188.
[30] Eugene Kennedy, *On Becoming a Counsellor*, p. 26.

In the very first session or even before, the growth facilitator and client set up a working alliance. They discuss the mutual expectations, set them down in a list of ground rules in two copies. Each of them signs both copies and then each retains the signed copy for reference. For practical purposes the growth facilitator as one in the position of director may already have the ground rules or contract set down and printed. Before going any further in their counselling relationship, he/she takes time to discuss it in detail with the client and to establish whether the client fully consents to it before both sign. Obviously, such a discussion implies that the working alliance must begin as inconclusive. The fact that you discuss it with your client before means that the client may question or reject a particular clause; or they may want something added. It also means that if the mutual expectations cannot be reconciled, you may both decide not to enter the contract at this stage.

It is important how a facilitator introduces the working alliance to the client. To one who is unfamiliar with such an alliance, signing of contracts might appear a useless formality and might give the negative impression from the start; that the whole relationship will be bogged down with formalities. Signed working alliances might be more tolerable in a contract with a 'commercial' or paid counselor; it might be more difficult for the client to stomach where the relation is more in the line of spiritual direction. And yet even there, clarification of mutual expectations is no less important. Perhaps, in certain cases one has to be content with spelling out the expectations on paper, without having to sign in duplicate.

What ought to be emphasized is that it is not helpful to postpone discussing the mutual expectations beyond the first meeting. The time when a future client formerly asks for your counselling services is the time to discuss the expectations.

What are these ground rules? They are no absolute ground rules. Otherwise there would be no point in discussing them. They have to be decided by the parties involved. However, in general one might consider the following to feature in the discussion:

- o   Fee, in case the counselling is paid for
- o   Time, place and frequency of sessions
- o   Duration of sessions
- o   Openness

o   Confidentiality[31]

Sometimes it is opportune to revisit the ground rules, particularly if one of the parties seems to have forgotten or neglected some of them. That is the whole purpose of preserving them. It is also possible to mutually modify them, if that is in the interest of both parties.

TIME MANAGEMENT

It is important in counselling to set down among the ground rules the duration of the session, the venue and time for beginning the session. Having fixed the time, it is vital to stick to it. The growth facilitator above all should be punctual to set the example to the client. The session should stick to the time agreed upon. The normal duration of a counselling session is 50 minutes, but circumstances can require an occasional adjustment.

Towards the end of the session the facilitator might remind the client how much time there is left. The helper should also see to it that no new and burning issues crop up just before the expiry of the duration of the session. This is done by concentrating on winding down with issues that are at stake. Winding down does not mean that this particular issue must be concluded within the session. It is normal in counselling that the same matter lasts over several sessions. But at the end of each session there needs to be some form of wrapping the problem up for the next session, say by agreeing on some 'homework' for the week. On the other hand, where some concern being shared needs a little extra time, the counselor can negotiate the time boundary for this particular occasion. A person who is in tears and is in an emotional turmoil at the end of a counselling session might require a little extra time to calm down. However, this should not be habitual.

As the session comes to a close, as a helper you need to be discreet in checking the time. Looking at your watch constantly may give the impression that you are anxious to have the session finished and have no interest in the client. It is helpful to place a wall clock or any other clock

---

[31] "Never repeat what you are told and you will come to no harm; whether to friend or foe, do not talk about it, unless it would be sinful not to, do not reveal it; you would be heard out, then mistrusted, and in due course you would be hated. Have you heard something? Let it die with you. Courage! It will not burst you!" Ecclesiasitcus 19:7-10.

in such a position that you can conveniently and unobtrusively look at it in order not to distract the client. Even when there is not much to say you should strive to see that the session is terminated within the usual time boundary. Occasionally it might be necessary to end a session before the usual time. If a client who is aware of the time boundary wants to make a habit of coming before time, say in order to have a longer session, this must be checked in the appropriate manner.

PRAYER IN COUNSELLING

A growth facilitator who is a believer is aware that all that a human being can do is the sowing; it is God who causes what is sown to grow. It is the work of the Holy Spirit that ultimately brings about the growth of the individual, of course with the individual's cooperation. The facilitator is aware that effective counselling must take into account the role of God.

However, it is also common knowledge that misunderstandings about God and our relation to God are the source of numerous neuroses. For instance, prayer can be used as a means of escape from the necessary pain of facing reality. Secondly, when prayer is introduced imprudently and inopportunely in a counselling relationship, it can put off the client or jeopardize the relationship. Again, it might evoke transferential issues in the client.

The helper can pray for self in order to gain the necessary wisdom and prudence to help the client, as well as for the client to receive the necessary assistance in the process of growth. This can be done before, after or even unobtrusively during the counselling session. When it comes to praying over the client visibly, or praying with the client, here the facilitator must exercise skill and tact. Confusion must not be made of the growth facilitator's role. For this particular client the facilitator may be just a helper and not a pastor.

As a general rule you may pray with or for the client in their presence if the latter asks for the prayer. Secondly, you do so if you believe that this open praying is of help in the process of the counselling. Prayer should not be used as a substitute to counselling, when you have nothing else to say. You don't tell a client to start a decade of the rosary to fill up the remaining minutes of the session. The manner in which prayer is used in counselling marks the difference between counselling and spiritual direction. In the case where the client is a 'non-believer' or is very angry with God, the use of open prayer may even wreck the counselling relationship. The same may happen where the client is a believer of a different denomination from that of the growth facilitator, unless the prayer is framed in such a way that it is inclusive of the client's belief system.

On the other hand, prayer can be a very useful counselling skill where the growth facilitator perceives that it is one of the resources of the client. The helper can tap this spiritual resource for the benefit of the client. Where it is helpful clients can even be encouraged to pray by themselves. Beside its inner effects, prayer is one way of making clients aware that God is with them in their struggles. In the case of a client in whose life prayer plays a key role, its exclusion in a counselling relationship might even be detrimental.

ATTENDING

Attending means that I am physically and psychologically present for the client. It is a skill that we need not only in counselling, but in every human relationship, for teachers, mothers, formators, superiors, parish priests, matrons, etc. In other words, it is a skill of effective human relationship. Attending is setting aside time exclusively for the client. Clients might get the impression that you do not value them enough if on coming to sessions at the appointed time they find you watering your flowers or busy at your desk, or deeply involved in some other activity which you must then wind up while they wait. Having to interrupt the session frequently, even with a polite excuse, in order to answer the phone or the knock at the door betrays lack of attention. Switch the phone off, and, if necessary, put an indication at the door that you are engaged.

In attending we do not stop at minimizing external distractions during the session, but internal ones as well. In order to be attentive to others I need to have the ability to sort out my own emotional issues which would otherwise be in the way, blocking my ability to attend. Either I deal with them first or, if they rise in the course of the counselling session, I develop the ability to shelve them and deal with them later outside the session. A client might say something that evokes strong memories in me, or that stirs my anger. It would be inappropriate to vent out my raw feelings as they come.

Attending to another means being actively present to them with my facial expression, eyes and body language. It is not difficult for people to perceive that we are not listening to them or that we are distracted. It is even easier to perceive that during a counselling session, where it is important to the client to be listened to. We betray lack of attention in so many ways: giving inappropriate responses to what has been said, laughing or smiling at the wrong moment, fidgeting, constantly forgetting what has been told us before. In some ordinary circumstances attending is all that is required from the helper. This is the case, for instance, in certain moments of bereavement, or with a dying person, or even with deep friendships. People appreciate just your being there with them. On the other hand, your absence may deal a great blow to them. Attending is being fully present, giving quality time.

In attending you convey the message to the other: I am present to you, I am with you. I am prepared to listen to you fully. The other person can pick up the message whether or not we are attentive to them. This they can do both consciously and unconsciously. When people pick up half-hearted presence in you, they may become distrustful and less open to share.

There is no standard posture a helper must assume in a counselling session. There are those who prefer to take a relaxed posture, perhaps leaning back in a sofa and crossing their legs. This might give the client permission to relax as well. Many others find it more attentive to face the client squarely, while leaning slightly forward in a straight chair. In general, a facilitator should keep eye contact with the client, since there is much that is revealed through body language which the helper cannot afford to ignore for a more comprehensive understanding of the client. Moreover, eye contact sends a message to the client that one is attentive. However, keeping eye contact does not mean staring. One can do so in a discreet and not threatening manner.

LISTENING

In the novel "The Purloined Letter" someone 'hides' a controversial letter which is urgently being searched for by pinning it on the wall in the sitting room. Everyone looks in all impossible places apart from the obvious. It is amazing how often we see or hear without understanding. People can for a long time be the cause of the suffering of those they love, without being aware of it, simply because they are bent on doing good to the beloved and never stop to listen to what the latter really wants or needs. There is a person to whom you narrate your failure or misfortune and who immediately tells you of personal successes in the same area. It is as if to say to you, "you see? I am better than you." So, you shut up. Another to whom you try to talk to about your problem keeps interjecting with 'sorry', 'oh, that is terrible', 'really?', or immediately launches in giving you advice or telling you not to worry, giving you examples of much graver cases. You can feel like shouting and saying: "will you stop jabbering and try to listen?" The more usual and polite reaction is to stop sharing, and to keep the matter to yourself. That is sad enough when it happens in ordinary relations. It is more unfortunate when it happens in a counselling relationship. Yet it happens quite often.

Activity 11: Testing our quality of listening

Very often we are not aware how much of bad listeners we really are. There is a simple experiment to test our listening ability. A number of people sit in a circle or a row. One person is given a sentence on a piece of paper, reads and understands it. This person whispers the same sentence to the next, and the next person does the same to the neighbor until the sentence is transmitted to the last person. This one tests aloud what he or she has heard against the original sentence. It is amazing how often it happens that the original statement has been distorted, sometimes beyond recognition. The same happens all the time through communication.

Frequently Jesus concluded what he had to say with the words: "let him hear who has ears to hear". This was not said in order to insult his listeners, implying that some had ears only for decoration. It was expressing the sad fact that often people hear and seem to have understood, but in actual fact for some reason or other they have not.

Listening leads to understanding, and understanding is perhaps the most important skill in counselling. As Kennedy and Charles observe in their book, "understanding is at the heart of all good therapy. It is, interestingly enough, a quality that cannot possibly harm others, and it is also something of which all humans are capable.

You will listen and listen again, but not understand, see and see again, but not perceive. For the heart of this nation has grown coarse, their ears are dull of hearing, and they have shut their eyes, for fear they should see with their eyes, hear with their ears, understand with their heart, and be converted and be healed by me. (Mathew 13:15; Isaiah 6:9-10)

Understanding transmitted through the discipline of counselling skills helps bewildered people to see themselves in better perspective."[32] We can improve our understanding by taking time to study how to improve our listening skills.

Listening is said to be active when the listener conveys to the communicator what has been understood. Active listening is a two-way process involving both receiver and sender skills. Effective listening can only be assessed by the recipient. That is if I as listener have not managed to convey that I have listened, the cycle of communication has not been complete.

Listening to Words

What do we listen for? In the first place we listen to the words said. Words have meaning, and we strive to understand the meaning which the client is communicating. It is possible not to hear what a person is saying: it may be because the person is speaking too softly, or too quickly; or there may be other noise in the background which impedes our hearing, we may be distracted by some other thoughts that we miss what is said, we may be making an effort to think of what we are going to say next, or the story that the client is narrating may be so long and involved that we are lost in the details. There is nothing wrong with expressing to the client that there is a point we have missed. In fact, contrary to what we might think, people appreciate if we ask them to repeat or clarify what we have not understood. This tells them that we have been listening to the rest of the story. It affirms what they know instinctively that we are not super-humans or machines, but rather that we are ordinary human beings capable of being distracted. As we shall see ahead, there are other skills that help us check whether we have understood correctly the words said. We can paraphrase or summaries them and then check with the client whether that is what they really meant.

Listening to Feelings and Emotions

Some kind of emotional reaction is associated with virtually every situation. It is useful to elicit, clarify, and discuss feelings before moving to more cognitive (i.e., problem solving) matters. One of the first questions we can ask after the counselee has explained his/her problem is: "How do you feel about that?" Often the spiritual counselling session

---

[32] Eugene Kennedy and Sara C. Charles, *On Becoming a Counsellor*, 1977, p. 19.

will involve little more than the expression and clarification of feelings. Frequently people just want to share their joys, successes, commiserate about their failures, or cry over their losses (status, physical losses, losses of relationships, etc.) If we attempt to solve the problems before feelings are clarified this is seldom successful. The unresolved feelings often get in the way of discussing alternatives. The counselling session can deteriorate into a "yes-but" situation.

Listening to feelings and emotions is much more difficult and at the same time much more important than listening to words. It is difficult because, while we perceive words with our ears and we have no problem understanding their meaning if we speak the same language with the client, we often have to decipher emotions indirectly, mainly through gestures and postures. The difficulty is compounded by the fact that a client quite often instinctively or deliberately tries to hide emotions. People are not proud of feeling jealous, ashamed or angry. Listening to emotions is important because often healing consists mainly, and sometimes exclusively, in dealing with the cause of a particular emotion.

Activity 12: Listening to your own feelings

If you are to listen to the feelings and emotions of clients, you should first be familiar with your own emotional states. A number of emotional states are listed below. You are asked to describe what you feel when you experience these emotions. Describe what you feel as concretely as possible: How does your body react? What happens inside you? What do you feel like doing? Consider the following examples.

When I feel accepted, I feel
o *Warm inside*
o *Safe*
o *Free to be myself*
o *Like sitting back and relaxing; I can let my guard down*
o *Like sharing myself*
o *Some of my fears easing away*
o *At home*
o *At peace*
o *My loneliness drifting away*

How do you feel when you are angry, affectionate, accepted, afraid, anxious, attracted, bored, belonging, competitive, confused, defensive, disappointed, free, hopeful, hurt, inferior, intimate, jealous, joyful, lonely, loving, rejected, repulsed, respect, sad, satisfied, shy, suspicious, superior, trusting?

In order to understand the language of emotions we need also to be familiar with reading bodily communication. Below are a number of bodily gestures we might observe and try to understand.

o   The way a person is sitting, sudden change in the posture, body movements.

o   Use of one's hands and fingers: tapping on a chair, wringing of hands, scratching one's head, biting nails, clenching fists, twisting a handkerchief, covering the face or the cheeks with the hands, banging the table with a clenched fist.

o   Facial expressions: smiles, frowns, raised eyebrows, twisted lips, having a blank look, closing eyes, looking on the ground or at the ceiling, crying, glaring at you, avoiding your eyes.

o   Voice-related behavior: lowering the tone, shouting, speaking too fast, spacing words, emphasizing, pauses, silence, stammering, coughing unnecessarily, and stopping in mid-sentence.

o   Automatic physiological responses such as quickened breathing, skin rush, or paleness or red looking, sweating or perspiring of hands, or the brow, blushing, trembling, twitching of the nose, biting of lips.

o   Physical characteristics like deterioration of health, loss or gaining of weight, change in complexion. If we are very sensitive with each other in the community, we can read each other's warning signals.

o   General appearance: good grooming of the hair, the manner of dress… Neglect of one's grooming or a sudden interest in it may be an indication of something going on in that person's life.

Listening to Experiences and Behavior

The words and the bodily postures of the client should tell us in the first place what happened or is happening; what the client experienced or is experiencing. Secondly, they tell us how he or she reacted or is reacting. If we can communicate in a succinct way that we have understood the situation, the feelings and the reaction of the client to that situation, then we convey that we have understood. We might respond with a statement like: "you are feeling... because..." or something similar in different words.

Listening with Empathy

Feltham and Dryden define Empathy from the point of view of counselling, as "the attitude and skill of following, grasping and understanding as fully as possible the client's subjective experience as if from the perspective of the client."[33] As in the case of listening, it is not enough to understand clients from their subjective point of view, empathy requires that we communicate that understanding, if it is to be effective as a counselling skill. Sometimes clients appreciate even the effort that one is striving to understand and empathize, even with partial success.

There are people who are naturally empathic; people we usually describe as sensitive. They are attentive to other people's emotions, even when these do not complain openly about their problems. We all value friends who are like that. That is why empathy is an important skill to cultivate, not just for counselling but also for ordinary relationships.

Even though closely related, empathy cannot be equated with listening, even effective listening. Empathic listening might also be called loving listening. We can imagine a situation in which a person is a very able listener but without love. This person can understand the words said, can read all the bodily language, can identify the feelings, but then uses that understanding of the other for exploitation. This person could be called a good listener but not empathic. Empathic listening implies listening in a manner that values and cherishes the other, even though one may not agree with some of the other's point of view.

ADVANCED EMPATHY

There is a person who is said to see through you, someone you feel you cannot hide the truth from, even if you wanted to. People are said to have penetrating eyes. For some this is a particular gift, something that is part of their personality. Others acquire it as a result of living long with you. A person gets to know you very well to the extent of being able to tell what you are thinking before you say it. Whereas one who is able to read your mind can be perceived as a threat in a lawsuit, such a person is

---

[33] Feltham and Dryden, *Dictionary of Counselling*, London: Whurr, 1993.

a blessing in the counselling context. It is a blessing when the counselor can use such knowledge, not to manipulate but to direct the client towards growth. This skill is similar to empathy in as far as it is understanding of the client from within as it were; however, it goes beyond, for it includes seeing what the client is not able or willing to see of self at the moment. It is called Advanced Empathy.

Like all other counselling skills Advanced Empathy can be learnt or enhanced. There is nothing magical or paranormal about it. It is based on other skills already seen such as careful attending and listening, both to what is spoken and to all the non-verbal communication.

The aim of applying Advanced Empathy is to help the client see personal blind spots, other possible alternatives, implications and consequences of certain decisions or actions, what has been overlooked or ignored, recurring patterns, self-defeating behavior, connections, unconscious personal strengths and potential; and then to move on to make better-informed decisions. The growth facilitator must avoid using Advanced Empathy to show off personal skills and capabilities, at the expense of the client.

Quite often when you communicate to the client a hunch that is negative, unpleasant or disagreeable, the initial reaction will be of denial or even anger. That is why it is most important to cross-check with the client at every step whether you have understood correctly. This must be done in a manner that is tentative and sensitive: "From what you have said I seem to gather that… I wonder whether that is true", "it would seem to me, judging from the fact that… is that correct?" "Am I right to assume that…?"

Sometimes it is helpful not to insist when the client turns on the defensive as a result of receiving advanced empathy. Give allowance to the possibility that you are mistaken, and be open to being corrected by the client. If you had misunderstood, possibly due to lack of knowledge of certain facts, accept; if necessary, apologies. Even when you perceive that you are correct, still you can let the point drop for the time being and then bring it later in a different way, or when the client is more disposed to receive it. It may be appropriate to sweeten the client, mixing challenge with empathy. Find a point of affirmation or understanding, without, however, sounding patronizing or flattering. In spite of the immediate reaction of denial, the client is likely to think about the challenge alone after the counselling session, especially if it touches a sour point. Sometimes a well-disposed client brings up the issue after thinking about it.

Activity 13: Applying Advanced Empathy on Self

As usual, in learning a counselling skill it is helpful to start with self. Describe a situation in your own life, say a problem you are trying to solve. Write down the surface and obvious reasons why this is a problem. Then try to go deeper and identifying underlying issues. An example:

We had an argument with colleagues at table. My point of view was that the choice of Church leaders should be based on merit and not on consideration of where a person comes from; of tribe, nationality or race. I insisted that such considerations are basically ethnocentrism and racism, and that they only impoverish the Church, and reduce us to the same level with corrupt politicians. Moreover, in our case it is worse, for we profess the good news of Christ, in whom there is no longer Greek or Jew. I lost patience when one of the colleagues insisted that the Church must be local, and I retorted not waiting for him to finish, that it is universal as well. It is all right if a local candidate has the requisite qualities, but if a foreign candidate is more qualified, then we must not insist on the locality of the Church. I felt justified and self-righteous, and a little disdainful of those who seemed to defend or at least condone the alternative view.

When I looked closer at myself, I realized that while I still held the same opinion, I could have been gentler in putting it forward. I should have given the chance to the colleague to express himself to the end. I might have been more convincing if I had adapted the attitude of a questioner wanting to know, gently challenging. I could have acknowledged all that was positive in the other's argument, before putting forward my objections. I also realize that it is not every day that I argue so forcefully like that. I had some amount of stress in me created by a recent personal problem, and I needed some form of off-loading, and the argument created the occasion. My colleague might remember my temper more easily than my argument and that serves no good purpose.

A keen person, using Advanced Empathy, could have gone beyond the argument and observed the way I was expressing myself, as well as my non-verbal communication, and then asked me what was *really* my problem. The immediate reaction from me to such a question might be "what do you mean asking me 'what is my problem'?" If such a person went on to tell me that he or she was not referring to what I was saying but to the way I was saying it, probably I would there and then have denied saying that the person was diverting the argument. But this intervention might have helped me later to see the real issues underlying the loss of temper.

FEED BACK

Looking at myself in a mirror while seated in a barber's chair always gives him a queer sensation. I look slightly different from the way I conceive myself, particularly when I see my reflection reflected in another mirror. I am more used to seeing the front part of the face, and not the side or the back of the head. The same feeling comes when I see myself on a video recording or hear my voice on a cassette recorder. It does not sound quite like me; like the way I consider myself. And yet this is the image others have of me all the time. That is what they see and hear of me. It is healthy to see that side of self now and then, in order to balance the personal image. That applies also to our personality in the process of growth.

Closely related to Advanced Empathy is Feedback. Feedback from others helps us to see ourselves as they see us, to hear ourselves as they hear us. Sometimes people find it embarrassing to point out to another person such trivial matters as "you have a piece of food on the side of your mouth" or "your zip is open", even when they know that by pointing out the detail they are saving the other person much greater embarrassment. It is harder to tell another person that your mouth, your arm pits or your shoes smell, yet 'small' things such as those can even wreck a marriage.

Feedback is both an act of courage and love. It is an act of courage for it is often perceived by the receiver as criticism, and we know that no one likes to be criticized. Criticism, even one meant for the good of the person criticized, often evokes angry feelings, and sometimes even shatters relationships. The person who challenges therefore

I tell you most solemnly, you are not looking for me because you have seen the signs but because you had all the bread you wanted to eat. Do not work for food that cannot last, but work for food that endures to eternal life, the kind of food the Son of Man is offering you, ... (John 6:26-27).

undertakes some risk. At the same time, it is an act of love for it aims at the good of the one challenged.

One who truly loves challenges those they love. A touchy Jew might have found it humiliating to be told to his face by Jesus that he and others were looking for him not to hear what he had to say but to get free bread from him. Yet Jesus said this not to humiliate them but to invite them to something greater than ordinary bread.

Useful feedback must have as its motive the good of the person it is given. It should not be made out of frustration. Nor should it be made out of a desire to demonstrate one's higher knowledge or moral superiority.

Quite often we hurt people and continue hurting them simply because we are not aware that we are doing so. In some cases, the situation would change if the one being hurt would pluck the courage to make the other party aware, in the appropriate way, of the harm done. The alternative view of self which Feedback provides is a useful tool in the process of growth. It helps the timid and self-abasing to acknowledge their strong points; the disrespectful to see their rudeness and its effects on others; the self-centered to face their egoism, and the talented that are unaware of it to acknowledge their aptitudes.

There are people who are beautiful but are unaware of this; people who are so convinced of their ugliness or malformation that they can hardly stand their image in a mirror. Sometimes it is therapeutic when another caring person makes them take a good look at themselves in the mirror and acknowledge their beauty. However, even making another person look in the mirror and see the beauty that you see may require some skills of persuasion. The simplest form of giving feedback is projecting to the clients their exact image, for instance repeating to them what they have said, or making them listen to their own voice. Often enough it sounds strange to them, but at least they can't reasonably deny it to be coming from themselves, any more than one would deny that a mirror image is one's image.

Whatever the manner of giving feedback, it must be given skillfully and caringly if it is to be effective. In counselling the motive of giving feedback must always be the good and growth of the receiver. In order to give meaningful feedback, the giver must be one who listens carefully and understands both what the other says and feels. Even when there is more to say, a giver of feedback ought to give only the amount the receiver can deal with at a particular time.

In most cases the feedback that clients need for their growth is that which regards things that are unpleasant about them. And yet it is important for their acceptance of such feedback, also to hear what is positive about themselves. This positive side must be given, not simply as a sugar-coating in which the painful feedback is wrapped, but as a result of genuine love and acknowledgement of the fundamental fact that the good and potential for good in every human being by far outweighs the negative; for we are all created in the image of God and by nature oriented to goodness. It is important to include both positive and negative observations in feedback. There needs to be a balance between support and challenge. Whenever you can, sandwich negative feedback between positive and check that both have been received.

Feedback must be about things that the receiver can do something about. It does not help to be told that your impediment in speech makes it difficult for others to comprehend you. But it does help when one tells you that "when you speak slower, I understand you better." Again, one cannot change mistakes made in the past, but can change present behavior or can resolve to behave differently in the future.

In giving feedback avoid focusing on the person but on the behavior. Feedback must not degenerate into criticism or judgment. Focus on particular behavior of the person and its consequences, and not on generalized statements on the personality of the individual. It is better to say that "when you shifted furniture in your room last night and on some other occasions, I got woken up and could not go back to sleep", than to say, "You are noisy and inconsiderate". This is not a question of being kind or polite; it is the truth. We are not reducible to our individual actions or behavior; we are capable of change.

The above example shows that a statement that aims at giving effective feedback tends to be longer and more detailed than one that is judgmental. Nonetheless one giving feedback must strive to be brief and concise, always remembering to give only what the receiver can handle. In trying to be polite there is the tendency of being lengthy and vague, and in the end, also ineffective. Think of what you want to say before you say it in order to avoid being windy.

One of the ways of training yourself in the art of giving feedback is by learning how to value and receive it yourself. One who is capable of receiving negative feedback and using it for personal growth also knows that it is worthwhile to take the courage to give feedback to others, and that it is important to be sensitive while doing it. People around us are constantly observing our behavior, whether intentionally or otherwise. Many of them dare not tell us what they see and observe about us; perhaps because they are subordinate and consider giving us feedback an act of impertinence or disrespect. Or perhaps they are intimidated by our possible reaction, fearing to offend us. Quite often, instead of talking to us – something that would be much more useful to us – they talk about us to others. The way we respond to others' feedback very much influences their courage or lack of courage to give it to us.

When someone tells you something about yourself, especially something negative, strive to receive the message and think about it. If it is true thank the person and try to change the situation. You do not have to accept every feedback and to act upon it. Know that others can be mistaken about you. Test it against other's opinions and against your own feelings and knowledge of self. Take what is true, not what pleases you.

When opportune you can also solicit feedback. For instance, a lecturer can give a questionnaire to the students to evaluate the course and the manner in which it has been delivered, and to suggest ways of improvement. If some do not want to be identified as those who gave the negative feedback, they can be given the liberty not to sign their names. Respond to the reasonably suggested changes. If you do not, you give the message of lack of respect for the opinion of those who gave the feedback. In soliciting feedback, you need to be careful not to ask to hear what you want to hear. Avoid asking for feedback only from those whom you know will flatter you, or only speak positive about you.

Listen to negative as well as positive feedback. Value the good about you. Do not give way to the Destructive Critic in you that exaggerates your mistakes and underrates your capabilities. Listen to your feelings which at times can be hurt by feedback. Irritation by what people say is often an indication that there is some truth in what they are saying.

PARAPHRASING

Paraphrasing is a particular form of giving feedback. You reflect back to clients what they have just said, using different words, with the purpose of calling greater attention to the meaning of what they have said or are saying. In paraphrasing you need to avoid two pitfalls. On the one hand you must not "put words in the mouth of clients", or give your interpretation of what they have said. In paraphrasing you must avoid altering the meaning of the client's words. On the other hand, you must avoid "parroting," or simply repeating what the client has said. When you do this, often enough an irritated client will retort: "that's what I just said".

When paraphrasing is appropriately applied it is more likely to evoke such exclamations as "exactly!", "yes, that's what I mean", "precisely!" and then the client may go on to say more. Good paraphrasing makes the client feel understood, without realizing that you are saying what the client has just said using different words. But clients feel understood precisely because they *are* understood. Too often in a dialogue a person narrates a painful or exciting topic only to realize that the 'listener' was all along thinking of another painful or exciting topic from his or her own life. Quite often the counter experience of the partner in a dialogue belittles or competes with the narration of the first speaker, thus blocking the way to further self-disclosure. A response with a paraphrase therefore, is an indication of listening and can even be a means of expression of empathy.

Consider the following responses to a housewife sharing something regarding her marriage:

Housewife: I'm completely worn out. I go to the garden daily, collect firewood, get water from the well, and look after the children. My husband simply sits around after gardening and listens to his radio or washes his bicycle. In the evening he goes to drink and comes back late and drunk to demand for food.

Response 1: That is not so tragic. At least he does not beat you!

Response 2: Mine too is more or less like that, but thanks to God he does not drink.

Paraphrase: you are exhausted going out to work as well as looking after the house and children without any help or consideration from your husband.

EXPLORATION

Exploration is the skill by which the counselor obtains from the client information necessary for the growth process of the client. It is the art of asking meaningful questions in the most effective way. It also includes skills by which information is attained without explicit questions, for instance through a raised eyebrow, a nod, a repetition of a phrase just said, or the use of phrases such as 'go on...', 'and so...', 'and then...' etc.

Asking questions is a common feature of our day-to-day interaction. We ask questions for all sorts of reasons and in all sorts of fashions:

○ There are questions we ask for the purpose of getting to know another person better. New acquaintances might want to know the other's name, where they live, what they do, etc. Such questions are important for people building a relationship. But when untimely, or depending on the way they are asked they can be too intimate and disconcerting. At the beginning of a counselling relationship a counselor might want to know the general background of the client, in as far as this often has a bearing on the present behaviors and attitude of the client.

○ There are questions that put the one asked on a spot; that embarrass the respondent, whether this is intended or not; questions for instance that put a person's technical expertise in question. "You say you are a teacher (doctor, counselor, musician, etc.) how come you do not know...?" When such questions are asked deliberately, they serve the malicious purpose of the questioner. When they are inadvertent, they betray a lack of sensitivity. Good counselors do not purposely put down clients for the fun of it. They strive to increase their sensitivity, to avoid hurting the feelings of clients, unless this is unavoidable or unless it is a calculated move for the eventual good of the client.

○ Sometimes people ask questions without paying much attention to the answer given. People who feel uneasy in the presence of an inferior tend to ask questions for the sake of filling in the conversation gap. They do not pay much attention to the answers, for that is not the purpose of the question. Instead, they may be thinking of the next question while the respondent answers. It is irritating to be asked the same question over and over again, particularly by the same person. For instance, someone asks after your name and you mention it. A few moments later the same person asks "what did you say your name was?" and you give it once again. Then that same person addresses you with a different name afterwards. Questions of that nature betray a lack of listening or even a lack of interest in the answer on the part of the questioner. While listening is an important tool throughout the counselling exercise, it is particularly required when an answer is being given to a question you have asked.

o There are questions that are meaningless: that ask the obvious and that are quite often annoying to the person asked. It can be upsetting to be asked whether you felt grief at the loss of your mother. The person who was grieved at the occasion finds it unnecessary; while another person who for some reason was not upset might consider the question a form of accusation. It is not enough to consider the answer you want to arrive at without taking into account the effect of your question on the client.

o Some questions can be asked purely to satisfy the curiosity of the questioner. That may be all right in ordinary conversation among friends, but not in counselling. A counselor must shelve many personal feelings during the counselling session. Among these is idle curiosity.

o There are questions that touch a raw nerve; that cut us to the quick. Italians have a proverb that the tongue rubs where the tooth hurts. You ask an apparently innocent question only to be surprised by the intensity of the response. For a counselor this may be an indication of an area in the client's life worthy of further investigation. At the same time, it may not be very wise there and then to pursue the inquiry in that area. It may be more prudent to reserve it for a more opportune time. It is natural that people feel uncomfortable to talk about the very issues they bring for counselling. These issues must eventually be confronted if there is to be genuine growth. However, a too hasty search for growth might make you lose the client all together. It is particularly helpful if probing questions are followed my affirmation and empathic statements.

o In court defendants are asked questions with the intention of bringing them to admit something. Some questions can sound like an interrogation, even when they are not meant to be. Often questions that begin with "why" may sound interrogative. In general, 'why' questions are not helpful in counselling. More will be said about "why" questions later.

o Some questions may be quite helpful, but they may be posed in a manner that puts off the person being asked. It is as important to know the right questions to ask and the proper manner of asking them.

o There are questions that affirm the respondent; questions that invite another person to speak of the things they are proud of. It is possible for a counselor to affirm the client, not by a statement but with a question. In answering it the client is brought to speak about things that are elevating to self.

As we can see from the above list, not all questions are inducive to the growth of another. Some are damaging to the growth process. Others are helpful. That is why it is important to know the right questions to ask and when and how to bring them forward. We might first discuss questions that are not helpful in the counselling context, before going on to questions that are helpful.

Closed Questions

Do you like children?

Are you happy in your marriage?

Do you think you have a drinking problem?

Questions like the above are good for questionnaires where the respondent does not have to phrase the answers. They may also be useful in court where a prosecutor wants to pin down an elusive defendant. But they are not very helpful in the counselling session. They can all be answered with a 'yes' or 'no', especially when the client is not in the mood to cooperate. The counselor then is compelled either to ask another question or to use some other skill, in order for the session to move forward. These are called closed questions. They can be trying for the counselor and tiring for the client.

Of course, even in a counselling session there can be room for closed questions which require a 'yes' or 'no' answer. A closed question can be a necessary prelude to open questions. In order to investigate a client's marital relationship, it is necessary first to establish whether or not the client is married. You might then first ask whether the client is married or not. What is important is to know that such questions should be minimized. You need to think of ways of rephrasing closed questions in such a way that the client can say more about the issue. There are better ways of asking whether or not a client is happy in marriage.

'Why' Questions

You came late again, why?

If you do not love him, why did you marry him?

Why do you laugh when you are narrating something sad?

Another form of exploration that is not very helpful in counselling is the too frequent use of 'why' questions. "Why" questions put counselees on the defensive. "Why" implies that an explanation is being demanded. 'Why' questions usually yield the following results:

o   The client feeling grilled and interrogated

o   The client feeling that the helper is intruding – possibly wanting information for his/her sake and not the client's sake

o   They cause the client to lose track thus becoming distracted

o   The client may feel that the helper asks questions without necessarily hearing the answers

o   They may cause the client to give up and let the helper take over.

As in the case of closed questions, 'why' questions can also have a place in the counselling context. At a certain stage it may be necessary to challenge the client with a 'why' question. Even when you do not use the word, a question or probe may still be a 'why' question. To simply state: "you came late again!" implies the question "why?" and demands an explanation. At times such a challenge is called for. Of course, it can be softened: "I realize you came late again; I wonder why." What is important to remember is that the use of 'why' questions should be kept to the minimum and that when they are used the counselor knows their likely effect on the client and considers this to be timely.

Open Questions

An 'open' question is one which invites the client to speak at length. Open questions challenge clients to think. Questions like "what made you choose that vocation?" "How do you spend your day?" "Can you say more about that?" cannot be answered with a short 'no' or 'yes' answer: they invite the client to go on speaking. Open questions give a chance to the counselor to listen not only to the answer to the question, but also to what is said unintentionally. They allow greater room to study body language and non-verbal communication. The use of interrogative adjectives such as 'how', 'when', 'what' 'where' can be helpful in the formulation of open questions.

RELUCTANCE AND RESISTANCE

There are two kinds of problems in counselling situations: 1) the concerns clients bring with them and 2) difficulties with the helping process itself. Resistance/reluctance on the part of clients is one of these difficulties.

Reluctance

I loved playing instruments from a very early age but I never had the opportunity to learn to play them until my late teens. A fellow student who also belonged to a youth band started giving me private lessons in playing the guitar. I was a very eager learner even if being left-handed I had to learn the guitar the 'right way'. The few lessons he taught me gave me enough to continue on my own until I could comfortably accompany simple music during liturgical services. But that took years. Later on, in my mid-twenties I got introduced to the organ and the piano, but still on a private basis. The success with the keyboard was less than that with the guitar. Eventually I acquired a guitar and a keyboard of my own to continue my lessons. I bought books and audio cassettes for guitar and piano lessons.

Quite early on I learnt that with music, as with many other practical skills, the important thing is to do a little practicing regularly, and not to bite big chunks at a time followed by long spells of no practice. But although I am convinced of this, I have never been able to keep a regular practice to my satisfaction. The temptation has always been to come back to these hobbies with full zest, carry on the drills for a few days or even weeks, occasionally being taken away by over-playing the pieces I have learnt so well, and then getting bored by these and by the dry drills, thus breaking off again for long spells. I can often speculate on how much I could have learnt by now if I kept a minimal but regular practice. Then I start again and the whole cycle is replayed.

This is an illustration of reluctance in our lives. We all have things to which we aspire, which we never quite achieve, dreams we know we can achieve and which we strive after, but are kept back from achieving completely by some pain we are reluctant to undergo consistently.

A man had two sons. He went and said to the first, "My boy, you go and work in the vineyard today". He answered, "I will not go", but afterwards thought better of it and went. The man then went and said the same thing to the second who answered, "Certainly, sir", but did not go. Which of the two did the father's will?' (Matthew 21:28-31).

This reluctance ranges from simple things such as hobbies to life goals and fundamental convictions. People who come to counselling for the most part genuinely want to grow. But since all genuine growth is painful, they are frequently reluctant to embrace the inevitable pain involved in authentic growth.

Reluctance in clients may take on different forms. One may talk about safe and low priority issues. Another may be unsure what they really want. Or it may be that they don't work hard enough. Or again they set unrealistic goals and then excuse themselves for not attaining them. Or they may be over-cooperative: 'yes' men or women, without dealing with the issues at depth. The second boy in the gospel story who accepted to do the father's will but then did not budge is a typical example. Or they don't take responsibility for themselves; they blame others, systems, institutions, see everything in the negative, etc. People may do all this, not intentionally but habitually.

The different forms of reluctance require different skills to confront. If a client's reluctance is due to lack of confidence and trust in the counselor perhaps due to past betrayals, it is then necessary for the counselor with time to strive to win the confidence of the client. Reluctance due to a sense of shame or due to the fear of change will also require different approaches.

Resistance

Resistance is more active than reluctance. It is the reaction of a client particularly in situations when they feel coerced. In Catholic seminary formation it is required of every seminarian to have a spiritual director who accompanies the seminarian on his internal and private spiritual journey. Whereas seminarians are free to choose the spiritual director they like, they are not at liberty not to choose one, for spiritual direction is deemed essential for spiritual growth of the seminarian. That requirement that each has to have a spiritual director and present the name to the General Spiritual Director makes some who would have preferred not to have one resistant in the course of direction. Such a seminarian goes for spiritual direction merely to fulfill a requirement and not out of genuine conviction of a need for his own spiritual growth. In such cases it is incumbent on the spiritual director to win the confidence and trust of the seminarian and to break the resistance.

Resistance is usually a form of power struggle. Resistant clients often present themselves as not needing help. But then others get the problems. Again, with any pressure they feel abused. They do not feel any willingness to establish a relationship with the counselor. Some are resentful. They deceive or trap the counselor or the formator. Some make an active attempt to sabotage the process. They play games.

How to Deal with Reluctance/Resistance

o   Look at the situation objectively. Is the client showing reluctance/resistance at all or is it you that think this is the case? It may be that what you think to be reluctance or resistance is only a natural response to a difficult situation, where a contrary response would have been foolhardy. Or for instance, you may have come to the conclusion that a client is hiding something from you. Acting on that conclusion you might try all sorts of ways to get to know what it is that the client is hiding. In such a case the client's reaction might be construed as resistance. If your conclusion is based on insufficient facts and is erroneous the only way out of the impasse is for you to correct your error. Growth and change are painful, and hesitation in undertaking painful decision is only natural.

o   If it is indeed reluctance or resistance, ask the reasons why. Is it possible that you and not the client, are the source of the problem? Is it the manner of your approach that is the cause of the reaction? Look at the quality of your interventions. Did you ask the wrong questions? Did you ignore something important? Is there a better approach you can consider?

o   Be aware of your reaction to the reluctance/resistance. What emotions does it evoke in you? Do you feel despised? Challenged? Incompetent? Do you feel angry? Frustrated? Impatient? Do you feel like giving up on the client, or do you tend to be aggressive? How are you handling these emotions within the counselling session? Do you express them in ways that might sabotage the counselling relationship, or are you able to handle them effectively?

o   Accept and work with a client's resistance. Do not ignore it, but neither should you allow yourself to be intimidated by it. Start off with the frame of reference of the client. Knowing your client well will help you know how best to deal with the resistance. It may be better to leave the point of contention for the time being and consider other matters. You may come to it later at an opportune moment or using a different approach. In some cases, it may be better to hammer on the sore point and let the anger out of the client.

o   See reluctance and resistance as normal things. Help the client to see the positive side of their resistance. Consider reluctance as avoidance, which is not necessarily due to ill will. Avoid such thoughts as "they shouldn't do that!"

o   Paraphrase or mirror back the resistance/reluctance to the client. You might even consider switching roles for a moment. Let the client play counselor and you the client. Act out the resistance and let the client see it from a different perspective. Using this skill might require you to do some explanation before the actual exercise. A resistant client is likely to ask in the middle of the actual exercise what all this farce is about, especially when he or she starts feeling cornered.

o   At times you may need to confront reluctance and resistance with the skill of immediacy. Point it out to the client using concrete examples. Invite the client to say what he or she thinks about what you have said.

o   If all else fails, and if the resistance is such that you cannot help the client in any meaningful manner, admit it and consider the possibility of terminating the relationship. It is possible for a client to close self to the possibility of growth, and if such a thing occurs the best course of action is for you to admit defeat, rather than go on wasting each other's time and money.

IMMEDIACY

Stephen was a senior member of our association. He kept custody of some of the assets of the association including a farm tractor. For a long time, the tractor was grounded and partly on account of that the association was low on funds. I was secretary to the association. In one of its meetings, it was decided to assess the economic advantage of keeping the tractor, and if advisable, to sell it off. Stephen was not in that meeting. As expected, I circulated the minutes of the meeting and posted a copy to Stephen as well. After sometime I was surprised and a little disconcerted by receiving a letter from Stephen, addressed to me personally, in which he was complaining that he had been misjudged. I kept the letter and forgot about the affair. A week or so after I received another letter from him, more pungent than the first one, sounding as though I was to blame for what had been said about him. My immediate reaction was one of anger. But later on, I calmed down enough to decide on a course of action.

I got hold of both letters along with the minutes of the meeting and arranged a meeting with Stephen. I shared about feeling hurt by what sounded like a personal attack, when I had only done my duty of recording the proceedings of the meeting and of circulating the minutes to the members. I admitted that I could have phrased the minutes in a manner less hurtful to him. I explained the concrete details that had been discussed and that I had to present in the minutes. I suggested that if he was not satisfied with what had been said about him the proper forum to air out his complaint was in the next meeting. If he could not wait for that he could see the leader of the association. To my surprise Stephen was apologetic, and from that day on we actually became friends.

Immediacy is direct mutual talk. Sometimes it becomes necessary in relationships to bring salient issues to the surface and to talk about them openly. The usual tendency is to keep quiet about matters we are unhappy about, accumulate anger by degrees, which anger is bound to come out in some unhealthy way.[34]

In the counselling context the responsibility of being immediate is on the leader or counselor. It is exercised when we hook to a phrase just said, or when we capture body language and explore what is going on behind the particular gesture. You observe a situation and then explore it. One of the functions of immediacy is to strengthen the working alliance. A typical statement of immediacy includes self-disclosure on the part of the counselor, indication of how the counselor is contributing to the problem, some concrete challenge, say in the form of what you suspect to be happening but are not sure, and an invitation of the client to discuss the matter with you.

Immediacy is called for when something is going on in a relationship which at least one party is aware of but is hesitant to bring to the surface; something that is likely to have adverse consequences. For example, one can apply immediacy when a meeting is starting to lose direction, when there is tension between a counselor and a client, when there is growing attraction between client and counselor; attraction that is ethically unhealthy or that threatens to sidetrack the counselling process.

The counselor needs to have a certain distance from what is happening in order to deal with it. For instance, in the last case mentioned, if the counselor and client are both attracted to each other, imprudent attempt to use the skill of immediacy might yield the opposite of what is intended: consolidating the attraction and bringing it to a higher level rather than breaking it to continue with the counselling process.

Immediacy demands the possession of many other skills such as attending, listening, empathy, exploration, as well as strengths such as maturity, self-control, love, respect and courage.

SELF-DISCLOSURE

Self-disclosure is the skill by which a counselor reveals part of personal experience for the purpose of helping the client. This can be achieved in many ways. Clients may need to know that what they are experience is not something unique or insurmountable. It has been experienced and

---

[34] See "Unhealthy expression of Anger" on page 74.

overcome; therefore, it can still be overcome by someone else. In some cases, clients might even consider the ways a counselor used in confronting the problem as helpful in their own situation. Self-disclosure can also help the client to know that the counselor is not some kind of super-person, but one who has gone through their difficulties and therefore understands the pain entailed in them. A hesitant client may find it easier to open up after the self-disclosure of the counselor.

However, a counselor needs to apply particular prudence in exercising self-disclosure. Every experience is unique, every person is unique too. What worked in one's experience does not necessarily work in another's. In self disclosure there is the danger of wanting to show off, of patronizing the client, and of belittling the client's experience. In self disclosure the counselor may really be saying that what you are going through is nothing at all. We have seen much worse and gone through it. There is also the danger of scandal and of eroding the counselor's capacity to role-model for the client, depending on the kind of experience the counselor chooses to share.

Self-disclosure must be motivated by the good and growth of the client. It should be brief. The counselor needs to guard against the temptation to share more than is necessary. It should not be given to gain sympathy from the client, thus switching roles. It must be timely and appropriate.

DECISION MAKING AND PROBLEM SOLVING

The Nature of Decisions

We all have to make decisions much of the time. Some decisions are easy. Most people do not have to agonize over what to wear or when to wake up or whether to talk. Some are much harder, for instance the decisions to choose a career, to commit one's life with another in marriage, to undergo a serious operation, to go for a medical check for HIV. Decisions can also be clear or vague. With regard to decisions between right and wrong where the right and wrong courses of action are known, the question is not so much which course of action to take. It is rather whether or not we have the strength of will to make the right decision. On the other hand, decisions between two or more good courses of action may be harder to make. It is hard to decide which is better among good options, and perhaps harder to decide which is worse among bad options.

We rarely have only one thing at a time to decide on. Life does not dish out one problem at a time for us to work on. The usual situation is that while we are busy with dealing one matter another gets in the way. We then have also to make the decision regarding what to tackle first and what to keep for later.

Sometimes having made a decision we keep wondering whether we made the right one, or regretting when we are sure we made a false one. Consequently, we may find it agonising to make a similar decision in the future, fearing to make another mistake. People who decide to trust and find that they have trusted the wrong person will find it harder to decide to trust when caught in a similar situation.

It is very important that we make the right decisions and that we follow them through. Every choice has consequences, good or bad. Even apparently minor choices have a cumulative effect that can have serious consequences in our life. And then there are decisions that can have much more far-reaching repercussions. People do not become heroes or saints by a single act, nor do they become villains by a single choice. Repeated small choices leaning in a particular direction usually pave the way to serious decisions. That is why every single decision is important. The decisions we make in turn make us who we are: they lead to actions and omissions, shape our attitudes, harden into habits, establish our personality, bring about or erode our happiness, and, eventually, determine our destiny.

Having to make decisions is not an easy thing. The inability to face the pain entailed in decision making leads to a life of constant doubt. The postponement of decisions in order to avoid the pain involved has the opposite effect of making us live with constant worry. The stress increases as we approach a time when the decision cannot wait any longer. The procrastination may mean that we make decisions when it is too late, and therefore we make the wrong choices. On the other hand, decisions made too quickly can also lead to wrong choices. They lead to regret later, to self-blame or blaming of others. In fact, looking back in our lives the most regrettable moments are due to wrong decisions we made. Repeated wrong decisions eventually result into failure in our duties, disappointment to others and a diminution of our self-esteem. They can lead to depression or despair.

On the other hand, the ability to make the right decisions gives us self-confidence. The courageous endurance of the pain involved strengthens the will. Right decisions yield success in whatever undertaking we may be involved. The person who habitually deliberates and decides knows what to do even when he or she has made a wrong decision. The mistake turns into a lesson, a useful tool for future decision-making. People who do not flinch from making decisions are self-driven, resolute and resourceful. Others find them reliable and look to them for guidance. They assume responsibility for their actions.

Steps Involved in a Typical Decision Making

Acronyms can be useful memory aids. There is one that summarizes the major steps involved in a typical decision-making process. The person who wants to make a decision, does just that; *DECIDES* (each letter of the word standing for a step). The person:

Defines the Problem

Establishes an Action Plan

Clarifies values

Identifies alternatives

Discovers probable outcomes

Eliminates poor alternatives systematically

Starts action

A more concise acronym suggests that if you must decide, then steer through your problems using the *OAR*: ask yourself: What are the "O;"? *Objectives* that you want to attain; what are the "A;" the *alternatives* you have? And what are the "R;" the *risks* involved? Both these acronyms can be helpful. However, it is important to point out that different decisions require different sequences of deliberations. Moreover, in actual life situations of decision-making it may prove impractical to follow some formula on paper, ticking off the steps as you go through them. Nevertheless, any combination of the steps below can be helpful in decision-making, depending on circumstances.

DECIDE TO ACT

The first and most important step is to decide to do something about the problem. Once that decision has been made usually the person can work out much of what is written below. When the prodigal son of the gospel (Luke 15:11-32) came to the decision to return to his father, he worked out what he would say. The real decision was in swallowing the shame and deciding to face the pain. The second important decision was to stick to the resolution during the process of the implementation. He might have had second thoughts: he could have chickened out, thinking about what his elder brother or the house servants would think of him. Actually he did not have to say all that he had planned. He did not have to ask his father to treat him as one of his paid servants.

PRAY FOR THE LIGHT OF THE HOLY SPIRIT

Even in the most elaborate and well-worked out decisions, there is always room for human error. We cannot foresee all the future consequences of our decisions. The "facts" upon which we base our decisions may be false. Decisions that seem excellent under all aspects can prove to be mistaken later in the light of new information.

In this human predicament the believer knows that God sees the wider picture, and that God's help is always there for the asking. God does not take away the responsibility for us to think or the pain to decide, but God helps us to have the strength to make the necessary choices. The life of Jesus was guided by a single driving force, namely to discern and to do the will of the Father. The tricks of the Tempter (Luke 4:1-13), trying to persuade Jesus to turn stones into food since he had the power to do so; the proposal to impress the hardened religious leaders by a miracle, jumping down from the pinnacle of the temple, and the suggestion to subdue all the kingdoms of the earth, might have seemed wise by human standards. The suggestion from his own apostle Peter (Matthew 16:22), that Jesus finds a way of avoiding the ignominy of the cross was well-meant and sounded reasonable. None of these, however, corresponded to the will of the Father, and they were rejected as soon as they were suggested. A follower of Christ cannot dispense with the assistance of the Holy Spirit in decision making, especially because our intelligences and our wills are much weaker than we believe them to be.

Decisions made under the guidance of the Holy Spirit might now and then seem erroneous when judged by human standards, especially by those who do not believe. However, they can never lead to ultimate ruin of the one who makes them. On the contrary, they always lead to triumph in spite of any appearance to the contrary in the short run.

ARTICULATE THE PROBLEM

Some problems are quite obvious but others manifest themselves to us as a continued annoyance or worrying. We need to define them before we can deal with then effectively.

Very often people try to find solutions to the wrong problems and then of course they cannot find the solutions. Among many traditional African cultures, the quickest diagnosis for all sorts of problems is to go to a soothsayer. Fortune-tellers are well-accomplished and well-trained cultural psychologists who work out a solution by telling their clients what they want to hear, or by guessing the answers from what the clients tell them. People go to oracles with all sorts of problems: to obtain jobs, to bring back lost spouses, to obtain healing for incurable diseases, to get rid of enemies, to grow wealthy, to catch thieves, to find marriage partners, to pass exams, etc. What they do in effect is to fail to articulate their problems maturely and to look for appropriate solutions to these problems. Instead, they create more problems of wasting meagre resources in payment of the soothsayer, of having to undergo complicated exercises ranging from walking naked in the night to human sacrifice, of fuelling hatred against those they erroneously believe to be the causes of their problems.

Definition of a problem demands rigorous self-examination. It requires humility, especially when we are part of the problem. It is humbling to admit that the reason why you cannot obtain a job is that you do not exert yourself enough, that you lost a spouse because you are selfish or quarrelsome or dirty, that you can't pass an examination simply because you do not have the intelligence for it, however much you apply yourself. However, if the solution to a problem demands a personal change from the one trying to solve it, no amount of effort to change the environment can remove the problem.

In an effort to articulate our problems it may be helpful sometimes to write down our reflections on the matter. Writing helps us think more coherently. Try to focus on the facts of the matter and not just your impressions.

As much as possible view positively the problem at hand; see it in terms of opportunity rather than problem. It is said that a pessimist sees the difficulty in every opportunity, and that an optimist sees the opportunity in every difficulty. Try to be an optimist and not a pessimist.

CONSULT

Quite often that which seemed a major problem becomes easier if it is discussed with a caring friend. Or it may be that in our isolation we see only one course of action, whereas there are many others. Talking with a friend can help us discover other courses of action. Frequently new ideas do not even come from the partner with whom we share our problems, but from ourselves. As we talk to a good listener, we are struck with new insights. Sharing with another person reveals to us prejudices that we harbour but are not aware of. To benefit from consultation, we need to be resilient with feedback, particularly when it is negative.

IDENTIFY ALTERNATIVES

Brain storm: write down as many possible courses of action as can come in the mind, including the most ridiculous. Among the many choices there is one that gives us the immediate but not necessarily long-lasting satisfaction. There is also one that is the best choice but not necessarily the easiest. Avoid the natural tendency of selecting the alternative that corresponds closest to the status quo, for it is not necessary always the best. Carefully weigh the possible positive results from each alternative and the risks involved. One way of doing this is to set down each option on paper and below it draw two columns, one headed "Pros" and the other headed "Cons," then within the columns list the possible advantages and disadvantages.

Having identified the different alternatives and weighed them carefully the next step is to decide which of them is the best. Unless you have to, do not make a decision while you are under strong emotions, for instance when you are angry, depressed, desperate, or frightened. Even when you do make a decision under such circumstances, it is good to delay the implementation if possible.

WORK OUT A PLAN OF ACTION

Make your plan to fit within available resources of money, of available time, of personnel, etc. Think ahead about what will be the indicators that the problem is being solved. In working out a plan of action be realistic about difficulties involved.

LEARN TO LIVE WE IRRESOLVABLE PROBLEMS

Not all problems have solutions to them. At least these solutions may not be immediate. The lack of solutions reminds us that we are finite. Here is where decision making differs from problem solving. While we cannot solve all problems, we have to make decisions all the time, even with regard to what we cannot solve. In some cases, the best course of action is to accept to live with the unresolved problem. This is what Paul came to realise after, that the thorn in the flesh would not be removed in spite of his pleas. The cross is very much a part of Christian living.

HELPING OTHERS SOLVE THEIR PROBLEMS

In the context of counselling one person helps another make a decision. It is important to point out right away that the counselor must avoid giving advice in the process of helping the client make a decision. We do not have the same thoughts, feelings and experiences as our counselee and, therefore, advice coming from our own experience is often inappropriate. It is easier for counselees to act on the decisions which they themselves made during the counselling session. Obviously, we can provide helpful information. When we give advice, we deprive the counselees of the opportunity to develop their own brain-storming and decision-making skills.

The process of helping another come to definite decisions in their life follows closely the steps described above. All we need to do is to apply the different counselling skills discussed above, to help the client articulate their problems, identify possible alternatives, weigh the risks involved, work out an action plan, accept to live with problems they cannot change, etc.

Part V

RE-CREATING IN THE IMAGE OF GOD: HELPING A GROUP

We have now come to the fifth and last part of this book. To recapitulate, we saw that regardless of how we are or how we feel about ourselves, we were all created and destined to be good, lovely and loveable. We can regain that inner beauty and goodness in ourselves through our efforts assisted by God and by others in cooperation with the circumstances of our life. We are also called to play a role in the restoration of that beauty in the lives of individuals we meet, either in ordinary encounters of family, friends, enemies and strangers, or through pre-arranged and well conducted counselling sessions.

We can also facilitate the growth of others on a larger scale through organized group meetings, and that is the burden of the present section.

WORKING WITH GROUPS

The Necessity of Cooperation *211*
What is a Group/Community? *214*
Formation and Running of a Group *215*
  Recruiting of Members 215
  Preparing People for Group Membership 216
Some Elements of Group Process *218*
  Participation 219
  Roles 219
  Influence 223
  Feelings 225
  Eye Contact 226
Stages in Group Development *226*
Dimensions of Behavior & Intervention Strategies *229*
  The person who talks too much 229
  The person who talks too little 229
  The angry person 230
  The Person who fools around 230
  The Person who is over-intellectual and theoretical 230
  The Person who is Self-disparaging 231
  The person who is anecdotal 231

THE NECESSITY OF COOPERATION

There are few things that fascinate me in the world of nature as social insects. And in my part of the world, I am quite familiar with termites. They are the plague and affliction of the poor peasant. They destroy certain crops like maize, sugarcane and sorghum. They bring down houses made out of wood, if that wood has not been treated or coated with oil. With their mounds scattered all over they render farmland difficult to work with a tractor or simple hoe. These mounds can be as high as two meters or more, and as hard as baked bricks. Even when you are able to break down the ant hill, its soil is usually infertile for crops. If you intrude on their habitats termites willingly die a martyr's death by biting mercilessly and instantly drawing blood.

But if you do not have a grass-thatched roof or a maize garden, termites are fascinating creatures to study. They have a lot to teach to humans. They have a very high level of co-operation and co-ordination. The termite community begins one rainy day when the white ants fly from a mother community. It would seem as if God made these creatures purposely to feed other creatures. The day the white ants fly many other creatures have a feast. Birds of every kind swarm around happily eating one insect at a time. On the ground there is much traffic including ants ten times smaller than termites, frogs, snakes, and bigger mammals, all gathering in the booty. The few termites that survive this decimation go into pairs and enter the ground to form new colonies. It is as well that they are so reduced otherwise the whole landscape would soon look like an enormous egg-tray of termite knolls.

Soon enough the future queen (the female of the solitary pair) starts her career of producing babies, for the royal family will very soon need them for their very survival. Probably she begins with a few workers, for a palace has to be built, food has to be brought, children have to be ferried away and the homestead has to be kept clean. These workers are the least menacing of the ant family, for they do not bite at all. They simply go on working. And yet they do all the work of the ant hill including that which ruins peasants. I don't know whether they ever take a rest. I have never seen one standing still. If you dig a part of a live ant hill you are very likely to find it rebuilt the next morning. It is these soft-bodied, harmless workers that do the job. The queen also produces soldiers which have heavy, hard heads disproportionately bigger than the rest of their bodies, carrying two formidable mandibles for defense. These do not move much. They are stationed strategically in the ant hill to guard the colony.

211

Some go out of the ant hill to guard the workers on their daily cores. At a certain stage the queen produces the feathered ants which are destined to be eaten or to further the colony. These do not seem to have any work in the colony apart from waiting for the day when their mission begins.

Termites are so organized that they are said also to colonize some other insects which secrete a substance they need for one of their projects. Any other intruding insect is executed without trial. Those they colonize are captured and given a particular place in the ant hill. They are fed in the same way as a human farmer feeds his cattle with hay. Then the secretion is ferried away to be processed according to termite technology.

Anyone who has dug an ant hill to destroy it knows how much work it involves. It is futile to think that you have destroyed it until you get to the royal pair; the queen who is much more distended due to the nature of her vocation and the king who retains his original size and appearance as if he does regular jogging. The hardest place to get to is the palace. It is infested with the biggest-headed soldiers ready to do their once-in-a-life-time job. Once any of these bites, the jaws lock once and for all, and that is the end of him. As children we used to hold them by their harmless bellies and make them bite the edge of our shirts in a row, knowing that once they have bitten, they are rendered harmless. They cannot even go away.

There are a few characteristics about termites that are worth highlighting as a prelude to studying human group work.

1. The impact of united action: unless you have very good sight you may not be able to see an ant at a ten-meter distance. But you can see an ant hill at a distance of a kilometer. The effectiveness of the ants in all that they do does not depend on their numbers; there are millions of other insects which don't make such an impact on us. It depends on their high level of cooperation. As individuals we may be insignificant; as a united group we form a formidable force.

2. In the ant hill each task is equally important, and each member-insect works to the best of its ability. There are no menial jobs and no noble tasks. All the members depend on the queen and king for their life. In turn the life of these two depends on the work of the others. Since ants are such a behaviorist diet for many creatures they would not survive against predators if they did not have the strong jaws of the soldier ants to protect them. The queen cannot move about to look for her own food.

212

The worker ant cannot bite back in defense. The soldier cannot fly. The flying ant cannot build an ant hill. Each depends on the other.

3. Each role requires heroic self-giving. The worker-ants slave themselves to death for the ant hill. They go out of the ant hill in search of all the necessary supplies. The soldier's suicidal bite would make the coward abnegate his role. The queen and king are trapped by their subjects in a palace whose exit is too narrow for them. The day the flying ants go out of the ant hill is for the majority of them the first and last day for them to see the sun, if they are lucky to see it at all.

There is a variety of gifts but always the same Spirit; there are all sorts of service to be done, but always to the same Lord; working in all sorts of different ways in different people, it is the same God who is working in all of them. The particular way in which the Spirit is given to each person is for a good purpose… just as the human body, though it is made up of many parts, is a single unit because all these parts, though many, make one body, so it is with Christ… nor is the body to be identified with any one of its parts… God put all the separate parts into the body on purpose. If all the parts were the same, how could it be a body? As it is, the parts are many but the body is one. (1 Corinthians 12: 4-20).

It would seem that the all-wise Creator who made these tiny insects co-operate so well by instinct arranged that those he made in his own image achieve such unified action by something higher besides instinct; that is reason and will. We saw in the first part of this book how we humans are also social by nature.[35] We have only to look around us to see how much humanity has achieved through cooperation. And yet many of the world's woes are also due to dysfunctional human relationships, from broken families to wars, with all the inevitable repercussions of neuroses, fixations, traumas, social inequalities, refugee situations, malnutrition. In order to live harmoniously we have to supplement what is given by nature with what we acquire through conscious effort. Among humans, peace, harmony and cooperation are learnt; they are not purely instinctual the way they are among termites.

All right! Suppose you accept all that is said above. You are convinced that it is important for each one of us to be an effective member of the community or group where you are. You want to contribute more positively. The question naturally that you are likely to ask yourself is, where do you begin? And the answer is: first assess how much or how

---

[35] See "Inter-Personal Reflection of God's Image" on page 34.

little you contribute: get to know where you stand. Do you belong to any community or group? How well or poorly is your community or group functioning? Are you satisfied with the role you play or is there room for you to do more or better? Are there opportunities for you to join or initiate a group?

A rudimentary knowledge of the basics of Group Dynamics is helpful in our participation in or initiation of groups/guidance of groups. But first we need to understand the difference between a community and a group.

WHAT IS A GROUP/COMMUNITY?

A family has been defined as the smallest community. In our families we experience love – or the lack of it. There are roles and responsibilities duties and rights, but the emphasis is on *living* not on *doing*. A family is a community. Besides the family, people also choose other communities. There are religious communities in which men and women *live* a particular ideal, a particular charism. They have roles and responsibilities, but the emphasis is on *living*. That too is a community.

We can also think of groups. In school children form groups such as of Scouts or Girl Guides or Young Farmers. Adults join Lion's or Lottery Clubs or Labor Unions. These have common interests as well as role differentiation. We refer to these as groups and not communities. Members to these groups may be living in different communities.

A community is a group, although a group is not necessarily a community. The keyword in a community is 'living'. A group on the other hand is a collection of individuals who interact and inter-relate in a face-to-face manner *around a common goal*. They remain in relationship with one another long enough to influence one another, establish clear identification of membership and act in a unified manner. Like communities, groups can give one a sense of solidarity, significance and of belonging. In a community, as in a group, most if not all the skills mentioned in the previous chapter are important. Learning the skills of group work is also a preparation for functional community living.

Many of us live or have lived in communities: nuclear families, extended families, religious orders, priests in a presbytery, etc. Communities can give answer to our basic needs of love, of mutual support and they can enhance our reciprocal growth. But functional communities do not just happen; they have to be cultivated. Dysfunctional communities can become a source misery and even despair for some of their members.

While much of what has been said so far can be of help in building health communities, a lot more can be said about the subject. Here we restrict ourselves to discussing the formation and running of groups.

People living in communities can also be members to different groups: social clubs, religious devotions, farmers' associations, organizing committees, cooperatives, support groups, trade unions, political alliances, student guilds, etc. We can decide to initiate groups for a specific purpose in answer to our needs.

Different groups have different guidelines in accordance to their nature and purpose. The regulations in a study group cannot be the same as in a group for married couples or parish council. Nevertheless, groups do have common elements which, when followed, lead to the achievement of the purpose for which they are formed. It is these common tenets that we look at below.

FORMATION AND RUNNING OF A GROUP

Recruiting of Members

The person who wants to start a group must in the first place be clear of the purpose of the undertaking. To persuade and motivate others about an idea the initiator needs to be convinced and enthused of the same. Moreover, the initiator must also have the ability to convey what he or she has in mind. The purpose for which the group is created must answer some need of the would-be members; otherwise, they will perceive it as a waste of their time and resources. Below is an example:

Today there are many young people who on finishing their studies find that they cannot obtain a job. Everyday several pages in the newspapers are dedicated to job advisement. Yet to their disillusionment, many job seekers discover that the majority of the publicized jobs are occupied even before they are advertised. They are put in the newspapers as a fulfillment of the requirement of the law, and not because firms are actually looking for employees. There is stiff competition for the few genuinely available jobs: on turning up for interviews people find that there are hundreds, sometimes thousands vying for the same job. In this intensive competition upright employers look out for the exceptionally good. Those who are less upright give out jobs, not on the basis of merit but of personal connection to the employer, or in view of some ulterior motive. There is even the saying that what matters is not "know-how" but "know-who." Other employers demand a certain length of experience, but one needs to have had a job in order to acquire experience. Practically a person who is neither exceptionally good, who is not ready to bend personal principles in order to meet the underhand demands of unscrupulous employees, and who has not had any prior work experience practically has no chance of getting employed.

Observing that the difficulty of finding jobs is a widespread phenomenon, and bearing in mind that "two heads are better than one," a job seeker or one who wants to help job seekers might want to start a group of people in the same predicament whose aim is job-creation. The purpose is good. The reasons to support the purpose are factual and convincing. The need creates a strong motivation. The question is how to start.

One of the best ways in recruiting new members for a group is through personal contact. Interested candidates may be invited to an initial talk, after which individuals are invited to make personal initiative towards joining the group. Every necessary detail with regard to the nature of the group should be made clear to the interested members. Expectations should be clarified so that candidates whose needs are better served elsewhere leave without further waste of their time. Any necessary sacrifice be the members for the cause of the group should be made known to the prospective members, so that they can decide whether or not they are willing to incur this sacrifice.

Preparing People for Group Membership

Once all the potential members have understood the purpose of the group, they are ready to establish a *Working Alliance*. In the Working Alliance the expectations of all parties should be clearly set out. One way to do this is to suggest to the members some basics and let them make further suggestions. Explore, clarify, and challenge where necessary, the mutual expectations.

It is important to know that a Working Alliance is not just a contract, but a relationship.

The Working Alliance is set out concretely in the form of *Ground Rules*. Copies of these may be distributed to the individual members and/or the ground rules may be displayed in some prominent place within the meeting room. More complex groups may need a more elaborate set of group rules or *Statutes*. In the Catholic Code of Canon Law, canon 304 lays out a norm required of Catholic groups or *Associations of Christ's Faithful* as they are referred to in the code:

> All associations of Christ's faithful, whether public or private, by whatever title or name they are called, are to have their own statutes. These are to define the purpose or social objective of the association, its center, its governance and the conditions of membership. They are also to specify the manner of action of the association, paying due regard to what is necessary or useful in the circumstances of the time and place.

The formulation of a working alliance or ground rules or statutes takes into consideration the fact that a group is composed of individuals, each with a different intellect and will, each with a different character, each with personal interests and dislikes, and all subject to changing feelings and moods. Harmonized common action of such a composition demands some kind of regulation. Provision can be placed within the working alliance, of the possibility of its revision at certain intervals, if changing circumstances make it no longer relevant to the interests of the group.

Members need to know what they have to do in order that each of them gains the most out of the group. In a Growth Group, for instance, they should be aware of these essentials:

o Basic group interaction skills like listening, empathy, caring confrontation, concreteness, affirmation, etc.

o Focus: when you come to the group sharing: what do you want from the group today?

o Flexibility: John comes in intending to share something about time-management. But Jane's sharing about her grieving experience reminds John of his own unshared grieving. John should then feel free to switch from time-management to the problem of grieving. Or Jane's grieving takes up all the time that there is not time left for John to share what is on his mind. Let him learn that even taking time to listen to others and to help them towards growth is part of one's growth as well. John should learn to consider as worthwhile even the fact of helping another deal with his or her issue.

o   Attention to personal feelings during participation in the group; owning these feelings as a first step to dealing with them in a healthy way.

o   Playing an active role in the group: the more participants put in it, the more they gain from the group for themselves.

o   Giving honest feedback to each other.[36] Feedback should be specific, behavioral, and it should allow room for the recipient to maneuver.

o   Openness to feedback from others.

o   Readiness to carry out allocated tasks outside the group: insights for growth acquired in the group should be acted upon.

SOME ELEMENTS OF GROUP PROCESS

In all human interactions there are two major ingredients – content and process. *Content* deals with the subject matter or the task upon which the group is working. In most interactions, the focus of attention of all persons is on the content. In the example given on page 215 above, Content is the task of how to get self-employed and to earn a living under conditions where it is very difficult to get a job. Questions regarding what to undertake, how to get an initial capital, what each member is required to do, etc. belong to Content. Similarly, in the context of a Growth Group the issues that members bring to discussion such as coping with grief, with fears, stress, or decision making; all this are part of Content.

Group *Process,* on the other hand, deals with such items as morale, feelings, tone, atmosphere, influence, participation, styles of influence, leadership struggles, conflict, competition, cooperation, etc. In most interactions, very little attention is paid to process, even when it is a major cause of ineffective group action. Sensitivity to group process will better enable one to diagnose group problems early and deal with them more effectively. Since these processes are present in all groups, awareness of them will enhance a person's worth to a group and enable the person to be a more effective group participant. Below are some guidelines to help one analyze group Process.

---

[36] See "Feed back" on page 199.

Participation

One indication of involvement is verbal participation. Look for differences in the amount of participation among members.

o   Who are the high participators?

o   Who are the low participators?

o   Do you see any shift in participation? E.g., highs become quiet, lows suddenly become talkative? Do you see any possible reason for this in the group's interactions?

o   How are the silent people treated? How is their silence interpreted? Consent? Disagreement? Disinterest? Fear?

o   Who talks to whom? Do you see any reason for this in the group's interactions?

o   Who keeps the ball rolling? Why? Do you see any reason for this in the group's interactions?

As a group member, pay attention to your own participation process in relation to others' participation. Listen to yourself. Are you among those who speak most or least? Is this helpful to the group? Does it give you some form of satisfaction? As one guiding a group be equally attentive to the participation of each member and respond accordingly for the good of the member and for the overall good of the group.

Roles

With time the members interacting in a group tend to play characteristic roles. Each of us in fact has a characteristic role we play in group activity. Some of these roles are: rescuer, entertainer, optimist, controller, bully, generalizer, persecutor, panic monger, pessimist, victim, blamer, worker bee, do-er, placator, facilitator. Obviously, we can now and then shift roles or even play more than one role. At different times it may be necessary to play one role and another at another time. In order to grow in group interaction, it is important for someone to observe the roles one plays and to try to deliberately shift to roles one does not easily play, but which are positive.

The roles we play in groups may be due to the influence of our own first group; the family. It is possible to identify among those mentioned above roles that were typical in our first community. We may model such roles if they were played by people we esteemed. Or we may find such roles irritating, disdainful or intimidating; depending on the feelings similar roles in our first community evoked in us.

At the same time our roles in groups reflect the roles we play in ordinary life. People who like to talk about themselves in ordinary conversation are likely to do the same at meetings. Those who are kind bring that kindness in group interaction. Some of these roles are positive and if we become aware of them, we are happy to have them and want to continue playing them. Others are negative and the only reason we keep playing them is that we are not aware of them and of the effect they have on others. Once we are conscious of this, we become ashamed of them and wish to act differently. The crucial point then is to be conscious of the roles we play, so that we may decide whether to enhance them or to drop them.

During a Group Dynamics session, a lecturer divided us in three groups of seven. She then gave to each group a sheet of manila paper, a pair of scissors, glue and pins. She told us that each group had 30 minutes in which to make a boat. She stood there watching us and we looked at each other inquisitively. All sorts of questions and comments were asked: where does this lead to? Is it not one of those endless games, another waste of time? How do we begin? Who is the artist among us? Le us decide what kind of boat to make. Let us make a sailing boat with a mast. It is already 10 minutes and we have not yet started. Give me the pair of scissors. Hold the paper while I cut. Before you cut it without any plan recall that we have only one sheet…

At the end of the appointed time the lecturer told us to stop. Surprisingly we had patched up quite a beautiful boat and we were quite proud to display it. But the lecturer showed little interest in the product of our common activity. Instead, she wrote on the black board a heading *Group Task Roles* and then she asked each of us to write in the personal notebooks answers to the questions: 1) who was the Initiator or Contributor: who proposed new ideas to the group? 2) Who played the role of Coordinator, distributing tasks? Who was Procedural Technician or Handyman of the group? 3) Who was the Energizer prodding the group into a decision and attempting to stimulate the group to greater activity? Etc. She wrote another heading: *Group Process Roles* and under this she wrote the questions: 1) who was the Encourager accepting the contributions of others by listening, praising and understanding others' points of view? 2) Who was the Harmonizer attempting to reconcile disagreements, mediating differences between members and reliving tension? 3) She wrote a third heading: *Individualistic Roles* and under it she wrote the questions: 1) Who was the Aggressor lowering the status of other group members, rejecting suggestions, valuing ideas of others, attacking the group or the issue being worked on? 2) Who was the Recognition Seeker working in various ways to draw attention to self? 3) Who was the Playboy with a nonchalant attitude that interfered with group functions and belittled the group task? 4) Who was the Dominator who tried to assert personal authority by intentionally controlling and manipulating the whole group?

With this last group of roles, I felt a little humbled recognizing myself in some of them, and I learnt that I was not alone. I realized that this exercise had the capacity to help me to recognize the good roles as well as the undesirable ones I unconsciously play in groups, and the desire to enhance the good roles while minimizing the negative ones.

RESPONSE AND EXPECTATIONS

We respond to others according to the roles we see in them or they themselves assume. To each role we have a different response, and from each role we have different expectations. To a doctor we take our symptoms of disease and we expect a diagnosis and cure. To a teacher we bring our questions expecting answers. To a friend we take ourselves and we expect acceptance. And to a mother we take our hurts expecting comfort. Similarly, we tend to respond to people in accordance with the roles we see them play. The one who plays the role of a mechanic we expect to fix our gadgets, whereas the one who plays priest-confessor we take our confessions.

In any group members tend to assume specific roles after sometime. The particular role label is partly determined by the person's own behavior, partly by the rest of the members. Individuals tend to act according to the members' expectations, according to the kind of role they have assigned to the particular individual. An experiment to show the different roles people play set out as follows:

Six volunteers were invited to come forward and discuss a topic. The topic was suggested: an introduction to the idea of having an award of "Student of the Year". The seven members were to discuss whether or not such an idea should be introduced and how. Before the discussion labels were to be placed on the foreheads of each of the participants. The labels were pre-numbered from one to seven. Each was free to choose which number. The labels were tied on their foreheads in such a way that the rest of the participants could see what was written apart from the person carrying the label. The participants were to react to each other according to the label each individual was carrying and not so much according to their ideas. The different labels were "Stupid", "Expert", "Boss", "Joker", "Insignificant", and "Dependable".

As the discussion went on it was obvious how people began to act according to the label they had been given. The one labeled stupid withdrew and did not participate much, because each time she said something people sneered. The joker was also put down because each time he suggested something others burst out laughing. The insignificant was equally confused because no one paid any attention to whatever he said. The expert's ideas were welcomed and she was encouraged to say more. The boss was treated with respect whatever she proposed.

At the end of the discussion each one was asked to guess what kind of label they had been carrying, and they answered fairly accurately.

The lesson of the experiment is that participants should not allow themselves to be slotted into any label. It is good to experiment by playing different roles at different times. If you joke all the time and members get to label you as such, they will not take you seriously even when you have something serious to say. The one who assumes the duties might find himself overloaded when he would want to have a break. Others feel he is supposed to take on that role. Even the "expert" might reach a time when he feels the role given him is weighing too much on him when others could share some of the responsibility. In turn we tend to act according to the labels people have placed on us, unless we make a conscious effort to break free.

In a healthy group or community each member takes on the responsibility of promoting the values that sustain and enhance the group or community. It is not enough to say that this is not my duty or role. It is everyone's duty to promote the common good and this means at times shifting of roles.

Influence

Jesus had now finished what he wanted to say, and his teaching made a deep impression on the people because he taught them with authority, and not like their own scribes. (Matthew 7:28-29)

Influence and participation are not the same. Some people may speak very little, yet capture the attention of the whole group. An influential member's silence may itself be a message. Others may talk a lot but are generally not listened to by other members. Some of the things to observe in groups with regard to influence are: which members are listened to most? Which members attract least attention from others? Is there any shifting in influence? Who shifts? Do you see any rivalry in the group? Is there a struggle for leadership? What effect does it have on other group members?

The ability to exert influence depends on a number of factors. Some people are charismatic leaders. They exert influence without much effort. They are what we frequently refer to as born or natural leaders. They effortlessly emerge out of the crowd. One may have the ability to influence others through natural charm, a warm smile, a pleasant tone of voice or a combination of these. But influence can also be acquired. Chief among the qualities of an influential person is the authority other members see in that individual. Authority in turn is of different types.

- o There is the authority of experience. People respect the opinion of the one who talks out of experience.

- o There is the authority of learning. When the subject is such as requires knowledge, the expert in the field is respected for that proficiency.

- o There is moral authority. Particularly in matters regarding moral rectitude one who is upright exerts greater influence.

A person may also influence others by the quality of verbal skills: the ability to present issues with clarity and/or the use of concrete examples that everyone can understand.

Influence is not always positive. It can also be negative. Ringleaders in strikes can be people capable of exerting negative influence, where a strike is not justified or is unfairly damaging to an institution. Negatively influential individuals in a group can be damaging to the group's cause.

For instance, they can easily sabotage or block ideas that do not conform to their own opinions. A wise leader identifies early enough people who wield strong influence in the group, whether positively or negatively. Those who influence others negatively can be harnessed to do the same in a positive way. It is injudicious to compete with or fight those who are influential in a group. It is much wiser to win them on one's side.

Although most of us naturally prefer to be influential to being in the background, it is also true that truly influential people do not aim for that quality for its own sake. Often the ambition to be influential earns the very opposite of what it clamors for: scorn and contempt, and jealousy within oneself towards those competed with. Authentic influence is a bi-product of well-focused effort towards the group's objectives. It is the result of concerted effort to acquire the skills of group membership or leadership. A person who listens to others, who affirms and empowers others, who recognizes personal limitations, who talks to edify, who keeps quiet when there is nothing to say, is likely to be influential even without consciously striving to be so. To such a person it is not important who is influential in a group; what is important is that the objectives of the group are attained.

When influential people are aware of their power of persuasion, they may even choose not to exercise it as long as the desired goal is achieved in some other way. If they are leaders, they prefer to direct the members toward the goal they have in mind, without themselves bringing their own ideas directly. If someone else brings forward their own opinion, even in a defective way, they build on that until it looks as if that other person is the initiator of the same idea, even when they know it is not true. In all this they do not act to manipulate others but to empower them.

Similarly, a member who is aware of the power of influence can minimize that power as long as the group goals are being achieved. Such people introduce their own ideas with a complement to another person: "I agree with Jo…" they pose questions in a polite form even when they are convinced of being right: "can you enlighten me on… Correct me if I am mistaken, but…" They keep silent in order to allow others to take the floor, particularly those that are less influential than themselves.

Feelings

During any group discussion feelings are frequently generated by the interactions between members. These feelings, however, are seldom talked about. Quite often people talk heatedly over one issue when actually the underlying feelings that generate the heat are quite different. In groups as in any other human interaction feelings constitute a major element. Feelings are an indication that there is energy in the group, and that is good, not only when feelings are positive (enthusiasm, joy, mutual appraisal, affection, excitement, warmth, etc.) but also when they are negative (anger, irritation, defensiveness, competitiveness, etc.). A healthy group is not one where feelings are never generated, but where they are dealt with effectively.

Whether acknowledged or ignored feelings have a definite effect on the group. They may provide motivation or sabotage group goals; they may create sour working relationships, lead to divisions within the group or formation of clicks; feelings can lead to prejudice and rejection of people's ideas apriori on the basis of opinions held about those people. People talking from strong feelings may have their rationality obscured and become quite adamant on issues that appear quite obvious to the rest of the group. Feelings of attraction and infatuation may lead to pairing within the group, and this in turn might lead to other feelings of jealousy or even hatred. Feelings of inferiority and superiority may find expression in subservient and condescending talk among members.

Because feelings play such a significant role, it is important in the first place to recognize them. Observers may have to make guesses based on tone of voice, facial expressions, choice of words, gestures, silence, and many other forms of non-verbal cues.[37]

Having recognized feelings, you need to decide how best to deal with them in the actual situation. You may judge that the best thing is first of all to empathies with the person or persons having those feelings; show them that you understand how they feel. In certain situation the best course of action might be to ignore the feeling, at least for the time being, and go on with the group's business. For instance, you might avoid giving a chance to a person who talks too much or one who brings down the morale of the group by seeing everything in a negative way. In a different situation it might be better to confront the feeling with the skill of

---

[37] See also "'Disagreeable' Emotions" on page 70.

immediacy. People who depict signs of boredom might be challenged whether they find the discussion unhelpful. Or again it may be better to deal with the cause of the feeling and not the feeling itself. A member who obviously seeks attention might be given that attention outside the group: you may take time to talk to them individually.

Eye Contact

The skill of Eye Contact can be used both in one-to-one counselling as well as in group facilitation. In facilitating a group, a leader needs to make good use of eye contact. Eyes can gather important information about the participants of the group. You can encourage someone to speak through the use of your eyes, you can also reduce the monopoly of one person by avoiding encouraging them through eyes. It is important not to keep eye contact with one person alone, for then the others feel neglected. Learn to look at people when you talk and when they talk. As facilitator you need to scan the participants with your eyes now and then in order to know what is going on. Obviously, the scanning should be done in such a manner that it does not look artificial or threatening. Through scanning you also notice who wants to speak. Often people get discouraged if they want to speak and the leader does not pay attention to them. Some are too timid or polite to speak without permission, and yet this permission they will not ask verbally but through their eyes or through the raising of their hands which also can be missed by one who does not scan with the eyes. It is also important to note the various reactions of the members at others' interventions: nods, disapproval, confusions, boredom, disagreement, deep emotion, irritation, etc. You can then check with the people whether what you observe corresponds to what they are feeling.

In groups facilitated by two people one who is not talking at any particular moment has a better opportunity to scan the reaction of the participants with his eyes. The two facilitators complement each other in such a way that each one covers a particular arc of the group with their eyes which their co-facilitator cannot cover from the position where they are seated.

STAGES IN GROUP DEVELOPMENT

Like an organism, groups go through a number of stages of development. It is important for a leader to be familiar with these stages at least in general, and to know what is needed at each stage. Otherwise, the behavior of group members may appear incomprehensible, and the bewilderment this causes to the leader may be reflected back to the members. Below is a simplified outline of these stages.

Orientation: This is a phase of exploration. People get acquainted, get to know each other. We learn how the group functions. We define our goals, clarify our expectations and find our place in the group. In this phase we often have a lot of anxiety and insecurity. It is also a time of testing our limits, what is acceptable in the group and what is not.

At this stage the person forming a group has the following responsibilities

- o Create a trusting and safe climate
- o Set boundaries
- o Clarify group roles
- o Deal with members' fears and concerns
- o Make sure that everyone participates in the interaction so no one feels excluded.

Transition: This is characterized by anxiety. People are also quite defensive. We have doubts whether we want to share beyond our public image. Anxiety arises also from the fear of being misunderstood. People may need some structure to deal with anxiety. People are not sure about the expected behavior. Testing continues also in this stage.

At this stage the person forming the group has the following tasks:

- o Noticing signs of resistance and communicating to participants that some of these resistances are both natural and healthy
- o Create a climate in which participants can deal with their resistance openly
- o Modeling appropriate behavior especially in terms of confrontation, respect and disclosing ongoing reactions.

Working Stage: This is characterized by exploration of significant problems, and the desire to bring about change. People start developing leadership skills. People are much less dependent on the group and more on their mutual resources.

At this stage the leader of the group has the following tasks:

- o Providing reinforcement of desired group behavior that fosters group cohesion
- o Help members consider options and alternatives for dealing with difficult situations
- o Encourage members to keep in mind what they want from the group and to ask for what they want

Consolidation and Termination: Members look at what they have learnt from the group. They may also start distancing themselves as an unconscious desire not to terminate. It is also the time to wind up unfinished business.

At this stage the leader has the following tasks:

- o Prepare the members for the eventual separation by reminding them of it a few weeks before it comes
- o Evaluate what members have achieved in the course of the sessions, and to what extent this corresponds to their original expectations
- o Avoid starting on business that time will not allow to bring to a meaningful conclusion
- o Reinforce changes which members have made
- o Ensure that any unresolved issues among members or between members and leaders are attended to before the group terminates
- o See how the members propose to work on what they have attained
- o Find an appropriate way for the members to say goodbye to each other

DIMENSIONS OF BEHAVIOR & INTERVENTION STRATEGIES[38]

Training in group facilitation would be incomplete if it stopped at making one aware of the things to observe in a group process without giving help in improving that process.

The following are some tips for facilitators on handling particular hard role-players in a group.

The person who talks too much

o Highlight a point made by this person and invite other people to comment on them. If he/she persists, he/she can then be interrupted with the statement, "It would be valuable to know what others in the group think."

o Make a point of sharing round the available time among all group members, perhaps in the form of equal time activities.

o Avoid eye contact; although this may have the unintended effect of making the person more anxious or even hostile.

o Give the person a specific task such as recording on the board/flip chart. This reduces the time for talking.

o Give helpful feedback; make the issue public. It is important to praise or affirm the individual's contribution while at the same time drawing attention to its effects on the ability of others to meet their needs

The person who talks too little

o Make a particular effort to value any contributions that are made; work to build up the person's confidence.

o Allow preparation time.

o Direct questions at this person; although this may have the unintended consequence of making him/her anxious and more reluctant to contribute.

---

[38] Gerlinde Wilberg, Unpublished *Lecture Notes on Group Dynamics*, Institute of St. Anselm, England, Oct. 2002.

o Check out occasionally that the person is content with this silence and reassure that it is OK to be silent.

o Work in pairs ensures that the person will make some contribution. A person who finds it difficult to speak in a large group (of say twelve people) may be articulate and loquacious in a pair, trio or small group of four people.

The angry person

o Accept the feelings expressed as valid, i.e. that is how that person feels. Communicate that you understand this fact.

o Avoid getting into "fights"; do not retaliate or allow disagreements to escalate.

o Develop ground-rules which make aggressive behavior less acceptable. Draw attention to occasions in which other participants get "put down" rather than affirmed.

o Confront the anger with immediacy: "you sound irritated, is there anything that is bothering you?"

o Become aware of the issues which generate the angry response; try to understand how the response helps the individual to cope.

o Find ways to indicate to the person that he or she is valued for himself/herself and does not have to prove him/herself by being competitive.

The Person who fools around

o Get in touch with what is being avoided by this behavior and find ways to communicate this to the individual.

o Ensure that the topic of the role of humor receives appropriate discussion within the group.

o Do not reinforce the inconsequential behavior by rewarding it with laughter or attention.

The Person who is over-intellectual and theoretical

o Encourage concreteness and specificity by challenging over-theoretical statements; ask for examples.

o Encourage group members to state if they do not understand what is being said and involve other group members, e.g. "Can anyone help here?"

o Share your perception that they are making issues more complicated than necessary.

The Person who is Self-disparaging

o Avoid encouraging them by contradicting their self-disparagement.

o Call the bluff by taking them at their own word; agree with them in their auto-denigration.

The person who is anecdotal

o Ask them to clarify the points which they make so that their more general relevance is made apparent to the individual as well as to other members of the group.

o Thank them for their contribution, summaries the relevant parts of what they have said and ask for comments from the group.

EPILOGUE

The Lord Jesus told his disciples: *"I am the way, the truth and life. No one can come to the Father except through me"* (John 14:6). Without any reference to Jesus Christ, so many books on the market today offer some form of *way* to achieving personal wholeness and fulfillment. By doing this the writers believe or make believe that they are in possession of *truth*, and that their readers, by following what they say, attain fullness of *life*. Such books contradict the words of Jesus to the extent that they claim to lead to God, while ignoring the only Way, Truth and Life.

In the course of writing this book I have asked myself over and over again, whether this is not just another of those books, perhaps with scattered references to the teachings of Jesus to lend it credibility. However, I would not have submitted it to publication if I was not convinced that it is not. Yes, it is a merger of common sense, some psychological principles and scriptural teachings. Yet it is a legitimate approach to wholeness for non-Christians, non-Catholic Christians, as well as Catholics, for three reasons:

1. We are all created in the image of God. We are all creatures with the capacity to know the truth. Common sense, human wisdom and scientific discoveries are all gifts of God. They can be misused against God, or they can help us to get closer to him. In this book they have been used as a way of coming closer to God.

2. Christ commanded us his followers to go out to the whole world and proclaim the good news. One way of doing this effectively is to start where the persons to whom the good news is brought are. In fact, the best way of reaching those who do not believe strongly in the Christian faith or who do not believe it at all, but who believe in psychology and common sense, and who are interested in attaining wholeness, is to start on their ground. This is what this book has attempted to do.

3. For many centuries until now, the approach of the Catholic Church in training its priests has been to

subject them to a course in Philosophy, both Christian and non-Christian, as a preparation for Theology. The Church believed and still believes that critical thinking and human wisdom laid a firm foundation for revealed truth. Following the same reasoning, I think that this book lays a foundation for benefiting from God's own plan of leading mankind back to himself through the Church.

For that reason, *In God's Own Image* can be regarded as the first part of another work entitled *If You Only Knew the Gift of God*, which elaborates how the firm faith in, the proper celebration and the consistent living of the Eucharist are commensurate to following *the way* Christ has marked out, getting to know *the truth* he has revealed, and attaining *the life* he has offered.

About the Author

Simon Peter Kyambadde Muwambo is a Catholic Priest in Uganda. He studied Sacred Liturgy at the Pontifical Institute of St. Anselmo, Rome. He further studied Counselling at the Institution of St. Anselm, Cliftonville, England. He then taught Sacred Liturgy and Counselling at St. Paul National Seminary, Fort Portal. At present he is Director of St. Augustine Institute for National Ongoing Formation of Priests in Uganda, as well as Advisor to the Liturgical Commission of Jinja Diocese.